The Era of Great Disasters

MICHIGAN MONOGRAPH SERIES IN JAPANESE STUDIES

NUMBER 89

CENTER FOR JAPANESE STUDIES
UNIVERSITY OF MICHIGAN

THE ERA OF GREAT DISASTERS

Japan and Its Three Major Earthquakes

Iokibe Makoto

Translated by Tony Gonzalez

University of Michigan Press
Ann Arbor

Copyright © 2016, 2020 by IOKIBE Makoto
English translation © 2020 Japan Publishing Industry Foundation for Culture (JPIC)
Originally published in Japan by Mainichi Shimbun Publishing Inc., in 2016.

For questions or permissions, please contact um.press.perms@umich.edu

Published in the United States of America by
the University of Michigan Press
Manufactured in Japan

First published July 2020

A CIP catalog record for this book is available from the British Library.

ISBN 978-0-472-07467-9 (hardcover : alk. paper)
ISBN 978-0-472-05467-1 (paper : alk. paper)
ISBN 978-0-472-12725-2 (ebook)

Contents

Digital materials related to this title can be found on
the Fulcrum platform via the following citable URL:
https://doi.org/10.3998/mpub.11422327

Preface to the English Edition

Japan is blessed with beautiful and varied nature, yet it also experiences frequent natural disasters. Both aspects are the result of a single historical reality. Around twenty-three million years ago, the eastern edge of the Asian Continent broke off and headed seaward, forming the Japanese archipelago. However, this offshore trip was blocked by the movement of another plate heading northward into the Pacific Ocean. The Pacific Plate, which travels at a geologically remarkable speed of ten centimeters per year, halts the southward motion of the Japanese archipelago, submerging beneath it and pushing it upward to form mountainous islands. This submergence periodically produces earthquakes and tsunamis along the Japan Trench—the Great East Japan Earthquake being one notable recent example—and furthermore compresses the archipelago from both sides, causing cracks (active faults) all along it. When the Pacific Plate slides beneath the Japanese archipelago it also brings with it a large amount of seawater, which in combination with high geothermal heat produces magma and creates a volcanic belt along the mountain ranges in northeastern Japan.

In addition to the Pacific Plate, the Philippine Plate moves northward at four to five centimeters per year and submerges beneath southwest Japan (at the Nankai trough). Its northeastern border forms the Sagami trough, which continues to dive beneath the Kantō plain, causing for example the 1923 Great Kantō Earthquake, the topic of the first chapter in this book. Continued squeezing by these two oceanic plates seems to be the prime source of active faults in Japan and continues to produce an upward movement of several millimeters each year, forming mountains such as Mount Akaishi in Japan's Southern Alps.

One might wonder why people would live in such a dangerous area, but natural disasters are extraordinary events that seem to come only after the previous one has been forgotten. In normal times, the Japanese islands are both beautiful and bountiful, with good fishing grounds and rich farmlands. The people living here have accumulated over two millennia of expertise related to living alongside nature and its disasters. As a World Bank report on the 2011 Great East Japan Earthquake pointed out, such expertise greatly lessened losses during that event. For example, the elementary and junior high school students along the coasts evacuated to higher ground immediately after the earthquake.

This book focuses on the modern era of disaster response. As Japan's technical capability improved through post-Meiji modernization, so did its ability to respond to disasters. Yet the Japanese archipelago has entered a particularly active period of seismic activity since the 1995 Great Hanshin-Awaji Earthquake. Amid the resulting misery, Japanese society has focused more than ever on reducing disaster deaths. I am glad to have the opportunity to share a record of this work with people around the world through this English version.

This book focuses on three major earthquakes from Japan's modern history. The first is the Great Kantō Earthquake, which struck the capital region and caused 105,385 fatalities, the most of any quake in Japanese history. The second is the Great Hanshin-Awaji Earthquake, which killed 6,434 people in Japan's second-largest urban region, the area between Kobe and Osaka. The third is the Great East Japan Earthquake, which remains freshest in our memory. This magnitude 9.0 quake, the strongest in Japan's recorded history, struck off the Pacific coast of the Tōhoku region and caused a tsunami that took the lives of 22,010 people. It furthermore caused a serious accident at the Fukushima Daiichi Nuclear Power Plant that robbed surrounding residents of their homes and has put into question the future of Japan's nuclear power industry.

This book aims to comprehensively deconstruct each of these three great earthquake disasters. While all disasters are unique and multifaceted, I attempt to present a bigger picture while still paying attention to important particularities.

The first important point to understand is the physical mechanism of these disasters. How did tectonic movements shake the earth and stir up the ocean? How did each disaster damage society and people? Was it an isolated single disaster, or a complex compound one? Because I am a historian interested in humans and society rather than a natural scientist, however, my primary concerns are the human and social aspects of disaster. Disasters do not consist of nature unilaterally damaging human society;

they are instead the result of interactions between these two forces. For that reason, the types of disasters a society anticipates and the preparations it makes for them are extremely important. The nature of these preparations affects everything from the ability to cope with the immediate crisis to the prospects for completing recovery and reconstruction.

While individual disasters are unique by nature, certain common patterns emerge in Japanese society's response and revival process. The initial emergency phase centers on life-saving activities, with the first seventy-two hours said to be the most crucial. Self-assistance is fundamental to human survival in disasters, but when that is impossible, families and communities must step in. When even that is impossible, victims must wait for public assistance by frontline units such as police, firefighters, or the military. Earthquakes tend to cause fires and responding to them is as important during the initial stage as rescue operations. Such emergency relief work immediately following a disaster makes the difference between life and death, and to a very great degree determines the extent of casualties.

Another reality of cataclysm is that mere coincidence can separate life from death. Those who do survive suffer greatly. The Tendai Buddhist concept of "three thousand realms in a single moment of existence" teaches that all forms of good and evil exist within every person's heart. This teaching is manifested in situations of extreme chaos, such as the collective hysteria that followed the Great Kanto Earthquake and its fires, which resulted in vigilante killings of innocent Koreans and others from outside the local community due to a torrent of rumors. In contrast, extreme situations also give rise to many noble and self-sacrificing efforts to rescue others. Disaster zones can be worlds of both the worst evil and the greatest good. This book draws attention to examples in which the brilliance of humanity is revealed through extremes of misery.

The second phase of disaster response is a period of emergency relief during which local governments provide evacuation centers, food, and water to victims deprived of safe housing. Earthquakes disrupt lifelines such as electricity, water, and gas, so evacuees depend on the provision of goods from areas not affected by the disaster, including other neighborhoods, other regions of the country, and even other nations. Through this support, social infrastructure such as communication systems, roads, and utilities are generally restored within two to three months, and temporary housing is erected. Within a few months, survivors who have been living without privacy in emergency shelters are able to recover their family life—if their families have survived—though perhaps in somewhat cramped quarters.

The third phase is one of waiting. While survivors live in temporary housing, cities and permanent dwellings are rebuilt. Simply reconstructing homes in their original locations typically requires only one to three years, but rebuilding entire towns through land readjustment projects or relocation to higher ground can take from five to ten years.

Conflicts have arisen over the best approach to reconstruction following each of the three earthquake disasters examined in this book. Should the goal be to restore things to their predisaster state, or should disasters be considered opportunities for "creative reconstruction" that aims to improve on what was?

After the Great Kantō Earthquake, Home Secretary Gotō Shinpei (1857–1929) advocated a revolutionary creative reconstruction plan for transforming Tokyo into a splendid imperial city to match Paris and Berlin, but landowners and financial conservatives fiercely opposed him. Gotō's reconstruction budget was drastically cut, but Tokyo somehow reemerged as a modern metropolis. After the Great Hanshin-Awaji Earthquake, too, Hyōgo prefecture governor Kaihara Toshitami (1933–2014; in office 1986–2001) proposed a creative reconstruction plan, but the central government limited the use of national funds to restoration only, and refused to allow the use of public money to rebuild private property such as homes. Undeterred, Governor Kaihara used prefectural debt to fund some creative reconstruction projects. The administration of Prime Minister Kan Naoto (1946–; in office 2010–11) also debated announced policies for creative reconstruction after the Great East Japan Earthquake. The establishment of a new reconstruction tax enabled projects along parts of the Sanriku coast that have resulted in towns that are remarkably safe against future tsunamis. This transformation in social consciousness toward a more progressive approach to reconstruction is a central focus of this book.

In April 2016, as the final touches to the original Japanese version of the book were being added, the Kumamoto Earthquake struck. When I was a professor at Kobe University in 1995, the Great Hanshin-Awaji Earthquake occurred, and in 2011, when I was the President of the National Defense Academy near Tokyo, the Great East Japan Earthquake hit, and I became involved with the reconstruction of the Tōhoku region. It was when I was serving as Chancellor of the Prefectural University of Kumamoto (from 2012 to 2018) that the Kumamoto Earthquake struck. Some people have called me, unfortunately, "the earthquake man."

I became the chancellor due to my longtime professional friendship of some forty years with Kabashima Ikuo, the governor of Kumamoto prefecture, whom I had met when we were both studying at Harvard University in 1977. He invited me to serve as chancellor starting in April 2012 after I finished the presidency of the NDA that March. Two days after the main earthquake in Kumamoto (the first one had struck on April 14, followed by the main one on the 16th, telephoned to ask me to prepare a recovery plan. We established an experts group, and submitted a report one month later. The goal was to not simply restore Kumamoto to its pre-earthquake state, but to make an even better Kumamoto through a creative reconstruction approach.

Compared to the Great Hanshin-Awaji Earthquake, the destruction in the Great East Japan Earthquake was much larger, and worsened Japan's economic and fiscal situation. Despite this, the concern of the people throughout Japan for the disaster area was high and the public strongly supported the ambitious recovery plans. While natural disasters continue to occur one after the other, the upside is that many lessons are learned and knowledge about how to better deal with them is acquired and utilized the next time around. The reconstruction plan for Kumamoto following the earthquake there was just the latest reflection of Japanese society's maturity in this regard.

It is without doubt that my involvement with these earthquakes in recent years has affected the tone of the book in some ways. The chapter about the Great Kantō Earthquake is based primarily on historic research. Because I personally experienced the Great Hanshin-Awaji Earthquake, the parts related to it include my own experiences as well as interviews I conducted as someone responsible for the oral histories of the disaster, especially the firsthand insights of officials on the scene and at the national level. In the case of the Great East Japan Earthquake, as Chairperson of the Reconstruction Design Council I was able to introduce details regarding the making of the recovery plan. The Japanese version of this book was published in June 2016, based on a monthly column in the *Mainichi Shimbun* newspaper that ran for three years and eight months from 2012 through 2015. Research on disaster prevention comes primarily from the fields of science and engineering. As the foreword by Yamazaki Masakazu states, this book can be taken as describing the entirety of the history of earthquakes in human society.

I am quite pleased that the Japan Publishing Industry Foundation for Culture selected this book for English translation. Given that Japan is an advanced country with regard to disaster response, sharing our accumulated experience and expertise with other countries is a meaningful undertaking.

In publishing the English version, I added a new section on "Operation Tomodachi" following the Great East Japan Earthquake and Tsunami. Since the early years of the postwar period, Japan and the United States have continued to maintain a close alliance; we even worked together on domestic disasters in Japan in those early years, and on international disasters over the past fifteen years, but never on the scale of the relief efforts that followed the March 2011 disaster. It was not only the scale of the response, but the naming of the operation, which means "Friend," that symbolized the fact that the relationship had entered a new phase.

I am particularly indebted and grateful to Robert D. Eldridge regarding the English version. He provided advice on the English itself, as well as the need for additional explanations in some parts for the benefit of readers not familiar with Japan, essentially serving as the supervisor for the English version. In addition, I am thankful for the high level of interest shown in this project by Nakaizumi Kiyoshi and Komanoya Rico, both with JPIC. Furthermore, Seikai Yasushi kindly coordinated the translation and accuracy of the original text and the faithfulness of the English version, serving as my representative in many of the interactions in my place. This English version is a joint endeavor by all of them, to which I am truly thankful.

Iokibe Makoto
January 17, 2020
Twenty-fifth anniversary of the Great Hanshin-Awaji Earthquake

Foreword

Looking back on Japan's history, there have been so-called active seismic periods, times when major earthquakes appear with some frequency. There have been many such eras, including the period between the 869 Jōgan Sanriku and 887 Ninna Earthquakes in the ninth century, a series of events including the 1586 Tenshō and 1605 Keichō Earthquakes in the sixteenth and seventeenth centuries, and the Ansei Earthquakes in the mid-nineteenth century. Prompted by the more recent 1995 Great Hanshin-Awaji Earthquake, the author Iokibe Makoto has penned this book to ask whether Japan has entered into a new "era of catastrophic natural disasters."

Iokibe himself was a victim of the Great Hanshin-Awaji Earthquake in January 1995. At the time, he contributed to recovery efforts as a professor at Kobe University, and today serves as President of the Hyogo Earthquake Memorial 21st Century Research Institute established in commemoration of that disaster. Following the March 2011 Great East Japan Earthquake and Tsunami, the Japanese government invited him to serve as Chairperson of the Reconstruction Design Council in Response to the Great East Japan Earthquake, and he similarly played a leading role after the April 2016 Kumamoto Earthquakes as Chairperson of the Expert Group for Restoration and Recovery. Thus, there is probably no person better suited to intuiting the arrival of an "era of catastrophic natural disasters" and to inquire into what such an era may look like.

The appeal of this rare work consists of two intertwining threads. One is that this is a carefully detailed historical record, written by a skilled historian and rigorously supported through citations from countless eyewitnesses. Perhaps of even more interest to many, however, is the author's deep compassion for disaster victims, rescuers, and those involved in recovery and reconstruction efforts, and his ability to present his subjects in a way that instills a similar compassion in the reader. The 200-odd pages in this book realistically present misfortune, benevolence, and courage in a way that no novel ever could.

Reflecting the author's historical perspective, the first chapter describes the 1923 Great Kantō Earthquake, the second covers the 1995 Great Hanshin-Awaji Earthquake, and the third and fourth discuss the 2011 Great East Japan Earthquake and Tsunami. The reconstruction efforts following each of these events changed Japan's concept of disaster recovery, not to mention mitigation and reduction, and the systems and structures for administering reconstruction experienced revolutionary progress.

One hero during recovery from the Great Kantō Earthquake was Gotō Shinpei, whose ideas in today's language might be called "creative reconstruction." Rather than simply restore a destroyed Tokyo to its original state, his idea was to reform it as a modern capital city, creating opportunities for further development. As is well known, Gotō's plans suffered from drastic scale-backs due to financial difficulties, but the author describes how they provided considerable results nonetheless, thanks to the hard work of bureaucrats at various posts who were the successors to his teachings. Their endeavors realized Gotō's ideals to a considerable extent.

Chapter 2 is even more compelling, as might be expected since the author himself was a victim of the disaster described therein. His keyword here is "mutual aid," a depiction of how survivors helped others in their neighborhood community. Some 80 percent of survivors were rescued through such mutual aid efforts, leaving a legacy of countless beautiful stories. The activities of students from the (then) Kobe University of Maritime Sciences are truly touching, and the testimonies of municipal executives regarding the link between local festivals and disaster survival will remain long in my memory.

In reflection, we see a new philosophy of reconstruction that carries on Gotō's ideals of creative reconstruction, with guidance shifting from the central government to the hands of regional governing bodies. The late Hyōgo prefecture governor Kaihara Toshitami encouraged regional leaders through his independent establishment of the Hanshin-Awaji Earthquake Recovery Fund, and many research institutions and cultural facilities were later founded under similar ideals. This also marked the start of an "age of volunteerism," a spirit of mutual aid and spontaneous offering of individual service that spread throughout Japan.

In my personal view as a reader and resident of the Hanshin area, the hero of the fourth chapter is the author himself. While he writes of his experiences modestly, he well describes the tremendous confusion that the Reconstruction Design Council faced at the time, and we are able to observe the complex struggles that confronted the author as its leader. In facing down obstacles posed by a feeble government and the demands of self-serving committee members, the author faced many difficulties that literally kept him awake at night. The resulting "Towards Reconstruction: Hope beyond the Disaster" is a landmark document, a first-ever clear statement of creative reconstruction as a public goal and a declaration of the need for public funding to attain it. It was reflected as-is in public law, and assistance for private property—including the relocation of homes to higher grounds—became a legal guarantee for the first time.

The sixteen years between the Great Hanshin-Awaji and Great East Japan Earthquakes were a time of great change in the reconstruction and recovery environment. Both the police and the Japanese Self-Defense Forces have further enhanced their quick-response systems, and the Ministry of Land, Infrastructure, and Transport has better prepared for direct on-site recovery efforts. The author reliably describes how local governments intensified their consciousness related to disaster relief, with the Union of Kansai Governments, Suginami ward (Tokyo), Tōno city (Iwate prefecture), and others helping afflicted municipalities. Companies such as the Mitsubishi Corporation and Yamato Transport too made great contributions in their respective fields of expertise.

However, the author's brush most clearly depicts the humanity of individuals. Many Self-Defense Force members had family afflicted by the Great East Japan Earthquake—one even received his wife's telephoned cry for help immediately after the tsunami. Even so he heartrendingly continued his rescue efforts until receiving a second call in which his wife assured him of her safety, saying "I'm fine—you keep helping other people," a report that the author describes as "words from an angel."

Throughout the book, the author's love and hope for human beings remain undaunted. He believes in the potential for confronting an era of cataclysm and refuses to descend to cynical pessimism. In this sense, he is reminiscent of a great evangelist cheering on an ancient people, rescuing them from their bonds.

Yamazaki Masakazu

Introduction

1. Three Great Earthquakes

We are living in an unanticipated era of catastrophes. The 1995 Great Hanshin-Awaji Earthquake marked a shift in seismic activity on the Japanese archipelago from a relatively peaceful period to a highly active one. The 2011 Great East Japan Earthquake that occurred sixteen years later was a compound disaster in which a powerful earthquake followed by a massive tsunami caused unprecedented devastation. This is of particular concern because we cannot assume that this disaster represents a climax of earthquake activity during this period.

I experienced the Great Hanshin-Awaji Earthquake firsthand. My family and I were unharmed, but our house was completely destroyed. Kobe University—where I was a professor at the time—lost 39 students, including one of my own seminar students, Mori Wataru. In total, 6,434 people lost their lives in that event, something that was previously unimaginable against the peaceful backdrop of postwar Japan. Standing amid the destruction and misery of the disaster area, I was sure I would never again witness such a tremendous catastrophe—that such a thing would never again be allowed. Surely, I thought, we would rebuild and strengthen our society in such a way that we would never again experience such calamity.

As it turned out, that earthquake was not a once-in-a-lifetime event. Instead, it heralded a new era of catastrophic disasters.

There's an old proverb that says disasters come when we have forgotten the last one, but these days they do not leave time for forgetting. The

Great Hanshin-Awaji Earthquake was followed by the 2000 Tottori Earthquake (M 7.3), the 2004 Chūetsu Earthquake (M 6.8), and the 2008 Iwate-Miyagi Earthquake (M 7.2)—and that says nothing of landslides, typhoons, and other types of disasters. This series of disasters culminated in the 2011 Great East Japan Earthquake and its resulting enormous tsunami.

I wish to focus on three points here.

The first is that although we need to learn lessons from past disasters, our attention should not be dominated by the most recent major incident. Just as generals are said to fight their previous battle, focusing on a single past event allows nature to surprise us with new, unexpected avenues of attack. A stable disaster-preparedness stance requires that we keep at least three major precedents in mind. To that end, this book focuses on three representative earthquakes from Japan's recent history: the Great Kantō, Great Hanshin-Awaji, and Great East Japan Earthquakes. I examine these disasters with the goal of intellectually preparing for the many more earthquakes we will face in the future.

The three quakes I focus on primarily affected coastal areas, but we must also keep in mind large inland-type earthquakes such as the 1586 Tenshō Earthquake, which triggered a landslide that destroyed Kaerikumo castle and the surrounding town. It collapsed the Takaoka castle along the Sea of Japan and the Nagashima castle near the Pacific Ocean, and to the west it flattened the Nagahama castle near Lake Biwa.[1] Several active faults are believed to exist near the epicenter of this earthquake, and we must assume that the future will bring more movements in the Fossa Magna region and along the Japan Median Tectonic Line.

My second point of focus is nature's disregard for equality in her allocation of natural disasters. John Lewis Gaddis called the Cold War between the United States and the Soviet Union "the long peace," in the sense that no major wars erupted during this period. It was also a historically rare period of peace in Japan, thanks to security arrangements with the United States, the stalemate between the United States and the Soviet Union, and a postwar constitution that forbids warfare. Nature herself seemingly cooperated in this postwar cessation of hostilities, with the Japanese archipelago experiencing few major temblors. However, the end of the Cold War initiated a twenty-year period of seismic crisis, which began with the 1995 Great Hanshin-Awaji Earthquake. Such periodic alternation between quiet and active periods is a feature of the earth's inner workings.

My third focus is the question of whether the Great East Japan Earthquake was the grand finale to the period of seismic activity that began in Kobe. The vast region affected by the Great East Japan Earthquake and surrounding areas has experienced frequent aftershocks, and there remains significant concern that these movements have enlarged even faraway fissures, activating faults and volcanism across the country and raising the possibility of more catastrophes.

Recent years have brought rapid advances in our understanding of the mechanisms that lie behind earthquake occurrences, but scientific data remain scant, and new disciplines are only just arising. It is, after all, difficult to grasp what is happening so deep underground.

The Japanese archipelago is the meeting point of the Eurasian, North American, Pacific, and Philippine Plates. Japan's islands arose from the seams between these four plates. In simplified terms, the Pacific Plate slips under the North American Plate beneath eastern Japan at the truly rapid rate of ten centimeters each year. Some areas of the contact surface slip smoothly by, while others are stickier. When the latter type strains beyond what it can bear, the result is a sudden movement that becomes an oceanic plate earthquake and an accompanying tsunami.

This convergence of tectonic plates is a complicated affair, particularly beneath the Kantō region—so much so that it may be impossible to predict their interactions. Many factors will probably remain unforeseen until an event actually happens. Even so, scientists have made remarkable progress in earthquake research. Examples include new understandings of geophysical mechanisms, modeling by computer simulations, geological analysis of bore surveys, and precise measurements of the earth's movements through instruments installed underground and beneath the ocean floor. By combining these technologies with research on historical documents, scientists have been able to recreate past disasters and make predictions that were not possible until now.

To take one well-known example, the 1923 Great Kantō Earthquake was previously considered to have been a single large earthquake. However, a recent reevaluation of research by the Central Disaster Prevention Council showed that this disaster was actually three consecutive earthquakes that occurred over a period of six to seven minutes. Even the 869 Jōgan Sanriku Earthquake, an event from the ninth century, has fallen within our scope of reexamination.

Of course, not all of this data can be directly applied to the future, but analysis of past data provides a basis for clearer predictions of what may come. For that reason, I would like to review the periods of earthquake activity that we are aware of in the Japanese islands.

Because I am a historian and a political scientist, not a seismologist, this volume focuses more on Japan's history of dealing with these earthquakes

Map 0.1. Plate borders around the Japanese Archipelago
Source: https://www.static.jishin.go.jp/resource/figure/figure005048.jpg

than the mechanisms underlying them. What kind of tragic circumstances did those affected by the earthquakes encounter? How did frontline disaster response units and other sectors of government and society respond? How effective were political responses? What was the prevailing approach to recovery and reconstruction, and were creative solutions found? By answering these questions, I hope to explore our common destiny as those living in an era of disasters, and to consider how residents of this archipelago can live better lives, beyond the grasp of misery.

2. The Japanese Perspective on Natural Disasters

Before delving into modern theories of catastrophe, I wish to examine how the residents of Japan have related to nature and natural disasters throughout history.

Humanity has long engaged in agriculture, which is no less than the utilization of nature toward human ends. Nature on its own will produce fruit and grains, but human interventions such as irrigation make this phenomenon more efficient and geographically concentrated, improving the quantity and stability of natural production. This is true in both East and West, but human attitudes toward nature differ between those worlds.

The archetypal Western approach is to build stone houses that shut out nature. Nature is something to be excluded, avoided, suppressed, and conquered. Of course, Westerners love nature too, including it in their gardens and incorporating it in their city planning. However, in essence, they don't want to be controlled by nature. Rather, nature should serve human civilization, according to this view, and to make sure it does so, Western culture sets out to defeat it.

This isn't the case in Japanese culture. Since ancient times, the Japanese have been surrounded by the bounty provided by the four seasons. Nature is not an enemy to stand against. Traditional Japanese homes breathe the outside air rather than shut it out. Our homes were made from wood and grasses and earth. The inhabitants of Japan revered and coexisted with nature.

This contrast reminds me of my time at the National Defense Academy of Japan, where I had the opportunity to ride in both an F-15 fighter jet and a glider. The F-15 carves a path through the air, climbing at sharp angles in defiance of gravity. In contrast, a released glider can stay aloft for quite a long time, despite its lack of propulsion. The glider pilot told me there was a gently rising air current ahead and to the right of us, but I could see nothing. He was able to sense minute changes in air pressure on the craft and follow them to remain in the air. I believe that this is similar to the way that the Japanese long lived with nature.

From time to time, nature bares its claws and fangs and behaves with such violence that resistance is futile. One can only take cover and wait for the violence to pass. Thankfully, natural disasters are brief and transient.

The morning after a typhoon or a tsunami passed, the Japanese of olden days would hear the sound of hammers—houses being rebuilt in the same place, out of the same trees and grasses and earth as before—and life amid the bounty of nature would resume. This was the fundamental stance of the Japanese regarding natural disasters.

While the individual citizen may take a laissez-faire stance, however, the nation and society as a whole cannot. I once read a story about a young girl who had lost her family to a tsunami, screaming "I hate you! I hate you!" at the now-calm sea. Even if the government and its politicians can do nothing to ease such pain in the short term, they cannot ignore the issue forever. After all, it is only a matter of time before nature again turns violent, and the resulting human misery is compounded.

I believe that an unwritten contractual relationship exists between a government and its people. The people provide government with great powers, such as the ability to levy taxes and engage in military actions. But such powers are entrusted only so long as the government maintains public safety and promotes social welfare. Any government that fails to do so loses its legitimacy.

The degree of national tolerance varies by country and era, but this principle has a universality that spans both East and West. It is reflected both in the social contract theory of John Locke (1632–1704), and in the Asian concept of the Mandate of Heaven; should the powers that be fail to protect the common folk from foreign enemies or natural disasters, should farmers be forced to abandon their fields and become refugees, it is a sign that the government has lost the Mandate of Heaven, and should be replaced.

The government of an agricultural society must protect its land and farmers from natural disasters, and doing so requires flood control and irrigation. In the case of Yayoi Era Japan, some 2,000 years ago when agriculture got fully underway, this resulted in the rise of many small "countries." Initially, rural communities sought to increase and stabilize their harvests through irrigation ponds. Technological innovation in the Bronze and Iron Ages increased the scale of agriculture. Rivers were dammed, allowing for irrigation and flood control. This further increased the scale of agriculture and the concentration of power.

Afforestation and flood control ensure the economic survival of the people, making such tasks an important element for retaining the legitimacy of power. In the first half of the eighth century, when the monk Gyōki (668–749) built breakwaters and bridges to promote the well-being of commoners, governments began repairing the embankments along large rivers such as the Tenryū. Emperor Shōmu (701–56; reigned 724–49), a wise ruler of the time, followed Confucian and Buddhist thought in viewing disasters and plagues as heavenly warnings or punishments against rulers, and made every possible effort to accommodate those who were affected through good governance such as emergency relief, tax reduction, and amnesty.[2]

The 1611 Keichō Sanriku Earthquake was not particularly large, yet it produced an enormous tsunami. In the Sendai Date domain alone 1,783 people died, and there were over 3,000 fatalities in the Nanbu and Tsugaru domains along the Sanriku coast. (Since the Great East Japan Earthquake, there has been a movement among researchers to reevaluate the size and impact of the Keichō Sanriku Earthquake and Tsunami.)

In response to this, Date Masamune (1567–1636), a powerful lord with excellent planning abilities, poured resources into upgrading infrastructure along the Kitakami River and digging a canal. The Teizan Canal, which took Masamune's posthumous name, was a later realization of his original plans for a waterway along the inland side of coastal sand dunes connecting the Kitakami and Abukuma Rivers. It was both an economic artery for the transportation of rice and other goods, and a national land conservation project aimed at reducing tsunami damage. Indeed, in the 400 years between the 1611 Keichō Sanriku Earthquake and the 2011 Great East Japan Earthquake, no tsunami crossed the sand dunes and the Teizan Canal.

In the Higo region of western Japan, Katō Kiyomasa (1562–1611) improved flood control. The Shirakawa River flowing out of Mount Aso has long been a rapid river, and when waters ran high it was necessary to use the southern Kumamoto lowlands as a flood lake to protect the castle town. Kiyomasa strengthened Shirakawa River embankments using wall-building technologies also used in Kumamoto castle, and further improved Shirakawa River flood control through a water distribution network that directed the Tsuboi River to the castle moat. This enabled boats to travel as far as the Kumamoto castle moat from the sea, turned the southern Kumamoto lowlands into a grain-producing zone, and along with further rice field development is said to have raised local rice production from 540,000 to 730,000 *koku* (1 koku of rice equals about 280 liters). This flood-control project closely resembles modern national improvement projects aimed at enhancing safety, harvests, and water transport.

However, the most impressive land reconstruction projects for flood control were those implemented by the Edo shogunate in the Kantō region, beginning with those ordered by Tokugawa Ieyasu (1542–1616).

The Tone River flows into Edo (present-day Tokyo) Bay and was constantly overflowing. Extensive construction work redirected the river far away to Chōshi in the Shimousa area (today the northern part of Chiba prefecture and southwestern part of Ibaraki prefecture), transforming the low wetland area around Edo Bay into rice paddies and residential areas.

So, the powerful daimyō of the Warring States period were not only experts at warfare. To survive over the long term, they needed diplomacy to form wartime coalitions, but also the ability to develop the economy of their territory. When they reunified Japan toward the end of this period, Oda Nobunaga (1534–82) and Toyotomi Hideyoshi (1537–98)—both masters of nation-building and management—made the Kinki region their base. As they built new castles and cities, they depleted natural resources such as wood, exhausting regional forests. Tokugawa Ieyasu and his successors in turn abandoned the land that for a thousand years had served as Japan's capital city, instead utilizing the untouched Kantō wilderness surrounding Edo Bay to extract resources for large-scale civil-engineering works, thus building a new national center.

Political power and expansion led to the afforestation and flood-control projects needed in an agrarian society, and this power, supported by the steady supply of rice provided by an agricultural society, became the foundation for 250 years of peace. The Tokugawa regime was undoubtedly a politically mature agricultural society, but even with its numerous afforestation, flood-control, and rice-paddy development projects, the regime could support a population of only thirty million across the Japanese archipelago. This was perhaps the limit of a rice-based agricultural society.

From this perspective, we see that the government and people of Japan were long engaged in flood-control and irrigation projects aimed at developing agricultural society, and these projects reduced the country's vulnerability to disasters. Nonetheless, commoners living hand to mouth could not pick up and move to a sturdy house safe in the highlands just because a typhoon, earthquake, or tsunami destroyed their homes. Their only option was to rebuild the same house in the same location. Furthermore, despite ongoing advances in afforestation and flood-control technologies, there were limits to what these technologies could achieve, and it was often difficult to direct limited financial resources toward preparing for natural disasters that, as we have said, tend to come only after the last one has been forgotten.

In that sense, truly effective flood control was not possible until the advent of modern-day technological innovation.

3. Periods of Earthquake Activity in the Japanese Islands

The Japanese islands, which sit off the Asian mainland, were formed approximately 15 million years ago. Although earthenware from the Jōmon Era left behind by people has been found dating from about 13,000 years ago, it was only during the sixth and seventh centuries that the Japanese began to leave written records. What's more, it was only after the eighth and ninth centuries that records exist regarding the frequency of earthquakes, as appears in the *Chronology of Natural Sciences*,[3] edited by the National Institutes of Natural Sciences National Astronomical Observatory of Japan. It took a while, in other words, for those who could read and write to be found in all parts of the country, and thus to be able to record local events such as earthquakes and other disasters. Even if an earthquake happened, if no one was able to write about it, then the fact was never recorded. Below, I summarize the record of main earthquake activity over the past 1,300 years. Below are the years of specific earthquake activity during different eras.

Jōgan-Ninna Period: 863–87 (24 years)

Main events include the 869 Jōgan Sanriku Earthquake and Tsunami along the Sanriku coast, and the 887 Ninna Earthquake and Tsunami in the Nankai trough. Lead-up events include the 863 Ecchū-Echigo Earthquake, the 868 Harima Earthquake in the Yamasaki fault, and the 864 eruption of Mount Fuji.

The 869 Jōgan Sanriku Earthquake was very similar to the recent Great East Japan Earthquake, in that it was an offshore tremor causing a large tsunami to hit the Tōhoku region. Because of this, a Jōgan Earthquake scenario is being closely studied by experts. It also shifted faults that caused an earthquake in Kyoto, Japan's capital at the time. Eighteen years later came a related Nankai Trough Earthquake off Japan's southern coast. This was the 887 Ninna Earthquake and Tsunami, which finally signaled the end of this period of activity. Similarly, few researchers believe that the Great East Japan Earthquake will be the last major quake of the current period. Rather, they fear that there will be future earthquakes due to the stress built up along fault lines, and that after numerous inland earthquakes there will be an earthquake and tsunami originating in the Nankai trough in the next twenty to thirty years.

Tenshō-Keichō Period: 1586–1611 (25 years)

The Sengoku (Warring States) Era, particularly the Tenshō and Keichō Periods, was a time of great seismic activity. Within a span of just twenty-five years, four earthquakes of historic proportions struck Japan:

(1) In 1586 the inland Tenshō Earthquake struck the Hida region. Due to a large landslide, Kaerikumo castle and the town of 300 people surrounding it were completely wiped out. Moreover, the earthquake was so big that Takaoka castle near the Sea of Japan, Nagashima castle on the Pacific Ocean side, and Naga-hama castle on Lake Biwa were destroyed.

(2) In 1596, large earthquakes struck both sides of the huge fault called the Japan Median Tectonic Line. The first was the Keichō Bungo Earthquake on the western side, which caused half of Mount Takasaki on Beppu Bay to crumble and Uryū Island to sink. This was followed the next day by a movement of the Arima-Takatsuki Tectonic Line, resulting in the Keichō Fushimi Earthquake that collapsed Toyotomi Hideyoshi's Fushimi castle.

(3) In 1605 came the Keichō Earthquake and Tsunami, which evidence suggests was linked to a Nankai trough movement extending from the Tōkai region to Kyūshū.

(4) In 1611 came the Keichō Sanriku Earthquake and Tsunami, inundating an area that extended from the Sanriku region to Hokkaidō. The 2011 Great East Japan Earthquake and Tsunami, which came exactly 400 years later, was very similar.

For whatever reason, turbulent periods in political history such as the Sengoku Era, the Bakumatsu Period, and the periods of warfare in the twentieth century have been accompanied by similarly historic seasons of fierce earthquake activity.

Genroku-Hōei Period: 1700–1715 (15 years)

Main events include the 1703 Genroku-Kantō Earthquake in the Sagami trough and the 1707 Hōei Earthquake and Tsunami in the Nankai trough. Both were extremely large events, preceded and followed by inland earthquakes and even a violent eruption of Mount Fuji.

It should be pointed out that later that same century, in 1771, a large earthquake caused a massive tsunami that struck the islands of Ishigaki and Miyako in the Ryūkyū Islands (part of the longer Nansei Island chain). The Ryūkyū Trench, which lies on the eastern side of the Okinawan Islands and is very deep, follows the Japan Trench and Nankai trough and regularly causes earthquakes and tsunamis. The 1771 Meiwa Earthquake, which did not cause much damage itself, triggered a massive tsunami that did, reaching forty to eighty meters in height and caused the deaths of nearly 12,000 people (including those missing), or about a third of the local population. The disaster is known as the Great Yaeyama Tsunami, or the Great Tsunami of Meiwa.

Ansei Period: 1854–59 (5 years)

On December 23, 1854, the Ansei Tōkai Earthquake (M 8.4) shook Japan from the Kantō region to the Kinki region. This caused a tsunami that hit the southern coast from the Bōsō Peninsula to Ise Bay, causing between 2,000 and 3,000 fatalities and sinking the frigate *Diana* of Russian explorer Evfimii Putyatin (1804–83) in Shimoda Bay. Just thirty-two hours later came the 1854 Nankai Earthquake (M 8.4), which had an epicenter in the southern sea of the Kinki region and extended to the Chūbu region and Shikoku Island. The resulting tsunami measured fifteen meters high at Kushimoto and caused several thousand fatalities along the Kii Peninsula and the Shikoku coastline.

This Ansei Period Nankai Trough Earthquake did not immediately impact as broad a section of Japan as the Great East Japan Earthquake, but neither were its impacts limited to a narrow region. Instead, it played out over the course of a day and a half. It also lacked any semblance of a main quake–aftershock relationship; both earthquakes are estimated to have been M 8.4 events. It activated the Suruga trough, but that area has been quiescent in the 160 years since, even during Nankai trough events in 1944 and 1946. For this reason, experts have been watching the Suruga trough since the 1970s as an area in which a major event could occur at any time, and neighboring Shizuoka prefecture has taken exceptional preemptive measures against such an event.

Inland earthquakes occurred throughout Japan just before and after the Ansei Earthquake and Tsunami. On November 11, 1855, central Japan was rocked by the Edo Ansei Earthquake (M 6.9), which had its epicenter near the mouth of the Arakawa River estuary on northern Edo Bay. The resulting fires killed some 7,000 people, mainly in eastern Edo (Tokyo) locations such as Fukagawa and Honjo. In August of the following year, a large

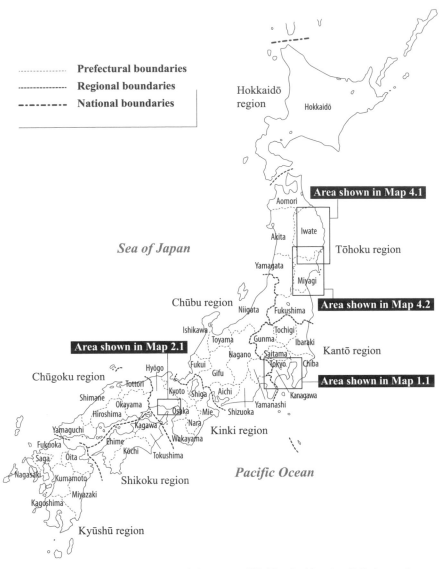

Map 0.2. Administrative and regional divisions of Hokkaidō, Honshū, Shikoku, and Kyūshū

typhoon hit the Kantō region, its strong winds and high waves causing extensive flooding and damage.

Global warming has increased the number of strong typhoons making landfall, so this sequence of events sends a foreboding message to disaster researchers. Indeed, "an era of catastrophes" is a better moniker for our times than "an era of earthquakes."

TABLE 0.1 Large earthquakes in Japan in recent years

Date	Name	Magnitude
January 17, 1995	Great Hanshin-Awaji Earthquake	7.3
October 6, 2000	Tottori Earthquake	7.3
March 24, 2001	Geiyo Earthquake	6.7
October 23, 2004	Chūetsu Earthquake	6.8
March 20, 2005	Fukuoka Earthquake	7.0
March 25, 2007	Noto Earthquake	6.9
July 16, 2007	Chūetsu Offshore Earthquake	6.8
June 14, 2008	Iwate-Miyagi Earthquake	7.2
March 11, 2011	Great East Japan Earthquake	9.0
April 16, 2016	Kumamoto Earthquake	7.3

Source: National Institutes of Natural Sciences National Astronomical Observatory of Japan (Ed.), *Chronological Scientific Tables*, etc.

In addition to the periods of historical seismic activity described above, one might add the twenty-five-year span from the Taishō to the Shōwa Period, which saw the 1923 Great Kantō Earthquake, the 1933 Shōwa Sanriku Tsunami, additional tsunamis in 1944 and 1946 at the east and west sides of the Nankai trough, and the 1948 Fukui Earthquake. However, some experts do not consider these events to be as closely associated as those in other periods of activity. In contrast, most would agree that the current period of high activity is just as remarkable as those of the past.

Heisei-Reiwa Period: 1995–

The 1995 Great Hanshin-Awaji Earthquake was followed by the Tottori, Chūetsu, and Iwate-Miyagi Earthquakes, then in 2011 by the largest earthquake and tsunami due to the Pacific Plate in recorded history. Since then, more earthquakes and volcanic eruptions have occurred, leading to the 2016 Kumamoto Earthquake and the Northern Osaka Earthquake in June 2018. As such, there is great fear that these inland earthquakes are a precursor to a Nankai Trough Earthquake in the next twenty to thirty years.

It goes without saying that although the period of Heisei ended in 2019, earthquakes, tsunamis, and other disasters do not obey any particular calendar.

ONE

The Great Kantō Earthquake

1. The Chain of Oceanic Plate and Inland Earthquakes

The mechanism behind earthquakes

Many readers will have no doubt felt an earthquake before, but most will have felt nothing beyond a 5 on the seismic intensity scale.

Such "typical" earthquakes generally start with a tremor that causes some rattling. You guess that an earthquake is coming and brace yourself as you wonder how large it will be. Some may cover their heads, or get under tables and desks as they should, or try to get out of the building if they can. The duration of that initial shaking is proportional to your distance from the epicenter. These slight but rapidly traveling "P-waves" (longitudinal waves) give advance notice of an earthquake. Suddenly, a strong shuddering occurs, signaling arrival of the "S-waves" (transverse waves). If the earthquake is of intensity[1] III or IV, you might think, "That was a pretty strong one," but you will be largely unperturbed. When an earthquake of intensity V Upper hits, however, it's a different story (see table 1.1). You feel like you're in danger, and seek shelter under a table as items start falling off shelves. Just as you think you're in serious trouble, the shaking starts to abate, and you are left with a stark reminder of the power of nature.

Most typical earthquakes give those experiencing them a warning, not a death sentence. But people in the Kantō region at the time of the Great East Japan Earthquake on March 11, 2011, had a very different experience. I had attended a meeting at the Ministry of Defense in Ichigaya, Tokyo, that day, and had just returned to the president's office at the National Defense Academy in Yokosuka when the initially weak, but long, fore-shocks hit. My first thought was that they signaled a powerful yet distant earthquake. A much stronger tremor arrived next, but it still felt within the range of a "typical" earthquake. However, at the point when a typical earthquake would have started to fade away, even stronger shakes arrived. The lights and the television blinked out. That's when I realized I was experiencing something new.

The Pacific Plate slips beneath the North American Plate, on which the Japanese archipelago rides, at the rapid rate of about eight to ten centimeters per year. In the Great East Japan Earthquake, a rupture that began 24 km underground and 130 km offshore from Miyagi prefecture extended north and south, causing further major ruptures in an offshore zone between Iwate and Fukushima prefectures that extended 500 km north to south and 200 km east to west. The earthquake had a magnitude of 9.0, making it the biggest earthquake ever recorded in the area around the Japanese archipelago.

Most large oceanic plate type earthquakes are not rupturing at a single fault, but rather span multiple faults in a wide area. The Great Hanshin-Awaji Earthquake that struck on January 17, 1995, was an example of earth-quake caused by single fault beneath; this M 7.3 quake followed a fault zone extending around 40 km from northern Awaji Island to the southern foot of Mount Rokkō. However, because this earthquake occurred in such close proximity (10–20 km) to the area between the major cities of Kobe and Osaka, its socially destructive power was much greater than that of the Great East Japan Earthquake. In the latter earthquake, the greatest intensity (the maximum level of VII) was felt 174 km from the epicenter in Kurihara city, Miyagi prefecture, and intensities of VI were felt across a broad swath of the three prefectures that comprise the Tōhoku region. Even so, nearly all of the approximately 20,000 fatalities were the result of the tsunami; only a few people were killed due to collapsing structures. In contrast, most of the several thousand fatalities in the Great Hanshin-Awaji Earthquake were due to building collapse, a statistic that illustrates the difference between offshore and inland earthquakes of equal intensity VII.

When an earthquake strikes from directly below, there is no leading shockwave like the one I described in the typical case—just a sudden jolt. The shock that hit my house during the Great Hanshin-Awaji Earthquake was so great I initially thought that an airplane had crashed onto it, or that we had been hit by a landslide. Further powerful jolts came as I struggled to wake up and figure out what was happening. I soon realized it was an

TABLE 1.1 Japan Meteorological Agency Seismic Intensity Scale

Human perception and reaction, indoor situation, outdoor situation

Seismic intensity	Human perception and reaction	Indoor situation	Outdoor situation
0	Imperceptible to people, but recorded by seismometers.	—	—
1	Felt slightly by some people keeping quiet in buildings.	—	—
2	Felt by many people keeping quiet in buildings. Some sleeping people may be awakened.	Hanging objects such as lamps swing slightly.	—
3	Felt by most people in buildings and some people walking. Many sleeping people are awakened.	Dishes in cupboards may rattle.	Electric wires swing slightly.
4	Most people are startled. Felt by most people walking. Most sleeping people are awakened.	Hanging objects such as lamps swing significantly, and dishes in cupboards rattle. Unstable ornaments may fall.	Electric wires swing significantly. Those driving vehicles may notice the tremor.
5 Lower	Many people are frightened and feel the need to hold on to something stable.	Hanging objects such as lamps swing violently. Dishes in cupboards and items on bookshelves may fall. Many unstable ornaments fall. Unsecured furniture may move, and unstable furniture may topple over.	In some cases, windows may break and fall. People notice electricity poles moving. Roads may be damaged.
5 Upper	Many people find it hard to move; walking is difficult without holding on to something stable.	Dishes in cupboards and items on bookshelves are more likely to fall. TVs may fall from their stands, and unsecured furniture may topple over.	Windows may break and fall, unreinforced concrete-block walls may collapse, poorly installed vending machines may topple over, and automobiles may stop due to the difficulty of continued movement.
6 Lower	It is difficult to remain standing.	Many pieces of unsecured furniture move and may topple over. Doors may become wedged shut.	Wall tiles and windows may sustain damage and fall.

TABLE 1.1—*Continued*

Human perception and reaction, indoor situation, outdoor situation

Seismic intensity	Human perception and reaction	Indoor situation	Outdoor situation
6 Upper	It is impossible to remain standing or move without crawling. People may be thrown through the air.	Most unsecured furniture moves, and is more likely to topple over.	Wall tiles and windows are more likely to break and fall. Most unreinforced concrete-block walls collapse.
7		Most unsecured furniture moves and topples over, or may even be thrown through the air.	Wall tiles and windows are even more likely to break and fall. Reinforced concrete-block walls may collapse.

Notes:

1. As a rule, seismic intensities announced by JMA are values observed using seismic-intensity meters installed on the ground or on the first floors of low-rise buildings. This document describes the phenomena and damage that may be observed for individual seismic-intensity levels. Seismic intensities are not determined based on the observed phenomena described here.

2. Seismic ground motion is significantly influenced by underground conditions and topography. Seismic intensity is the value observed at a site where a seismic-intensity meter is installed, and may vary even within the same city. In addition, the amplitude of seismic motion generally differs by floor and location within the same building, as shaking on upper floors may be considerably amplified.

3. Sites with the same level of seismic intensity will not necessarily suffer the same degree of damage, as the effect of tremors depends on the nature of the seismic motion (such as amplitude, period, and duration), the type of construction, and underground conditions.

4. This document describes typical phenomena that may be seen at individual levels of seismic intensity. In some cases, the level of damage may be greater or less than specified. Not all phenomena described for each intensity level necessarily occur.

5. The information outlined here is regularly checked at intervals of about five years, and is updated in line with actual phenomena observed in new cases or with improvements in the earthquake resistance of buildings and structures.

Source: https://www.jma.go.jp/jma/en/Activities/inttable.html, slightly edited by author.

earthquake, but nothing like the tame ones I had experienced before. It felt like a giant had lifted my home and was trying to rip it apart, with no intent of stopping until the house and everyone in it was destroyed. There seemed to be murderous intent in the earth's shaking. My house squealed as it deformed into a diamond shape, and even in the dark I could sense furniture flying about. Had I and the other three members of my family not been sleeping in a bed upstairs, I don't know if we would have survived. The phantom giant continued to shake my house for what seemed like several minutes. When I later read in official reports that the tremors only lasted twenty seconds, I could hardly believe it. Now I know the extent to which life-or-death situations distort time.

For those without firsthand experience of an earthquake occurring directly below them, I think it is particularly hard to understand what that first vertical shock feels like. The awesome power is so great that it can toss houses and trains up off the ground. In the Great Hanshin-Awaji Earthquake, a horizontal movement came while things were still up in the air, throwing a piano that was in a southern corner of our living room against the northern wall. The earthquake hit at 5:46 a.m., so thankfully the trains were not running yet; they were first thrown upward, and then the immediate horizontal shift knocked them off the rails so cleanly that they didn't even leave scratches. In two-story homes built in the traditional Japanese fashion, this upward-sideways motion toppled central supporting pillars. The many houses throughout my city that collapsed diagonally provided ample evidence of this process.

Earthquakes in which both types of tremors are felt

The above section compared the shaking during oceanic plate and direct inland earthquakes. So which kind did those feel who experienced the Great Kantō Earthquake of September 1, 1923?

Of course, residents of Tokyo did not experience the same thing as those living in neighboring Kanagawa prefecture, and even within Tokyo, those who lived on soft lower ground had a very different experience than those on higher ground. The Great Kantō Earthquake had characteristics of both offshore and inland earthquakes.

This earthquake was caused by a long fault in the shallow ocean area called the Sagami trough. In that sense, it was related to oceanic plates. Unlike the 2011 Great East Japan Earthquake, however, it did not occur far offshore, but rather somewhat inland from the Sagami Bay at the Shōnan coast. Modern research has suggested an epicenter approximately 10 km north of Odawara. This is some 100 km from Tokyo, but keep in mind that it was on a broad, trench-type fault. While the initial rupture occurred at Odawara, a second shock hit the other side of the bay at the lower Miura Peninsula around ten seconds later. Considering that the resulting tsunami reached twelve meters at Atami and nearly nine meters at the tip of the Bōsō Peninsula,[2] one can only assume that the second rupture had extended beneath Sagami Bay and triggered the tsunami.

The two shocks hit Tokyo as a single large earthquake consisting of a violent main tremor following the equivalent of a foreshock from 100 km away. The quake was so strong that seismograph needles across Tokyo, including at Tokyo Imperial University's Earthquake Research Institute, literally moved off the scale, making measurements impossible. The ground undulated so severely that it was difficult to remain standing. Initial estimates indicated a magnitude of 7.9, but recalculations in recent years suggest that it was around M 8.1.

Those experiencing the 1923 Great Kantō Earthquake endured a very long period of shaking. Just when they thought it was finally over, the residents of Tokyo were hit by another violent shock, an M 7.2 earthquake centered beneath the north end of Tokyo Bay that came just three minutes after the first one. This second direct hit rivaled the M 7.3 Great Hanshin-Awaji Earthquake. Numerous reports suggest that the second quake had stronger but less prolonged ground motions than the first. Such observations support an oceanic plate earthquake of around M 8.0 across a broad area, followed by a second brief earthquake beneath Tokyo. But even that wasn't the end: two minutes later, a third M 7.3 earthquake hit Yamanashi prefecture.

Earthquake prediction and scientific research

Criticism is sometimes directed at the large amount of government funds spent on the seemingly impossible goal of earthquake prediction. Indeed, no major earthquake disaster—including the Hanshin and Tōhoku events—has ever been scientifically predicted.

Abnormal phenomena are often viewed, in hindsight, as precursors to large earthquakes. For example, the classic *Great Tsunami of the Sanriku Coast*³ by Yoshimura Akira (1927–2006) claims that tsunamis in both the Meiji and Shōwa Periods were preceded by bountiful catches due to enormous schools of fish, and that remarkable variations occurred in the water levels of wells. However, I am aware of no such abnormalities before the 2011 Great East Japan Earthquake. While there are many possible signs of an impending earthquake, they do not always come, and when they do come they may not mean that an earthquake is imminent.

Although we have not yet succeeded in predicting earthquakes, research carried out toward that end has advanced greatly, and we have made marked progress in elucidating the mechanisms by which earthquakes occur. There have been other kinds of scientific advances as well; for example, the Great East Japan Earthquake led to a new Shinkansen braking system that safely stops trains on receiving an alert by the Earthquake Early Warning System.

Scientific advances have also helped to reveal the past. For instance, reinterpretations over the past two decades have contributed to our understanding of how the 1923 Great Kantō Earthquake occurred and developed.

Although seismograph needles in the Tokyo area were rendered inoperable during the Great Kantō Earthquake, needles in six other locations across Japan continued to function, and it was analysis of initial tremors (P-waves) from these that led scientists to realize that the event was a dual earthquake. Indeed, the first volume of the *1923 Great Kantō Earthquake Disaster Report*[4] (hereafter *Great Kantō Earthquake Report*), compiled in 2006 by a special investigative commission, is based on the results of research conducted in recent years.

Specifically, the epicenter was around ten kilometers north of Odawara and around twenty-five kilometers underground, causing a large underground rupture in the Odawara area. Another large rupture occurred beneath the Miura Peninsula approximately ten seconds later. Both earthquakes occurred along the Sagami trough, where the Philippine Plate slips at a rate of three to five centimeters per year beneath the North American Plate, on which eastern Japan sits. The Philippine Plate borders both the North American Plate and the Pacific Plate and is surprisingly shallow; recent research suggests that it lies about twenty kilometers below the area around Tokyo Bay. Contact surfaces between these plates move in a chain reaction. As described above, an inland fault triggered an M 7.2 earthquake beneath Tokyo three minutes later, and an M 7.3 earthquake in Yamanashi prefecture two minutes after that.

Personal reports support conclusions from the reanalysis of the Great Kantō Earthquake. The *Great Kantō Earthquake Report*[5] contains an account from an Odawara resident who reported hearing a sudden loud noise, accompanied by vertical tremors so powerful that items indoors bounced thirty-six centimeters high. The resident's house began to tilt and the floor collapsed. He crawled out, and when he made it outside the shaking was so bad he was tossed about. Then his house collapsed.

There were no foreshocks in the Odawara area, just a sudden upward jolt. This was exactly what we experienced in the Great Hanshin-Awaji Earthquake, and suggests that a large earthquake with a seismic intensity of VII started in this area. A contrasting report by teachers at the Fujisawa Elementary School at the base of the Miura Peninsula recounted the following:

1. The ground began to shake, but it didn't seem out of the ordinary, so they waited for it to subside.
2. Then came a violent vertical motion, and they realized this was something different. Cabinets fell, windows shattered, and specimens in the science classroom bounced about. They hurried to escape to the schoolyard through a window.

Figure 1.1. Ninety percent of Odawara was destroyed in the Great Kanto Earthquake (1923)

3. The air was filled with dust clouds. When they were able to open their eyes, they watched their school collapse. Somebody was crying for help.

The shaking in statement 1 indicates the arrival of P-waves from Odawara, forty kilometers away, which were weak enough to make people think they could wait the earthquake out. Statements 2 and 3 relate the arrival of the primary motion (S-waves) from Odawara, and ten seconds later a second earthquake directly beneath the Miura Peninsula itself, which collapsed the school building.

This earthquake is called the "Great Kantō Earthquake" because the damage spread far in the direction of the Kantō region, but from the perspective of earthquake mechanisms it could be called the Sagami Trough Earthquake, or, from the perspective of its epicenter, the Shōnan Earthquake.

2. Horrific Disaster Sites

Yokohama at the epicenter

Regarding the damage situation in Yokohama, which was closer to the epicenter than Tokyo and thus experienced more severe shocks, the *Great Kantō Earthquake Report*[6] shows that there was a clear difference in the rates of building collapse between hilly regions and areas of landfill over what had once been ocean or valleys. While the former had collapse rates of 30 percent, in the latter rates exceeded 50 percent, and even 80 percent in some areas. In addition to distance from the epicenter, therefore, the solidity of the underlying ground significantly affected the fates of the people and buildings atop it.

Another well-known work by Yoshimura Akira, *The Great Kantō Earthquake*,[7] quotes the memoirs of a foreign screenwriter who witnessed the event in Yokohama, where he had rented a house in the hilly district. The earthquake struck on his moving day, just as he, his wife, and a porter had crested a hill.

> There suddenly arose a roar and a mighty wind. The ground rocked back and forth as if crazed, throwing my wife and myself in different directions. Looking about, I saw everything around me shaking with a great noise. Homes collapsed, along with stone walls. The ground shook and heaved like the ocean, and it felt like I was floating about on a body of water. Finally, the earthquake ceased. When I came to myself, I found that I was grasping a hedge with one hand and holding my wife with the other. I saw a woman being pulled from beneath a collapsed house. She was still alive. I thought about death, and how if I were to die, I didn't want to be separated from my wife. Another strong earthquake then hit, and again the earth shook as if enraged. The Japanese were amazingly composed. Women and children gathered in a large nearby garden, but none caused a commotion or fell into a panic. Parents greeted one another, and children obediently remained near their mothers, even as the ground heaved like a ship at sea.

As this account shows, the earthquake hit hard, even in hilly areas, and after everyone thought the earthquake had ended another powerful one struck. This account also shows that, just as in the case of the Great Hanshin-Awaji and Great East Japan Earthquakes, the world was amazed by the calm, commendable behavior of Japanese disaster victims.

Of course, some may disagree, citing as evidence the massacres by vigilante groups that followed the Great Kantō Earthquake. This is an example of a pathological phenomenon in which survivors lose their mental balance due to the impact of a major disaster, shifting from excessive awareness of the damage to excessive defense. Such individuals always appear after a traumatic event, but only in small numbers. Both now and then, most Japanese quietly accept their circumstances, even when they are in the depths of misery, and demonstrate the strength of their social bonds by working to help others. (We will discuss the massacres in more detail below.)

Let me briefly summarize the disaster situation in Yokohama based on official findings, namely the *History of Yokohama City Earthquake Disaster*, Vol. 1.[8] Far from taking the cold tone typical of public documents, this report overflows with vivid scenes and emotions.

> There was a sudden rumbling like distant thunder, followed immediately by the ground heaving like large waves. . . . When I ran outside and saw all the things that had fallen to the ground, I wondered if this was the end of human life. . . . Many did not have time to run and found themselves trapped. . . . The Kannai area, at the city center, had been a landfill site since the port opened. The ground was therefore weak, and very many buildings there collapsed. . . . At the Yokohama District Court . . . over one hundred people died, including the Chief Justice. . . . Ninety workers at the Yokohama Post Office and around fifty at the Customs Agency were cruelly crushed. . . . Beautiful buildings such as the Oriental Palace Hotel and the Grand Hotel . . . collapsed, painfully crushing to death dozens of both Japanese and foreigners. . . . The narrow streets and old brick buildings . . . in Chinatown . . . led to the deaths of two thousand people, representing over one-third of the residents there [this district had the highest fatality rate in Yokohama]. . . . The firmer ground in the three hilly regions surrounding the city significantly reduced the damage to towns there, but there was extensive damage in the town of Yamate, where many Westerners resided. . . . This happened because much of the ground there was landfill, upon which large buildings such as hospitals, schools, churches, mansions, and hotels were built, and all of these collapsed. . . . Many Western educators and ministers were crushed within.

> Just after this fearsome earthquake drained people of energy, fires broke out at dozens of locations within the city. Some ignited immediately, others around an hour later. . . . According to a Yokohama

Local Meteorological Office investigation . . . fires broke out at 289 locations, and a strong southwesterly wind . . . fanned the flames . . . and by 5:00 p.m. . . . most of the city was aflame. Furthermore, large whirlwinds occurred in twenty locations. . . . The flames came so quickly that parents were forced to watch children trapped under debris burn, unable to rescue them. Husband and wife, brother and sister together shared unimaginable suffering.

All told, 24,000 people—5 percent of the population of Yokohama—died or were never found. As for homes, 20 percent collapsed, and 60 percent burned.

Tokyo during the combined disaster

Turning our attention to Tokyo, the *Great Kantō Earthquake Report*[9] includes many eyewitness accounts from eminent persons such as Watsuji Tetsurō (1889–1960), Imamura Akitsune (1870–1948), and Terada Torahiko (1878–1935).

For example, Watsuji recounts that the first tremors came as he was finishing lunch with his family. Because the shaking was so strong, he ran out to the garden. The second floor swayed some ninety centimeters. When it ceased, he and his family took refuge in an empty lot. The house across the street collapsed. Soon after, they heard an eerie rumbling, and the second set of strong shakes began. When they subsided, the family returned to their home to retrieve shoes and the like. The third wave of shaking came as soon as they returned to the empty lot.

Many of these eyewitness accounts concur that there were three earthquakes, and that the first set was stronger and lasted longer than the second. Terada reported that "the second earthquake was even stronger than the first, so I was surprised twice," and Imamura states, "I was surprised by the sudden, strong aftershocks. The one that came about three minutes after the first was particularly strong." That aftershock was actually an inland earthquake centered beneath northern Tokyo Bay. However, these testimonies come from people who were in the western half of Tokyo, on relatively stable ground, and did not lose their homes. The situation was much direr in the lowland areas between the rivers of eastern Tokyo.

The above-mentioned *Great Kantō Earthquake*[10] by Yoshimura includes the recollections of two boys. One is Masao, a fourteen-year-old watchmaker who was at an Asakusa movie theater with a friend, watching a Western. He states that as they were watching the cowboys' skillful gunplay and

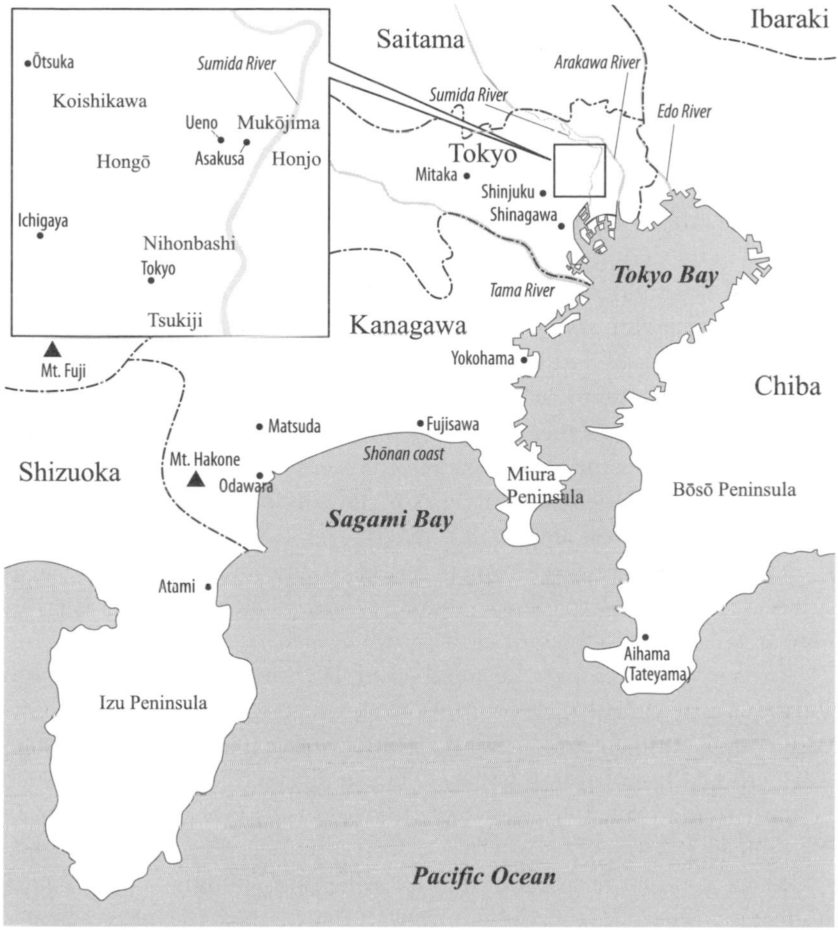

Otsuka

Koishikawa

Sumida River

Saitama

Arakawa River

Ibaraki

Sumida River

Edo River

Ueno Mukōjima

Hongō Asakusa Honjo

Tokyo

Mitaka

Shinjuku

Shinagawa

Ichigaya

Nihonbashi

Tokyo

Tama River

Tokyo Bay

Tsukiji

Kanagawa

Yokohama

Chiba

▲

Mt. Fuji

Matsuda

Fujisawa

Shōnan coast

Shizuoka

Mt. Hakone

▲ Odawara

Miura
Peninsula

Bōsō Peninsula

Sagami Bay

Atami

Aihama
(Tateyama)

Izu Peninsula

Pacific Ocean

Map 1.1. Main areas affected by the Great Kantō Earthquake

"listening to their cool talk," he and his friend "were suddenly launched into the air." Screams came from the balcony, which fell to the floor below. Theatergoers jumped from their seats and scrambled for the exit. Masao and his friend squeezed through the crowd and somehow made their way outside. He clung to a support post in front of a sushi shop, but the post was wobbling, along with the entire shop. When the tremors weakened, he escaped from the alley he was in, but the corner tempura shop collapsed, and beneath the rubble he saw a man whose eye had popped out of its socket. It was the first time he had ever seen a dead person. He ran toward a pond along a road that was flowing like a viscous liquid and encountered an unbelievable sight: the Ryōunkaku—a twelve-story building that was the symbol of Tokyo at the time—began listing, and its upper portion broke off and fell. The sound and vibration as it hit the ground sent shudders through Masao's entire body.

Another story comes from an elementary-school student who was in Honjo ward (present-day Sumida ward), the site of the worst destruction. September 1 was the first day of a new semester, so the children were released early, and he was playing at a friend's house. He left at around noon and was suddenly thrown up into the air and onto the road. Tiles slid off surrounding roofs, walls crumbled, and houses swayed and collapsed into clouds of dust before his eyes. His home, just ten houses down, was unreachable due to rubble blocking the road. Unable to proceed, he crawled to the main street and clung for dear life to a tree in front of a military uniform factory. Someone put their hand on his shoulder—one of the ten or so workmen at his father's metalworking shop—and informed him that his house was already destroyed.

The tremors were very strong in the Tokyo lowlands, possibly as bad as in the description of Yokohama above. By today's standards, it was probably an intensity VI Upper or closer to a VII quake.

Former estimates put the number of fatalities in the Great Kantō Earthquake at around 140,000. More recent research, however, has eliminated duplicate counts, reducing the number to 105,385. Of these, 11,086 were crushed by collapsing homes. The number of direct casualties such as these is approximately twice that from the 1995 Great Hanshin-Awaji Earthquake (5,502).[11]

There were more fatalities due to collapsing buildings in Kanagawa prefecture, where Yokohama is located (5,795), than in Tokyo (3,546). Adding in deaths due to tsunamis, avalanches, and collapsing workplaces,

TABLE 1.2 The Great Kantō Earthquake fatalities by prefecture [persons]

Prefecture	Crushed, etc.	Drowned	Factory damage, etc.	Subtotal	Burned	Total
	Nonfire				Fire	
Kanagawa	5,795	836	1,006	7,637	25,201	32,838
Tokyo	3,546	6	314	3,866	66,521	70,387
Chiba	1,255	0	32	1,287	59	1,346
Shizuoka	150	171	123	444	0	444
Saitama	315	0	28	343	0	343
Total	11,086	1,013	1,505	13,604	91,781	105,385

Source: Disaster Management Cabinet Office, *1923 Great Kantō Earthquake Disaster Report*, Vol. 1.

•Numbers used as-is from the source.

there were 7,637 casualties in Kanagawa and 3,866 in Tokyo. Earthquake damage in Kanagawa was thus approximately twice that in Tokyo.

Damage closely followed the pattern of being worst in concentric rings around the epicenter, with the effects of ground type playing a secondary role; as mentioned above, lowland areas of Tokyo near old rivers had rates of building collapse similar to those of areas in Yokohama closer to the origin.

The 11,086 fatalities by collapsed buildings exceed the total fatalities from the 1891 Nōbi Earthquake (7,273 deaths) and the directly related fatalities from the 1995 Great Hanshin-Awaji Earthquake (6,434 deaths, including disaster-related deaths). They alone would make the Great Kantō Earthquake the second-largest natural disaster in modern Japanese history, following the 1896 Meiji Sanriku Tsunami (21,959 deaths). Yet they only comprise one portion of the overall damage from the Great Kantō Earthquake, which was a compound disaster. While 13,604 people died as a direct result of debris or drowning, to 91,781 died in fires.

One reason for this was timing. The Great Kantō Earthquake hit just two minutes before noon, when many people were preparing lunch. Today we use electric and gas appliances, but at the time people prepared rice over open flame. It is therefore no surprise that collapsing houses caught fire at well over 100 locations throughout Tokyo. At least 70 to 80 of those could not be extinguished, and instead spread.

By the time of the Great Hanshin-Awaji Earthquake, almost no one cooked over open flames, and the earthquake hit in the early morning, when few people were cooking. Even so, some collapsing houses did catch fire. In fact, 256 fires were reported, 17 of which grew large. In some cases, the fires were caused by heating stoves or electric appliances; in others, shaking and collapsed homes caused shorts in snapping power lines that triggered fires. An unexpectedly common trigger was gas escaping from underground pipes and being ignited by electric sparks. In other cases, restoring power after blackouts also started fires.

We live in a different era from that of the Great Kantō Earthquake, and thus worry less about earthquakes causing fires. But this is a mistake. Seventeen fires spread in the Great Hanshin-Awaji Earthquake, and it was only thanks to the windless weather that day that these fires killed less than 10 percent as many people as collapsing buildings.

Conversely, strong winds were responsible for the fact that fire killed nine times as many people as building collapse in the Great Kantō Earthquake. The day, on September 1 afternoon, wind speeds in Tokyo were between ten and fifteen meters per second. During the morning, winds

Figure 1.2. *Whirlwind*, an oil painting by Tokunaga Ryūshū following the Great Kantō Earthquake. Figures are portrayed as if they've been thrown. More hands and legs stretch from the rubble at the bottom (From the collection of the Tokyo Memorial Hall).

were not so strong as to preclude leaving home. I know of no testimonies that describe strong winds before the earthquake hit. There was light rainfall in the morning, but it had cleared up by noon, when the shaking began.

The day before, on August 31, a typhoon had made landfall on the island of Kyūshū, on its way from the Ariake Sea to the Sea of Japan. On the day of the earthquake it turned back to hit the Kanazawa area, but weakened to a tropical depression by afternoon and was moving through the northern Kantō region toward the Pacific Ocean. A secondary depression had formed in the Chichibu area. As a result, winds exceeding ten meters per second blew as if to fan the flames throughout Tokyo, with their directions swiftly changing—southerly winds becoming westerly, then northerly.

Most frightening of all is that when winds fan a large fire, cyclones of flames can form. The heat creates an upward draft, which accelerates wind speeds and lifts urban detritus up into the air. The result is a black pillar of fire that writhes about, spewing flame. One of these cyclones landed on a large empty lot—the former site of a military uniform depot—where 40,000 people had taken refuge, bringing with them their prized family possessions. The entire area was reduced to a mountain of charred corpses within seconds.

In large cities, it is difficult to avoid fires caused by earthquakes. However, the true culprit in disasters like the Great Kantō Earthquake is strong winds. Tokyo's history is replete with large fires caused by windy conditions. Three fire sources combined with such winds were enough to wipe out all of Edo [Tokyo] in the Great Meireki Fire of 1657. Following that disaster, the Edo government improved both hard and soft fire-prevention systems to prevent large fires even under strong winds. Water systems, too, were improved, so most people probably believed that the great fires of old Edo were a thing of the past. They did not realize that those water systems would be destroyed and rendered ineffective in a large earthquake. Unfortunately, the firefighting techniques of Edo had been largely forgotten.

3. The Great Meireki Fire of the Edo Period

Sixty percent of the city in flames

A traditional Japanese saying holds that the most frightening things in the world are "earthquakes, lightning, fires, and fathers." Fathers are not quite so intimidating as they once were, and while lightning can be impressive, it does not cause large numbers of casualties. Most Japanese who experienced the 2011 Great East Japan Earthquake would probably not hesitate to add tsunamis to the top of the list.

But do tsunamis represent the most severe disasters ever to hit the Japanese archipelago?

As the casualty list in table 1.3 shows,[12] no single earthquake has caused more than 10,000 deaths independent of fires or other compounding factors, placing them in fourth place or lower. Second and third place, each with casualties on the order of 20,000 people, are held by tsunamis. The Great Kantō Earthquake is in first place, with over 100,000 fatalities, 90 percent of which were caused by fires.

As described above, the unfortunately timed arrival of a typhoon and tropical depression turned this into the worst disaster in modern Japanese history. As mentioned above, however, this was not the only time that wind-induced conflagrations have occurred in Japan.

Japanese towns were susceptible to fire for three reasons. First, people prepared their meals over open flames, so fire sources were part of their daily life. This was the case through the 1960s, when gas and electricity became standard home features. The second factor was the concentration of the population in large cities such as Kyoto, Osaka, and Edo. Finally, most Japanese homes were built using wood and grass, making them particularly flammable. Given these three conditions, it is no wonder that fires fanned by strong winds could grow out of control.

There were many large fires in Kyoto and Osaka, but there were even more in Edo. Tokugawa Ieyasu made Edo his primary base of operations in 1590, and established his shogunate there in 1603, three years after his victory at Sekigahara. After doing so, the shōgun ordered his daimyō to help build the city and castle of Edo through its *tenka bushin* (realm construction) projects. These were finally completed in the Kanei Period (1624–44), at which time the population of Edo was approximately 300,000 people.

During this time, in 1601, a fire in the Surugachō part of the Nihonbashi district developed into a major blaze. The fire spread by leaping from thatched roof to thatched roof, so the shōgun ordered that buildings switch to using wooden shingles. Of course, wood, too, is flammable, albeit not to the extent of straw thatching. Tile roofs would have been best, of course, but tiling at the time was quite expensive, not to mention heavy. In fact, the collapse of buildings in the 1649 Keian Edo Earthquake led to a ban on tile shingles.[13]

Then came the Great Meireki Fire of March 2, 1657.

TABLE 1.3 The six worst post-Meiji earthquakes

Rank	Year	Name	Magnitude	Fatalities [persons]
1	1923	Great Kantō Earthquake	7.9	105,385
2	1896	Meiji Sanriku Earthquake	8.5	21,959
3	2011	Great East Japan Earthquake	9.0	19,418; 2,592 missing
4	1891	Nōbi Earthquake	8.0	7,273
5	1995	Great Hanshin-Awaji Earthquake	7.3	6,434
6	1948	Fukui Earthquake	7.1	3,728

Notes: Fatalities of the Great Hanshin-Awaji Earthquake and the Great East Japan Earthquake are including disaster-related deaths.

Source: Disaster Management Cabinet Office, *1923 Great Kantō Earthquake Disaster Report*, Vol. 1, National Institutes of Natural Sciences National Astronomical Observatory of Japan (Ed.), *Chronological Scientific Tables 2017*, etc.

Following an eighty-day drought, Edo was as dry as tinder. A northwest wind that had been blowing since the day before had reached gale force. At 2:00 p.m., a fire broke out at the Honmyō temple in Hongō (it is sometimes called "the Kimono Fire" because legend claims it started from a kimono being burned there). It rapidly spread from north to south, jumping ahead of, cutting off, and burning many of those attempting to flee. The fire then split in two directions, one heading farther south, where it burned Nihon-bashi, and the other following the west wind to jump across the Sumida River. At the seaside Reigan temple, some 10,000 people sheltering there lost their lives. The flames finally died down at around 2:00 a.m.

The next day, however, another fire broke out in Koishikawa. A strong wind from the north carried the flames to Ichigaya and Banchō, and by early afternoon the main keep of Edo castle was burning. Mansions belonging to daimyō and bannermen were engulfed in flame, and at around 4:00 p.m. a westerly wind arose that saved the western keep. That night, a third fire broke out among the homes in Kōjimachi, and daimyō mansions surrounding the western keep and extending to Sakurada burned. The fire finally burned out after traveling south to Shibaura.[14]

In the end, just three fires burned down approximately 60 percent of the city of Edo, causing some 100,000 fatalities. This is an incredible figure, considering that Edo's population at the time was less than 500,000.

The shogunate's response

The shogunate's response to the Great Meireki Fire is of particular interest. Hoshina Masayuki (1611–72), regent of the fourth shōgun Tokugawa Ietsuna (1641–80), implemented emergency response measures such as providing porridge, releasing roasted rice from damaged stores, and enacting measures to prevent sudden price increases for rice and timber. He furthermore lent and donated funds and ensured that money flowed from daimyō, bannermen, and vassal families to the Edo townspeople.

The shogunate also engaged in urban-planning projects. The crowded, twisted streets of a wartime defensive city were reshaped into something more suited to the mass consumerism of a peacetime capital. The daimyō were commanded to reconstruct Edo castle, and were provided with replacement land to relocate from within the castle and along its moat to new locations in the suburbs. Along with the bannermen and vassals, temples and shrines were relocated from the castle grounds to Asakusa, Tsukiji, and Honjo. Tama-area towns such as Kichijōji and Mitaka were created as a result of these relocations.

Prior to the fire some 60 percent of the land in Edo belonged to samurai families, with the remaining 40 percent split between townspeople and shrines or temples. Postdisaster relocations relieved this congestion of land ownership within the city, expanded its borders, and, later, greatly increased its population.

Citizens too were relocated to allow construction of embankments and broad avenues along rivers and waterways, which acted as firebreaks. Firefighting at the time mainly took the form of tearing down downwind buildings before fire could spread, and these improvements heightened the effect of such efforts. Plastering of structures was also promoted as a fire-prevention measure.

More important still were the societal reforms that took place. In 1658, the year after the Great Meireki Fire, the shogunate had established four fire brigades called *jōbikeshi* composed of bannermen. In 1704 this was increased to ten brigades. Daimyō firefighting efforts were fortified, and brigades such as that in the Kaga domain performed remarkably well. Townspeople began to spontaneously form fire brigades in 1718, and two years later a formal system of forty-seven local brigades was established.

With this, firefighting systems had formed at the shogunate, daimyō, and townsfolk levels. Preventative measures such as nighttime fire-safety patrols began, each house maintained buckets and rainwater tanks for use in firefighting, and firefighters responding to alarm bells and drums from fire lookout towers came to be accompanied by *tobi* construction workers skilled at aerial work to help teardown buildings ahead of an approaching fire.

Some 100 large fires have been recorded in Edo's history, and large fires accompanied by strong winds did not cease in the Edo Era. However, there were no further disasters like the Great Meireki Fire. The population of Edo increased to over one million during the Kyōhō Period (1718–36), making it one of the largest cities in the world, but only the Meguro Gyōninzaka Fire in 1772 resulted in more than 10,000 fatalities, and very few had as many as 1,000. Clearly, Edo had become a mature city in terms of fire-prevention systems.

To avoid financial difficulties, the shogunate delegated most firefighting efforts to daimyō and townspeople. Daimyō and town councils did have financial difficulties, however, and maintaining full firefighting staff levels was difficult. The embankments and broad avenues that had been constructed as firebreaks were gradually enveloped by commercial activities. Even so, while there were unquestionably weaknesses in the firefighting systems of the late Edo Era, they nevertheless continued to successfully battle large fires.

Large fires also occurred after Edo came to be known as Tokyo, in the Meiji Period. Eight steam-pump-type trucks were mobilized to fight the 1892 Great Kanda Fire, but pressurized water mains were still incomplete. This caused the modern trucks to retreat against the force of the blaze. Fatalities were limited to twenty-five people, but the incident demonstrated that firefighting measures such as incombustible buildings and water supplies remained in an unfinished state.

Prior to the Great Kantō Earthquake, University of Tokyo assistant professor and seismologist Imamura Akitsune had predicted the arrival of a major seismic event, but his superior, Professor Ōmori Fusakichi (1868–1923), derided his prediction as lacking scientific basis. They agreed, however, regarding the danger of fires accompanying earthquakes and the lack of modern water systems. Indeed, the Great Kantō Earthquake immediately cut off the water system, and even a city as developed as Tokyo could not withstand the force of whirlwinds of flame. As noted above, the result was over 100,000 deaths, the largest number of fatalities since the Great Meireki Fire.

Another large fire fanned by strong winds hit Hakodate in 1934, resulting in the loss of 2,054 people and 20,000 homes. There have been far fewer large wind-fueled fires in the postwar period, with only the 1976 Great Sakata Fire occurring since the 1960s, and none at all since the 1980s.[15]

Even so, it is premature to state that Japanese city planning and firefighting systems have reached sufficient safety standards. There are limits to how well a wind-driven fire can be controlled once the water infrastructure has been destroyed, even with the increase in inflammable concrete buildings. If strong winds had been blowing off the Rokkō mountain range when the Great Hanshin-Awaji Earthquake hit, as they often do, then that disaster could have become a tragedy rivaling the Great Kantō Earthquake.

The population in the greater Kantō area has grown beyond reason, to the point where comparisons with Edo and its population of one million are meaningless. Still, people seem to merely hope that there will be no strong winds during fires. The problem extends well beyond Tokyo. Osaka, Kyoto—indeed, all Japanese cities—are vulnerable to multiple fires caused by earthquakes and strong winds.

4. Government Response to the Great Kantō Earthquake

The missing prime minister

It sometimes seems that nature has the bad habit of taking advantage of political weaknesses. The Great East Japan Earthquake came during an unstable period of regime change for the Democratic Party of Japan. The Great Hanshin-Awaji Earthquake, too, hit under the irregular circumstances of a Liberal Democratic Party–Japan Socialist Party–New Party Sakigake coalition, with Japan Socialist Party Chairperson Murayama Tomiichi (1924–) as prime minister (in office 1994–96). The worst case was the Great Kantō Earthquake, which came during a brief window in which there was no prime minister at all.

After representing the Japanese government at the 1922 Washington Naval Conference, Katō Tomosaburō (1861–1923) returned to Japan to become prime minister (in office 1922–23) and subsequently head up military disarmament and withdrawal from Siberia. He had gastrointestinal problems, however, and on August 24, 1923, died of intestinal cancer while still prime minister. Ambassador Uchida Yasuya (1865–1936) was appointed interim prime minister the following day, and the cabinet's resignation was submitted to the regent court on the 26th. Admiral Yamamoto Gonnohyōe (1852–1933) received an imperial edict to form a new cabinet on the 28th, but doing so proved difficult due to differences in opinion between two major political parties over the formation of a combined national-unity government. The Great Kantō Earthquake struck on September 1, the eighth day of this power vacuum.

Despite the temporary nature of his position, interim Prime Minister Uchida was pressed to provide a resolute initial response. It was impossible for the entire cabinet to convene that afternoon, so those who could attend held an extraordinary cabinet meeting in the garden of the prime minister's office, which was relatively safe even during the ongoing tremors. At the meeting, they discussed a requisition order for emergency provisions proposed by the Ministry of Home Affairs, and the establishment of an Emergency Earthquake Relief Bureau. However, both of these were major items requiring Privy Council approval, and it was impossible to convene senior counselors. Thus, due to procedural issues, countermeasures to address the emergency situation were not immediately taken. When bound by peacetime legal procedures, the Japanese government often tends to be slow in implementing bold measures, even when faced with a serious national crisis.

The undulating earthquakes that hit Tokyo had already taken the lives of over 13,600 people through building collapses and tsunamis. That alone made for a major disaster. By 1:00 p.m., fires were burning throughout the city, but still no one could have imagined that those fires would cause nine times as many casualties as had already occurred. As the fires spread and merged, they became so large as to be uncontrollable, and 44 percent of the main buildings of Tokyo burned to the ground. By 4:00 p.m., flames had reached the police headquarters. As the night progressed, the Home Ministry, Finance Ministry, Education Ministry, Communications Ministry, and Railways Ministry burned in turn, making the government itself a victim of the fire. The city burned throughout the night; it was not until the morning of September 2 that the fires finally ran out of fuel and died down.

The Japanese government could not just sit by idly, of course, even if approval from the Privy Council was lacking. Indeed, the mechanisms of the Japanese government were sufficiently autonomous to operate even without a prime minister orchestrating them from the top. The Ministry of Home Affairs, through its control of the police and fire departments, played a particularly important role in aiding the nation in such times of crisis.

The prewar Ministry of Home Affairs had such extensive authority that it could have been mistaken for the entire Japanese government. Security Bureau Director Gotō Fumio played a leading role in implementing the initial disaster response efforts of Home Minister Mizuno Rentarō. Beneath him, Inspector General Akaike Atsushi took general command of Tokyo's police, fire, and sanitation forces.

Personnel headed out to investigate the damage immediately after the earthquake ended, and based on their findings, the afternoon extraordinary cabinet meeting proposed the above-mentioned actions. Inspector-General Akaike also advised the home secretary and the director to enact martial law. All of these measures were delayed due to the difficulties in assembling the Privy Council, but the emergency requisition order and establishment of the Emergency Earthquake Relief Bureau were finally enacted at another extraordinary cabinet meeting on the morning of the 2nd.

The unprecedented seriousness of the events probably spurred on these actions. Another helpful factor was that Privy Council member Itō Miyoji (1857–1934), who attended the garden cabinet meeting, advised Interim Prime Minister Uchida that in emergency situations such as this, decision-making should be the responsibility of the Cabinet.

Not only the Metropolitan Police Department headquarters, but also 15 police stations and 254 substations and liaison offices burned down. Inspector-General Akaike argued strongly for martial law, insisting that it would be difficult to maintain security and respond to the emergency without dispatching troops. Martial law was indeed enacted on September 2, but it was in response to baseless rumors of attacks by Koreans.

Battling the flames

Following a typical earthquake, the first step is to rescue people buried under rubble. Lifelines are then established by opening roads and preparing food. Finally, medical facilities and services are deployed to evacuation sites. During the Great Kantō Earthquake, however, in many cases the fires came before people could be pulled from their collapsed homes. The lucky ones were immediately rescued by family or neighbors, but the rapidly advancing fire did not wait for rescue efforts by police, the military, and members of other public institutions.

In that sense, the entire day following the earthquake was a battle against fire. The fire division, which was under the jurisdiction of the police department, was a modern firefighting organization with 824 firefighters and thirty-eight pump fire engines—an effective force for combating fires in normal times. However, "the water sources that firefighters relied on ran dry," and "typhoon-like powerful winds quickly added to the strength" of the spreading flames, holding firefighters back.[16] In other words, Tokyo's fire prevention system "did not take into consideration that an earthquake and accompanying fires might cut off water supplies, so there was nowhere near the equipment and personnel needed to handle such a situation."[17]

The Tokyo municipal government's *Record of the Tokyo Earthquake and Disaster*[18] states that fires occurred at 134 locations, that initial firefighting efforts were successful at 57 locations, and that fires spread from 77 locations. Of those 57 successful cases, an estimated 34 were extinguished by residents and 27 were extinguished by fire brigades.

The expanding flames were not stopped despite the deaths of 22 firefighters and injury of 124 others, and by 2:00 p.m. citizens could do little but run for their lives. As mentioned above, at 4:00 p.m. the fires reached the site of the former uniform depot in Honjo ward and instantly incinerated 40,000 people. Another 1,000 people or more burned to death at the Tanakamachi Elementary School in Asakusa ward. Overtaken by the flames, 773 died on the Yokokawa bridge in Honjo ward, and 490 died in Yoshiwara Park. Another 370 drowned in the Sumida River at Mukōjima while trying to escape.

Records such as these show the terrors that masses of fleeing people experienced, but in fact open spaces were more likely to protect people than to doom them. Some 500,000 people took refuge in Ueno Park, and another 300,000 in the plaza in front of the Imperial Palace. The flames came close to both locations, but ultimately these areas remained safe havens at the peripheries of the blaze. In some cases, survival was a matter of miraculous luck. Fires surrounded all sides of Asakusa Park and the 70,000 people taking refuge there, but the ginkgo and other trees aided firefighting efforts using water from the pond there, and the rapid changes in wind direction were all favorable, keeping everyone safe. Yokohama Park was packed with 60,000 people, who were saved by the greenery there and by puddles that formed from broken water pipes.

Some of the people sheltering at the Honjo uniform depot brought furniture with them that later ignited, but many in Yokohama were "lucky" in that the sudden collapse of their homes prevented them from bringing items that might later serve as tinder.

Many natural disasters occur in Japan, but most are brief. The Great Kantō Earthquake, however, started with a broad rupture in the Sagami trough that induced a chain of fault-line earthquakes, so the duration of the sporadic earthquakes was long. Furthermore, the subsequent fires extended the disaster through the afternoon and night. Those who managed to survive the earthquake no doubt wondered why the gods were punishing them so mercilessly.

On September 2, government and private-sector organizations launched aid and recovery efforts. There was still no permanent prime minister, but the dire situation pushed politicians to act and contributed to the formation of the Yamamoto cabinet.

During this national crisis, Gotō Shinpei (1857–1929) showed the most vivid transformation. While he had once refused a position on the cabinet, he changed his mind, believing that circumstances demanded cooperative response from politicians, and he was appointed home minister. This was a commendable political decision, and one that embodied hope amid misery.

5. Vigilante Massacres

The perverse psychology of information blackouts

In the Japan of today, wars and massacres feel like a thing of the distant past. From a worldwide perspective, however, while there have been no global-scale wars in the past seven decades, there have been many civil wars and ethnic or religious conflicts, particularly following the end of the Cold War.

In November 2011, I visited the site of one such conflict—the former Yugoslavia. On a hill sits the House of Flowers, the mausoleum of the former president of the Federal Republic of Yugoslavia, Josip Broz Tito

(1892–1980; in office 1953–80). A display there shows events at which representatives of various ethnic groups gathered at the mausoleum to light its sacred flame. In that era, various ethnic groups not only coexisted, but even intermarried. This makes the home- and community-destroying ethnic conflicts that spanned more than a decade following Tito's death all the more painful.

Why did people living in harmony later massacre one another? The answer lies in deep historical wounds. As shown in *Oedipus Rex*, tragedy is difficult to avoid once the doors to the past have been opened.

The direct cause of the conflicts in Yugoslavia is said to have been a "they're coming" group psychology that creates a fear of imminent attack. Leaders (agitators) spouting hardline theories also played a large part in fanning the flames. The former Yugoslavia is not the only place where a lack of information has led groups toward what they consider a defensive first strike. Similar phenomena were seen among the Tutsi and Hutu in Rwanda, and in the massacres by vigilante mobs that occurred following the Great Kantō Earthquake, which is the main topic of this section.

Rampant thievery, looting, and violence in the confusion that follows a major disaster are a universal phenomenon. The peaceful and cooperative behavior that made international news following the Great Hanshin-Awaji and Great East Japan Earthquakes was the exception, not the rule.

In 1755, Lisbon—then the capital of a global empire—was levelled by a combined earthquake, tsunami, and fire, resulting in widespread public disorder. Under the mandate of the King of Portugal, the Sebastião de Carvalho Pombal (1699–1782) mobilized the army, which restored order by publicly hanging over thirty people accused of committing violent acts.[19]

After the 1906 San Francisco Earthquake—a terrible disaster that claimed 3,000 victims—fires continued for three days and looting immediately followed. Mayor Eugene Schmitz (1864–1928; in office 1902–7) distributed 5,000 handbills stating that illegal activities would be harshly punished, and later deployed 1,500 military troops to supplement the police force. Order was restored, though doing so required live fire on looters that resulted in two deaths.[20]

Considering such precedents, perhaps the events that followed the Great Kantō Earthquake should not be regarded as particularly exceptional. Yet how are we to understand this situation, in which rumors of "unscrupulous Koreans" resulted in vigilante bands actively hunting down and slaughtering them?

Yoshimura's *Great Kantō Earthquake*[21] states that "unfounded rumors generally begin as small truths that inflate as they pass from mouth to mouth, but the rumors of an imminent attack by Koreans that came in the wake of the Great Kantō Earthquake are unique in that they seem to have been based on no truth whatsoever," and "one can only assume that this great disaster triggered a psychosis in a majority of the people."

Yoshimura goes on to describe how the rumors originated in severely impacted areas of Yokohama, and how they spread. Yamaguchi Masanori, leader of the Constitutional Labor Party, incited evacuees to organize vigilante squads, and organized plundering started at around 4:00 p.m. on September 1, four hours after the earthquake occurred. Wearing red armbands and brandishing swords, they attacked shops and stole food and money. Some seventeen attacks were recorded. Fear of these attacks led to rumor-mongering, and as the rumors made their way north from Yokohama to Tokyo, the violence was misattributed to gangs of Koreans.

The Metropolitan Police Department's *History of the Great Taishō Earthquake and Fires*[22] provides a list of these rumors, which are analyzed in the *Great Kantō Earthquake Report*.[23] In addition to those that originated in Yokohama and spread north, rumors of a Korean attack also originated within Tokyo as a result of group violence in the northeastern part of the city. The list furthermore records rumors of arson, attacks, and rapes by Koreans arising on September 1 in several other areas, and all throughout Tokyo by the afternoon of the following day. In the Shinagawa district, there were rumors that most fires had been caused by human activity, namely bomb-throwing by Koreans and socialists working in coordination. All of these baseless rumors may have arisen from a subconscious belief among Japanese that the Koreans would one day seek revenge for having lost their country.

Police response

The police initially investigated the truth of reported rumors, and of course found them to be baseless. However, public refutations only served to anger the populace.

By September 2, police were receiving urgent, supposedly eyewitness reports of "lawless Koreans committing arson and looting" and "killing women." Lacking the manpower to confirm these reports directly, local police passed them on to the Metropolitan Police Department headquarters as factual information. After receiving so many corroborating reports, the Police Department, too, accepted them as fact.

At 5:00 p.m. on September 2, police headquarters unfortunately issued a statement saying that "some unscrupulous Koreans are committing acts of arson and other forms of violence, and arrests are currently being made in Yodobashi and Ōtsuka," and ordered local police departments to "take all measures necessary to secure the arrest of such Koreans."[24] No telephone or telegraph services were available in the disaster area, so this missive was delivered as a telegraph via the Navy transmitter at Funabashi under the name of Gotō Fumio, director general of security. "Koreans are taking advantage of the disaster to set fires throughout the city," it concluded, and made a nationwide call for "tight restrictions on the activities of Koreans."

The police themselves immediately questioned these conclusions. At 6:00 a.m. on September 3, an urgent notice by the Metropolitan Police Department stated that "most rumors regarding rioting by unscrupulous Koreans are nonfactual and erroneous; most Koreans are behaving appropriately, and care must be taken to prevent inappropriate persecution or violence directed toward them." While somewhat reserved, this notice did establish an official position that "most" of the rumors were false. On the same day, an update declared that "nearly all" of the rumors were false, that Koreans should be protected, and that violent anti-Korean vigilante groups should be arrested. On September 4, an extraordinary cabinet meeting revised the position of the Ministry of Home Affairs, ordering the "protection of Koreans" and a "prohibition on armed youth groups and vigilante groups."

This belated correction, however, does little to absolve the police of responsibility for spurring on the initial violence by vigilante groups.

Armed vigilante groups had set up checkpoints along roads and brutally beat or killed anyone they deemed to not speak fluent Japanese—not only Koreans, but also Chinese and even rural Japanese speaking in dialect. In extreme cases, these groups surrounded police cars or police stations where innocent Koreans were being protected, and not only killed the Koreans but beat the police who harbored them. Clearly, police systems for maintaining order during ordinary times had broken down.

Police confirmed the deaths of 248 Koreans and 58 Japanese and prosecuted known perpetrators. An investigation by the governor general of Korea (who was Japanese, since Korea was a Japanese colony at the time) determined that 832 Koreans had been killed or were missing, and paid surviving families restitutions of 200 yen per person (and 16 yen per person for Japanese victims).

With the support of Professor Yoshino Sakuzō (1878–1933), a separate investigation by the Committee for the Consolation of Korean Compatriots[25] composed primarily of Korean students initially found that 2,613 Koreans had been killed.

Dispatching the army proved to be the only way to quell the crazed mobs that arose among the unprecedented destruction. Provided with extensive authority under martial law, the military began working in earnest to restore order from around September 5. The Japanese army at the time comprised twenty-one divisions, and soldiers equivalent in number to nearly six of those were dispatched and played a decisive role in restoring order and aiding recovery from disaster. In afflicted areas where private-sector activity was difficult, the army's Corps of Engineers made remarkable contributions to the restoration of lifelines, including reopening 30 km of roads, 90 bridges, and 21 km of waterways; removing rubble at 72 locations; and repairing 880 km of telephone lines.[26]

In this sense, after the Great Kantō Earthquake the army played a role comparable to that of Japan's Self-Defense Forces after the Great East Japan Earthquake. Nonetheless, their record was marred by actions such as the killing of anarchist Ōsugi Sakae—along with his lover and young nephew—by military police led by Lieutenant Amakasu Masahiko (1891–1945), and the killing of labor union members by the 13th Cavalry Regiment at the Kameido Police Station.

We can attribute this to Japanese authority figures and society as a whole being less developed than they are today. However, it is impossible to say what delusions humans will succumb to when faced with the extremes of unimaginable misery and lack of information. Furthermore, when mass psychology becomes wrapped in extremism, probably few can maintain a healthy mind. One blessing of the modern age is that electricity can be quickly restored to disaster areas, allowing contact with the rest of the world through television and access to more accurate and balanced information via the internet. However, as we all know, the media and internet are not always accurate, and we should be careful, as we should in person, of believing rumors or other false information.

6. Constructive Recovery Amid Political Strife

Gotō Shinpei's grand plan

The recovery process following the Great Kantō Earthquake, the greatest disaster in modern Japanese history, was unusual in many ways.

Cabinet Minister Gotō Shinpei hoped to initiate an unprecedented, massive reconstruction plan. That plan, however, was in the end buried amid the bureaucracy and political strife of the Japanese government. Even so, through urban planning for the imperial capital, Tokyo was able to adopt the rational systems of a modern city. The final results can only be called an excellent example of creative reconstruction.

Yamamoto Gonnohyōe had been appointed prime minister by the Emperor on 28 August 1923, but political maneuvering stymied formation of his cabinet. The Great Kantō Earthquake on September 1 broke this deadlock. The damage to Japan's capital city had plunged the country into crisis, so this was no time for arguing—all had to work together to respond to the disaster. A man of high integrity, Yamamoto was filled with determination to see the country through this epic tragedy. Gotō was dissatisfied with the cabinet that Yamamoto was assembling, but declared his full cooperation nonetheless. Eager to avoid a single day with even two or three members missing, Gotō visited the home of Inoue Junnosuke (1869–1932) and convinced him to accept the post of finance minister, saying, "With the situation before us, we cannot afford to hesitate."[27]

A cabinet of just eight people was hurriedly formed in the afternoon of September 2, with some members serving multiple roles to make up for unfilled posts. Despite this being an extraordinary cabinet with no representatives from the Seiyūkai or Kenseikai political parties, it included major figures such as Den Kenjirō (1855–1930), Inukai Tsuyoshi (1855–1932), and Tanaka Giichi (1864–1929).

Up till that point, the world's greatest example of creative reconstruction after an earthquake had occurred after the 1755 Lisbon Earthquake. Following that disaster, Lisbon was transformed into a wholly new city under the guidance of Portugal's secretary of internal affairs, the Marquês of Pombal (in office 1756–77), to whom the King of Portugal gave broad powers over the course of twenty years.[28] The institutionalization of political plurality in modern times prevents something similar from occurring today, but emboldened by the support and trust of Prime Minister Yamamoto Gonnohyōe (in office 1913–14, 1923–24) and other major political actors, Gotō set out to accomplish such a task for the reconstruction of Tokyo.

After his investiture at the Akasaka Palace on September 2 by Prince Regent Hirohito (1901–89), Gotō proposed a reconstruction plan based on four principles: the capital would not be relocated, three billion yen would be allocated to reconstruction, the latest Western urban-planning ideals would be incorporated, and current landholders would be firmly dealt with.

The entire national budget at the time was less than 1.5 billion yen, so Gotō's proposed reconstruction budget would have been over twice that.

Figure 1.3. Yamamoto Gonnohyōe (far left) opening a Cabinet meeting on the grounds of the prime minister's office, following the Great Kanto Earthquake.

A simple conversion based on today's national budget equates this to some 180 trillion yen (approximately US$1.65 trillion). This is a tremendous figure, even compared to the ten trillion yen allocated for the Great Hanshin-Awaji Earthquake and the twenty-six trillion yen for the first five years of Great East Japan Earthquake recovery.

Gotō asked Tokyo Imperial University professor Honda Seiroku (1866–1952) to create a plan for Tokyo's reconstruction modeled on the urban planning of Barcelona. Based on that plan, the Home Ministry's Department of Urban Planning calculated that reconstruction would cost 4.1 billion yen.[29]

No matter how dark the times, people find hope as they walk through the tunnel of despair toward the light at the end. Gotō's bold plans promised salvation for the afflicted area. The problem was Gotō's political savvy for realizing such a bold plan. One interesting point in that regard was his initial prediction of resistance by landholders, and his aggressive attitude toward them. Setting issues of resolve and preparation aside, this probably did little more than increase the number of his enemies and alienate his potential allies.

Gotō presented his "Plan for Reconstruction of the Imperial Capital" at a cabinet meeting on September 6. The cabinet established a new independent institution for reconstruction and agreed that reconstruction would be financed through government bonds. Most surprising was his proposal that the national government purchase all land destroyed by the disaster (around 36.4 million square meters). Finance Minister Inoue expressed doubts about this, however, so the measure was shelved.

Regarding the new agency, Gotō proposed establishing a "Reconstruction Ministry" with authority over all reconstruction-related matters. However, each ministry opposed any reduction of its authority, and so after consultation with major ministers, an "Imperial Capital Reconstruction Bureau" was established with authority limited to urban planning and its execution in Tokyo and Yokohama. This meant that the other ministries would engage in reconstruction-related projects within their jurisdictions, for which they each stripped 800 million yen from the Reconstruction Bureau's budget.

After viewing the destruction firsthand, the young Prince Regent Hirohito was so moved by the plight of the country and its people that he delayed his wedding, originally scheduled for that autumn. He issued an imperial edict for the recovery of Tokyo on September 12. The document was based on a draft written by Privy Councilor Itō Miyoji, which sanctified Gotō's plan. In addition to keeping the national capital in Tokyo and establishing the new bureau, it also clearly described an aggressive approach to reconstruction: "The aim should be not only to restore the city to its previous state, but also to allow for future developments and to provide the city with a renewed appearance."[30]

Hirohito supported Gotō's plan throughout his life, and even sixty years after the earthquake expressed regret that it was never fully implemented.

Opposition by Itō Miyoji

On September 19, the Imperial Capital Reconstruction Deliberative Committee was formed as the ultimate authority on reconstruction. This was a large group, comprising the prime minister, home secretary, department ministers, leaders of the two major political parties, and representatives from the private sector. Plans for reconstruction drawn up by the Reconstruction Bureau were presented to this team of political power-players for formal approval.

After each ministry took its cut of the reconstruction budget, the Reconstruction Bureau was to receive one billion yen at the start of November, and the Ministry of Finance budget was calculated at 700 million yen.

At the second meeting of the Committee, Gotō came under unexpected attack for submitting a budget proposal of 703 million yen. This day marked the start of a long decline for Gotō and the Reconstruction Bureau's plan. It is ironic that this decline began within the very committee established to help Gotō realize the plan.

The three volumes of *A History of the Reconstruction of the Imperial City*[31] provide over 3,000 pages of details regarding the recovery process after the Great Kantō Earthquake, including many specific exchanges that took place in the Committee. The following, based on that work, provides just a glimpse of what happened.

The Committee's membership and positioning gave it the appearance of having utmost authority, but in actuality its activities were determined by the Reconstruction Bureau and the government; the Committee's true role was only to approve and authorize those decisions. Some Committee members were dissatisfied with this situation. House of Peers member Egi Kazuyuki (1853–1932) exemplifies the indignation that these elderly fiscal conservatives felt. He started the second meeting with an hour-long critical speech, saying, "If the government is to demand fiscal austerity, then proposals for a 55-meter-wide boulevard are extravagant in the extreme," and asserted that some people were "trying to take advantage of the confusion caused by the disaster" to implement long-term plans for the construction of Tokyo Harbor and the Keihin Canal.

The attacks continued with a three-hour speech by Itō Miyoji. Ironically, Miyoji was an old friend of Gotō's and draft writer of the imperial edict that so highly praised his reconstruction plan. Nonetheless, he was now declaring that he was "fundamentally opposed" to the plan proposed by the Bureau. Faced with foreign and domestic debt of 4.3 billion yen, spending another 700 million yen could lead to financial collapse, he insisted.

Miyoji's sentiments were similar to those of Egi, but his reasoning had ulterior motives. Japan was rushing to buttress its armed forces following the Washington Naval Treaty, and the military was afraid it would be forgotten should all efforts be directed toward recovery efforts in the capital.

Miyoji also stated that "[the recovery plan's] policy for purchasing over 3.3 million square meters of land at ridiculously low rates" had the potential for "violating constitutional rights to ownership," something that he would not stand for; he had assisted in drafting the Meiji Constitution, after all, and was often referred to as its "watchdog." His long speech demanding extensive revision of the plan greatly moved the politicians present, and his sentiments were mirrored by Seiyūkai party president Takahashi Korekiyo (1854–1936) and Kenseikai party president Katō Takaaki (1860–1926).

It was Shibusawa Eiichi (1840–1931), a Reconstruction Bureau member from the private sector, who halted the near-collapse of the restoration plan. "Even now, those suffering from this disaster are waiting in anticipation to see what becomes of this plan," he said, "so our failure to come to a decision would fail them as well. . . . It is highly important that we accomplish something." This reminder of the disaster victims delivered by a leader of the financial community forced the politicians to acquiesce. A majority voted in support of Shibusawa's proposal to form a special subcommittee that would pull together a plan, comprising ten members selected by Prime Minister Yamamoto.

This raised the question of who would lead the subcommittee. Yamamoto probably believed that the strong resistance Gotō Shinpei faced would prevent him from being an effective leader, and in the elitist world of Japanese politics it would have been poor form to select a private citizen such as Shibusawa, despite his apropos proposal that saved the situation. The prime minister thus selected Itō, the primary detractor of Gotō's plan. In doing so, he effectively abandoned that plan and initiated its burial.

The Imperial Capital Reconstruction Bureau and political restructuring

Under Itō Miyoji's leadership, the special subcommittee held its first meeting on November 25 at the prime minister's residence.

Shibusawa actively led the discussion. He regretted the delays in enacting a restoration plan, and since no more time could be lost, suggested "revising and implementing the government plan." Egi Kazuyuki opposed this, while major party leaders Takahashi Korekiyo and Katō Takaaki further opposed the construction of new roads—they claimed that existing roads could just be rebuilt with improvements—as well as construction related to the Tokyo Harbor and the Keihin Canal projects. While all three opposed any large-scale plans for reconstruction, Takahashi argued that the stability of daily life should be a high priority, while Katō insisted that the Reconstruction Bureau should cease its back-and-forth and leave actual decision-making to the Diet. In opposition to these arguments, Home Minister Gotō Shinpei raised the emperor's intent as indicated in his edict, which called for "not restoration but a regeneration" of the Imperial Capital, which was to be given a "renewed appearance." Shibusawa asked Committee Chair Itō to prepare a summary plan, but Itō considered the timing to be premature, and decided to continue the meeting on the following day.

The Committee reached consensus in the afternoon of November 26, following something of a paradoxical process. Rather than continue with his previous opposition, Itō asked for ways in which everyone could come together, to which Shibusawa replied, "We can only cast aside our minor differences and proceed with those things on which we agree." The committee set to work under this mantra, but already an Itō and Shibusawa coalition was starting to form.

Immediately after that, the committee took yet another unexpected turn. Citing frequent criticism of the government plan from outside the Cabinet, Itō stated that in the interest of smooth proceedings he wished for Cabinet representatives to leave the room. Gotō and the other Cabinet members were thus expelled. Now surrounded by minority-party members who opposed the government plan, Itō was able to conduct a frank exchange of opinions, after which Shibusawa asked for an arbitrated proposal. Saying that he had kept his own opinions to himself until he could hear those of the others, Chairman Itō solemnly declared that "we are left no choice but to amend the (government) draft," and presented ten proposed amendments.

While Itō had railed against the Gotō's plan just two days before, as a special committee member he suddenly found partial revision to be sufficient and made strong efforts in that direction. Shibusawa no doubt took the lead in its implementation, and their combined efforts seemingly served to reign in hardline opponents. It is possible that Shibusawa and Itō spoke privately during the shift from the Committee to the special subcommittee, and that Shibusawa was the more persuasive. It is furthermore possible that Itō's change of heart was won through an improved plan for compensation to landowners, discussed in further detail below. In any case, Itō's decision meant that the special subcommittee—and thus the Committee—would work toward revising the plan.

Original plans calling for central boulevards measuring forty-four meters and thirty-eight meters wide were scaled back to forty and thirty-three meters. On the other hand, the scope of land readjustment was expanded to twenty-three million square meters, thus covering most areas devastated by fires. The government would requisition one tenth of that land, and landowners would be recompensed for appropriated land in excess of that. The Tokyo Harbor reconstruction and Keihin canal projects that Shibusawa so earnestly promoted would be separated from disaster reconstruction and considered as independent issues.

Approximately 105 million yen was cut from the reconstruction budget, leaving 597 million yen. This would be funded by public bonds paid in six-year installments.[32]

The proposed budget for reconstruction from the Great Kantō Earthquake was presented by Minister of Finance Inoue Junnosuke at the 47th Extraordinary Session of the Imperial Diet, held on December 13, 1923. The Cabinet had approved this 597-million-yen budget and the amendments inserted by the Committee, leaving the Reconstruction Bureau no choice but to go along with it. The Ministry of Finance had also coolly assessed the plan, giving it a high level of validity.

However, deliberations in the Imperial Diet were less a discussion of the plan's validity and more a war of words. Some Diet members derided it, while others questioned its value or attempted to undermine any faith others placed in it. For whatever reason, Gotō and his plan were posited as clear enemies of the Imperial Diet. No one called for a return to sanity in the interest of the disaster victims, as Shibusawa had done.

During the debate in the House of Representatives, one member pointed out that Gotō had originally requested recovery expenditures of three to four billion yen; if Gotō now said he could make do with less than 600 million, wouldn't he say the same after further cuts? Another argued that "A large recovery grows larger, while a small one shrinks. It's like a rubber doll that expands or compresses as needed." A third dismissed the whole discussion as rubbish, questioning the very possibility of establishing the cost of recovery. He pointed out there was nothing in the budget for building the economy, industry, or society, all of which were needed for supporting the state and its people in the future. The plan, he claimed, was only about building roads and parks, and spending 250 million yen to purchase the land to do so. Not only that, but another 22 million yen in administrative costs to create an overblown Reconstruction Bureau! Why was such a thing needed? Why couldn't the Ministry of Home Affairs handle this?[33]

The Seiyūkai party, which held an absolute majority of seats in the House of Representatives, proposed and passed a measure to eliminate the Reconstruction Bureau and reduce the recovery budget by a further 130 million yen. The Bureau's duties were moved to a newly created Reconstruction Department, established as an extraministerial department under the Ministry of Home Affairs.

Budget reductions were accomplished by making the cities of Tokyo and Yokohama responsible for construction of all roads under twenty-two meters wide. However, this decision was reevaluated at the following 48th Ordinary Session of the Imperial Diet under the cabinet of Kiyoura Keigo (1850–1942), because it had become clear that neither city had sufficient financial resources to accomplish this, and therefore both required national aid. Another 105 million yen was thus restored to the budget in an act that was passed in the 49th Special Session of the Imperial Diet under the first cabinet of Katō Takaaki (in office 1924–26). In the end, therefore, implementation of the new urban plan required a budget of 600 million yen.

In his *Era of Imperial City Reconstruction: The Great Kantō Earthquake and Beyond,*[34] Tsutsui Kiyotada posits that one decisive factor behind Gotō's loss of leadership was the political battle over the proposed General Election Law, which would extend suffrage to all males aged twenty-five and over. Gotō directed much of his energy toward the reconstruction of Tokyo, but he also kept an eye toward the political restructuring he expected to follow enactment of the General Election Law. Gotō (along with the general public of his time) was highly aware of the immaturity and failings of the two major political parties. He hoped to drive out the conservative Seiyūkai, which held a dominant majority and opposed the General Election Law, and—together with Cabinet member Inukai Tsuyoshi and smaller parties and factions within the Kenseikai party—to form a new political party as an innovative central force.

The Seiyūkai party was of course adamantly against this, and Kenseikai president Katō Takaaki resisted efforts to split his party. Itō's speech in which he condemned Gotō's plan was a part of this struggle surrounding political restructuring. From the perspective of the two major political parties, Gotō had declared war on them.

Even so, cuts to the reconstruction budget and abolition of the Reconstruction Bureau would have been reason enough to instigate battles between Gotō and the other Cabinet members. Among the ministers, Inukai and his supporters called for a snap general election. In the interest of political survival, however, Gotō decided to submit to the emaciated budget, and Prime Minister Yamamoto went along with this plan. Mired in political machinations, Gotō probably had no chance of winning in a general election.

Of course, while the reconstruction budget was indeed cut, the initial proposed budged was very large—approximately one-third of the national budget (in terms of today's national budget, around thirty trillion yen [US$270 billion]). Perhaps this was part of the original calculus, and a way to obtain sufficient funding.

The Yamamoto Cabinet resigned en masse to take responsibility for the Toranomon Incident (an attempted assassination of Prince Regent Hirohito) in December 27, 1923, and with this Gotō left the political stage. The new Cabinet of Katō Takaaki enacted a 105-million-yen tax increase to help pay for the reconstruction budget, which had settled at just under 500 million yen. The six-year plan was extended to seven years, and in 1930 the imperial capital reconstruction project ended. Gotō passed away at the age of seventy-one, just one year before the project's completion, but he and the talented urban planners who worked alongside him had helped to build a new Tokyo.

The outcomes of recovery

The above section has described the process of recovering from the massive Great Kantō Earthquake. I would like to close this chapter with an analysis that goes beyond one-dimensional discussions of reconstruction versus revitalization to focus instead on what kind of reconstruction actually took place, and what was and was not achieved.

Following the year-end resignation of the Yamamoto Cabinet just four months after it was formed, Kiyoura Keigo, a bureaucrat-turned-politician associated with the faction of Yamagata Aritomo (1838–1922), was appointed prime minister and on January 7, 1924, created a cabinet based mainly around a House of Peers study group. This was the third successive nonpolitical or "transcendentalist" administration—following those of Katō Tomosaburō and Yamamoto—none of which were well received at first. There was widespread disgust with the inabilities of the two major parties, and public sentiment regarding rule by bureaucrats worsened. In response to increased criticism directed at the anti-Kenseikai cabinet, Prime Minister Kiyoura Keigo (in office 1924) dissolved the House of Representatives at the end of January.

The following general election on May 10 resulted in disastrous losses by factions in support of the government, and overwhelming victory by a three-party coalition of constitutional protectionists. The Kiyoura cabinet resigned in full after just five months, to be replaced by the Katō Takaaki coalition cabinet. As described above, the Imperial Capital Reconstruction Bureau was replaced by the Reconstruction Department, which was established as an extraministerial department within the Ministry of Home Affairs.

Although the organization was reduced in size, key figures therein found themselves in the spotlight. Most of these were transferees from the Imperial Capital Reconstruction Bureau: Naoki Rintarō, an engineer from the Reconstruction Bureau, served as department head, the Bureau's Land Readjustment Department Chief Inaba Kennosuke led the new land-preparation section, former Civil Works Director Ōta Enzō led the civil-works section, and former Accounting Department head Sogō Shinji (1884–1981) led the accounting section. Possibly the only executive without experience at the Reconstruction Bureau was construction section leader Kasahara Toshirō, who had headed urban-planning administration in the Ministry of Home Affairs. Most of these individuals were progressive administrators with a passion for building a new city who had participated with Gotō in the Urban Research Group or the Tokyo Municipal Research Council.

It was said that "Gotō had friends, not followers." He respected independence in the personalities and thinking of those around him, and had little need for rules and regulations. He did have growing influence, however, and an expanding network in the Tokyo municipal administration. This included Nagata Hidejirō (1876–1943), who was the mayor of Tokyo at the time of the earthquake, and Sano Toshikata (1880–1956), a professor of architecture at Tokyo Imperial University who joined Tokyo's reconstruction operation after serving as director of construction at the Reconstruction Bureau. Even after Gotō lost his standing, therefore, other specialists who shared his vision played large roles in the reconstruction of Tokyo.[35]

Each ministry was provided with a budget of around 800 million yen for recovery operations under its jurisdiction, and Recovery Department tasks were closely involved with urban planning in Tokyo and Yokohama. There were four primary task categories: land readjustment, road-building, bridge-building, and park construction. I present an overview of each below.[36]

While things had greatly improved since the time of the Great Meireki Fire, Tokyo remained a town of narrow alleyways and crowded buildings, so land readjustment activities involved reorganizing it into a modern urban layout with neatly organized major and minor roads. The Urban Planning Law of 1919 served as the legal basis for this work, but effective implementation under the circumstances of an earthquake disaster required enactment of the Special Urban Planning Law of 1923, which strengthened enforcement based on a proposal by the Reconstruction Bureau.

Landowners were required to surrender up to one-tenth of their land without compensation, but acquisitions beyond that were paid for. The average land acquisition rate was 15.3 percent per landowner. This might seem to be a reasonable approach, considering that redistricting would greatly increase land values, but it was the first large-scale land-readjustment project in Japan. When areas scheduled for implementation were announced in March, landowners protested confiscations and forced

Figure 1.4. Crowds filling the plaza in front of the Imperial Palace during "Imperial Capital Reconstruction Festival" (March 1930)

relocations. In response, proponents such as Gotō, Naoki, Sano, and other members of the Tokyo Municipal Research Council held over a dozen explanatory sessions, which by summer had quelled most of the protests.

Land readjustment covered some 30.4 million of the 36.4 million square meters of land that had burned. The Reconstruction Department took responsibility for approximately 20 percent of that area, and the city of Tokyo handled the rest. Most tasks involved road-building, with the Reconstruction Department constructing 52 primary roads with widths of twenty-two meters or more. Major present-day Tokyo arteries such as Shōwa Avenue and Yasukuni Avenue were created at this time. The city of Tokyo constructed 122 narrower auxiliary roads.

Bridge-building activities during the same period are particularly noteworthy. Wooden bridges burned during the fires, resulting in many fatalities along Tokyo's rivers. Civil Works Director Ōta rebuilt many of them using stronger steel structures, including the six large bridges crossing the Sumida River. He also created a Design Review Board that included artists, with the aim of creating bridges that combined good engineering and aesthetics. In all, the national government (the Reconstruction Department) built 112 bridges, and the city of Tokyo built 4,284.

Of particular value to later generations of Tokyo residents were park-building projects. Before the earthquake Tokyo had thirty parks covering approximately two million square meters. The Reconstruction Department built three new large parks, in Sumida, Hamachō, and Kinshi, and the city of Tokyo built fifty-two smaller parks, most of them adjacent to elementary schools so that they could be used both as extensions of the school grounds and as evacuation sites for students and area residents. Parks were planted with evergreen broad-leaved trees resistant to heat and equipped with water supplies such as fountains. This combination of attractive scenery and safety helped revitalize the city. The city of Tokyo furthermore built 117 three-story schools with steel structures and upgraded water and sewage systems.

The scale of national reconstruction efforts was reduced with Gotō's downfall, but the city of Tokyo nevertheless accomplished a good deal. Tokyo Mayor Nagata served as deputy mayor to Gotō when the latter was Tokyo's mayor, and the two shared a similar vision for the city. Gotō's plan therefore remained partially intact even after he himself was gone, contributing to the reconstruction and creative recovery of the city.

However, budget reductions made land reallocation and major road construction impossible beyond the bounds of fire-stricken areas. Road widths were also narrowed compared with original plans. It is difficult to say how many lives might have been saved during the wartime bombing of Tokyo had Gotō's more ambitious plans been realized, but one can see why even in the last year of his life, Shōwa Emperor Hirohito (reigned 1926–89) expressed regret that Gotō's plan had been scaled back.

Even so, when taken as a whole, reconstruction following the Great Kantō Earthquake went beyond mere "recovery," instead providing a fine example of creative reconstruction to rebuild Tokyo as a modern city, and furthermore providing a model for urban development throughout the country that lasted through the end of the World War II.

TWO

The Great Hanshin-Awaji Earthquake

1. An Earthquake Shatters Postwar Peace

A devil from the earth

Early in the morning on April 13, 2013, an M 6.3 earthquake with its epicenter beneath Awaji Island shook western Japan. This was reminiscent of the Great Hanshin-Awaji Earthquake that had hit the southern tip of the Nojima fault in the predawn hours eighteen years before, and media reports focused on the possibility of a connection between the two. The Japan Meteorological Agency denied any direct link, but some earthquake researchers have openly wondered whether both might be precursors to an even larger event, a massive earthquake and tsunami expected to one day occur in the Nankai trough. The thread of cause and effect is ever evolving, so the 1995 Great Hanshin-Awaji Earthquake cannot be set aside as disaster that resides solely in the past.

The Great Hanshin-Awaji Earthquake hit at 5:46 a.m. on January 17, 1995. This earthquake is of particular interest to me because I experienced it firsthand. While my family and I emerged unscathed, cracks developed beneath our home in Nishinomiya, a city in the Hanshin region between Kobe and Osaka. The entire structure shifted 25 centimeters horizontally and developed a tilt; a marble placed in a hallway will now roll down it at a surprising pace. At Kobe University, where I was teaching, we lost thirty-nine students, including one of my advisees. The earthquake shattered the peace of postwar Japan in an instant and gave me a direct encounter

54

with the destructive violence of a natural disaster. Some things can only be understood through experience, and the awesome power of an earthquake thrusting upward from directly below is one of them.

There were no forewarning tremors—I was awoken by being thrown straight up out of bed. At first, I thought an airplane had crashed into my house. A massive shaking followed immediately after, and I realized it was an earthquake, though unlike any I had ever experienced. It was as if some devil had arisen from the earth, seized my home, and was trying to rip it apart. The house squealed, and I could sense furniture flying about in the dark. All I could do was shield my six-year-old daughter, who was sleeping between my wife and me, in an attempt to protect her from this invisible monster. When the shaking finally subsided, it was hard to believe that we were still alive.

My student Mori Wataru lived in the Higashinada ward of Kobe, which experienced the largest number of casualties. Three days after the earthquake, as his father watched from the sidelines, members of the Japan Ground Self-Defense Forces (GSDF) pulled his body out from beneath a mound of rubble. His father later took me to survey the site, an attractive little two-story apartment building. Wataru had lived on the first floor. Everything within sight was a jumble of collapsed homes and larger buildings. Not that there was anything wrong with the structures in that area; the shaking had simply been overwhelmingly strong. The devastation was far beyond that in the area surrounding my home in Nishinomiya.

I saw a young woman sitting amid the collapsed buildings, holding a bouquet of flowers. Wataru's father introduced her as a close friend of his son's. She told me something of his situation before the earthquake. He had already found postgraduation employment at a major newspaper company but had expressed a desire to "impress the old man" (meaning me) with his graduation thesis. To that end, he had left his parents' home in Sakai (Osaka prefecture) to spend the weekend in his college apartment writing. There he met with the disaster. It was the academic version of dying at his post. I had always put great effort into my advising duties, but learning of the connection between Wataru's unusual devotion to his studies and his death made the situation all the more solemn.

The epicenter of the Great Hanshin-Awaji Earthquake was sixteen kilometers below the Akashi strait, near the northern tip of Awaji Island, just southwest of Kobe in the Seto Inland Sea. The Nojima fault moved along a fifteen-kilometer stretch in a southwestern direction from the epicenter and along the west bank of Awaji Island. The rupture site was exposed at the ground surface. Bedrock ruptured for about twenty to thirty kilometers in a northeast direction from the epicenter along the southern foot of Mount Rokkō, on the Honshū mainland between Osaka and Kobe. This section was covered with sedimentary layers, so fault lines were not visible on the ground.

This M 7.3 earthquake involving movement along forty to fifty kilometers of active fault caused extensive damage. It occurred in a band of high seismic activity that stretches across a densely populated urban region along the southern foothills of Mount Rokkō, where tremors of intensity VII were felt. While geographically limited, the occurrence of an earthquake so close to several major cities, including Kobe, Ashiya, and Nishinomiya, resulted in great devastation. The earthquake leveled approximately 105,000 buildings and killed 6,434 people, including disaster-related deaths. A cabinet decision designated "Great Hanshin-Awaji Earthquake" as the disaster's official name.[1]

Dwellings determined life or death

Because the earthquake struck in the predawn hours, when most people were still asleep, residential structures played a large role in survival. According to National Police Agency statistics,[2] 4,831 people (87.8 percent of the 5,502 direct fatalities) died due to building collapse or falling furniture. Another 550 people (10 percent) are thought to have died in fires, though in some cases burns may have occurred postmortem. The above deaths account for 97.8 percent of all fatalities. The remaining 2.2 percent (121 people) died outside, due to automobile accidents or falling objects.

A report, *A Survey of Fires in the 1995 Southern Hyōgo Prefecture Earthquake*, categorized fatalities according to the following building types:

1. Detached one- or two-story homes
2. Multifamily dwellings of up to two stories
3. Detached dwellings of three or more stories
4. Multifamily dwellings of three or more stories

According to this report, nearly half (48.7 percent; 2,377 people) of in-home fatalities were in category 1 buildings (low-rise detached homes). Among wooden homes, those built before new earthquake-resistance standards were established in 1981 were particularly prone to collapse, while almost no prefab or two-by-four structures built under the new standards collapsed. Category 2 (low-rise multifamily dwellings) had the second-most fatalities (36.6 percent; 1,788). The many apartment buildings and townhouses built shortly after World War II were hit particularly hard. By comparison, the midrise detached and multifamily dwellings in categories 3 and 4 together accounted for only 9.6 percent of fatalities (470 people). However, even some steel-reinforced-concrete buildings had collapsed floors or collapsed entirely. Others suffered such extensive damage that all residents were forced to evacuate. Still, midrise buildings were relatively safe.[3] The survey results thus support the public's general recognition that building safety is important.

According to a report published four months after the earthquake, there was a high correlation between building collapse rates and fatality rates. In an analysis of Kobe by ward, Higashinada ward (where my advisee Mori Wataru lived) had the highest rates of both building collapse and death, followed in turn by Nada ward, Nagata ward, and Ashiya city. Not until fifth place do we see a discrepancy, with Suma ward having more collapsed buildings and Hyōgo ward having more deaths.

In terms of absolute number of fatalities, the order was Higashinada ward, Nishinomiya city, Nada ward, Nagata ward, Hyōgo ward, and Ashiya city. While Nishinomiya was second only to Higashinada, its city limits extend to the northern area of Mount Rokkō, encompassing undamaged areas. With a population of 430,000, its ratio was thus lower than areas along the southern foothills of Mount Rokkō that experienced intensity VII tremors.[4]

As mentioned above, nearly 90 percent of deaths were due to structure collapse and only 10 percent to fires. This stands in stark contrast to the 1923 Great Kantō Earthquake, in which around 11,000 deaths occurred due to building collapse and over 90,000 due to fires. The difference was caused by wind. While near-typhoon-strength winds followed the Great Kantō Earthquake, the winds were calm after the Great Hanshin-Awaji Earthquake, preventing a compound disaster. Wind speeds in Kobe were 1 to 3 meters per second, and the speed of windward fire spread was only around 20 to 40 meters per hour. Research has shown that a wind speed of just 3 to 4 meters per second is sufficient to double the rate of fire spread. The Great Sakata Fire of 1976 occurred under strong winds of 10 to 12 meters per second, resulting in fire spread of 100 to 150 meters per hour.

This is not to say that few fires broke out after the Great Hanshin-Awaji Earthquake. In the first three days of the event, 256 fires broke out in the disaster area (204 on the first day and 26 on each of the second and third days). The 138 fires burning on the morning of January 17 were evenly distributed throughout Kobe: 26 were in Chūō ward, 24 in Hyōgo ward, 23 in Higashinada ward, 22 in Nagata ward, 19 in Nada ward, and 16 in

Suma ward. There were furthermore 35 fires in Nishinomiya city, and 13 in Ashiya city.

Some fires were due to human involvement such as oil stoves and electric or gas appliances being used for early-morning heating. Other fires were attributable to the earthquake itself, which caused electrical shorts due to the shaking of houses and power lines, or were caused by sparks when power was restored.

Fires will break out any time an earthquake brings down buildings. If there are also strong winds, fires will spread. Even without winds, multiple fires can overwhelm local firefighting capabilities, especially if fire hydrants are damaged.

Records of disaster-area experiences

Some things can be understood only by those who have experienced them. That experience brings with it a duty to communicate an accurate account to others, both domestically and internationally, and to future generations. To that end, researchers including myself have begun collecting oral histories from survivors of the Great Hanshin-Awaji Earthquake in three areas.

My group of interviewees includes first-line responders such as municipal leaders and heads of police, firefighting, and SDF organizations who immediately engaged in crisis management. Professor Hayashi Haruo of the Disaster Prevention Research Institute at Kyoto University has compiled a broader range of interviews from those involved in the recovery and reconstruction. Murosaki Yoshiteru, professor at Kobe University's Research Center for Urban Safety and Security at the time of the research, conducted interviews with 360 bereaved people regarding the circumstances under which their family members died.

These oral histories were collected as part of a project by the Great Hanshin-Awaji Earthquake Memorial Association (the present-day Hyogo Earthquake Memorial 21st Century Research Institute); it is scheduled for publication thirty years after the earthquake, but most participants gave us permission for early release.[5] In this book, I use these reports to present the experiences of survivors in their own words.

Of course, in addition to the oral histories that we collected, countless written and spoken accounts also exist. Those in *Accounts of the Great Hanshin-Awaji Earthquake*,[6] consisting of recollections from forty-six people and edited by the Japan Firefighters Association, are particularly interesting. The activities of fire brigades, which are voluntary citizens' organizations that cooperate with municipal fire departments, are deeply entwined with the experiences of ordinary people during disasters.

Reading the experiences of others makes clear that my own experience was not unique. Some even stated that they thought a terrorist attack had occurred. In some cases, not just furniture but trains and even homes were thrown up into the air by the amazing initial shock, which completely destroyed over 100,000 homes and took thousands of lives.

Traditional forms of cooperation

A traditional maxim states that "rain falls upon both sinners and saints," and the same is true of natural disasters. Circumstances, not merit, determine outcomes. For example, not a single local government leader died in the Great Hanshin-Awaji Earthquake, but this was probably because they all happened to live in areas with firm ground.

The only leader whose house was completely destroyed was Kokubo Masao, the mayor of Hokudan, on Awaji Island (the town has since merged with several others to form Awaji city). He was on the second floor of his home when the earthquake struck and said that the sound of the initial shock reminded him of a wrecking ball. He had not experienced such continuous, intense shaking since having ridden on a festival palanquin when he was a child. The first-floor exit was blocked by rubble, so he escaped through a bathroom window. His wife made it out as he was speaking with neighbors, and she noted that as mayor he should probably be at his office. However, getting there required traversing a 1.5-meter-wide alley blocked by rubble. He tried to detour down another narrow road, but it, too, was blocked by a collapsed house, this one with a family of three trapped inside. The entire town of Hokudan seemed to have been destroyed. It was a small town, where everyone knew everyone else. He recalled that his neighbors told him, "We'll take care of things here. You just get to your office."[7]

Hokudan was crowded with old wooden buildings and very close to the epicenter, and 39 of its 10,000 residents died in the earthquake. This was the second-highest rate of fatalities, following Ashiya. The town also had the highest rate of partially or fully destroyed buildings. It is no wonder that the mayor thought his town had been totally destroyed.

What truly drew attention to Hokudan, however, was the resilience of its traditional forms of emergency cooperation, which rely on local social connections. Residents buried in rubble were pulled out and housed or placed in shelter within the day, regardless of whether they were dead or alive. The mayor recalled how surprised he was by the townspeople's rescue activities in the first three hours after the disaster. He said that amid the misery of that day, he realized how powerful a community can be when its residents work to help each other. "These were families that interacted on a daily basis, so we knew the layout of each other's homes, and that allowed us to perform rescues quickly and efficiently."[8] Note that the official Japanese name for this disaster is the Great Hanshin-Awaji Earthquake, with the "Awaji" added through the enthusiastic efforts of Mayor Kokubo.

The modern city of Nishinomiya presents a contrast to Hokudan. Education Director (later, mayor) Yamada Satoru told of a story that in Nishinomiya, there was a clear distinction between districts with high rates of successful rescues and those with low rates. "It's simple," he said. "It all depended on if they had local festivals."[9] In other words, the extent of community ties was one factor separating life from death.

People shine in the midst of misery

The misery of a disaster site can induce despair even among rescuers. Maezawa Tomoe, chairwoman of the Hyōgo Women's Fire Prevention Group Liaison Council, told a story about her group going to Kobe to open a soup kitchen. It was so popular that long lines formed. When a small boy in an oversized jacket got to the head of the line, the server said, "Here, take one more for your mother." "My mother died in the earthquake," he replied. "Oh, one for your father then?" Then the woman standing behind him explained that the boy had just lost both parents. Taking pity on him, the server said, "Then you'd best eat their shares for them," and gave him a larger portion of meat.[10]

Another aspect of a major earthquake that those who are not on the ground often do not consider is the smell of the rubble. Ruins have a uniformly earthy odor, as if they have been soaked in mud. This is the smell that remains when houses and furniture and valued possessions have been wiped away by an earthquake and all has become a formless jumble—a smell I became familiar with in the Great Hanshin-Awaji Earthquake.

But I still had my family and my job. I had lost material possessions, but I had people who cared for me. One woman, a nurse, expressed a similar feeling when she told of the quake "having changed my sense of values."[11] After the violent shaking stopped, my wife Yoshiko hugged our daughter, who had been sleeping between us, and said, "So long as we have Haruka, I don't need anything else." Indeed, after the earthquake, she largely lost interest in the plates that she had so eagerly collected before.

Another family was trapped in their collapsed home in Kobe city's Nagata ward, with a fire approaching. The owner of an adjacent rice warehouse decided to tear the house down, reminiscent of the fire-control methods of the Edo period. He tied a rope to the roof, and with the help of fifty or so people pulled it down. "We weren't able to save the family, but at least we kept their bodies from being burned."[12]

There were even worse situations. A volunteer fireman mentioned a two-story apartment building in Ashiya that had collapsed, trapping a young girl beneath a beam. A fire was rapidly approaching those trying to help her. She waved to her mother and said "Goodbye!" Fire brigade members shouted "We're on our way! Hang in there!" as they poured water onto the flames and tried to charge in. But the beam couldn't be moved, and the fire grew. Others held her mother back, saying "If you go to her, you'll both die."[13]

There was a television broadcast of a father facing the burnt ruins of Nagata ward, hands pressed together, saying "I'm so sorry I couldn't help you." He, his wife, and their two children had been caught in their collapsed home. He had somehow managed to escape, and his wife made it out too, though she was injured. When he called out to his children beneath the rubble, he got no answer from his daughter, but he heard his son's response. He pulled away what he could, and finally uncovered his son's hand. He dug further, and pulled at his son's arm, but he was pinned beneath something heavy. The fire was approaching rapidly, and the man had no heavy equipment to aid his efforts. As it grew hotter, his son said "Dad, you have to run." The man hesitated—his son was here, alive; he was holding his hand. How could he let go? His son spoke his last words: "Thanks, Dad, but it's okay. At least Mom's safe." On television, the man bowed toward the burnt ruins, saying "He was a better man than his father."

Any of us survivors could have ended up in his shoes, living out the rest of our days with the image of a lost child. In many cases, a major disaster does much more than just "change our sense of values." But even amid inconceivable destruction, the brilliance of the human spirit shines through.

2. Front-Line Responders

Disaster mitigation through self, mutual, and public assistance

In a disaster-stricken community, there will always be those who are quick to condemn government authorities for what they consider to be inaction.

The sight of a disaster area littered with corpses makes people want to assign blame, even when it is the result of an extraordinarily large natural disaster. We cannot help but wonder whether some different social response might have prevented things from turning out so badly. The government's purpose, after all, is to ensure the safety and welfare of the people. That's why it is entrusted with the power to collect taxes, and to develop agencies to enforce laws. As described in the previous chapter, the scope of government authority historically expanded in tandem with the expansion of agricultural society. Controlling floods and erosion and performing other services to protect the well-being of citizens is a fundamental governmental duty.

However, this duty is generally limited to predictable events, such as annual rainy seasons or the arrival of typhoons. We might furthermore expect the government's duties to extend to coping with disasters that strike once every decade or two. But should governments be held responsible for preparing for an earthquake or tsunami that might occur only once in a thousand years? Or even a hundred? Would the public happily bear the tax burden that such preparedness entails?

Nature's capacity for destruction is so great that total disaster prevention is impossible. The best we can hope for is to mitigate disasters to some degree by taking steps to minimize damage. Minimizing the loss of human life is particularly important. When a once-in-centuries disaster strikes, we can only get out of the way and try to survive. Later, when it is time to rebuild and recover, the support of the entire nation is required. Humanity should not neglect ongoing efforts toward disaster mitigation, but neither should we expect to completely control nature.

No matter how we prepare for disaster, at any time nature can unleash a furious attack that buries us beneath rubble. Developing self-reliance and mutual aid systems is thus vital. Elements of self-reliance include strengthening one's home against earthquakes and securing furniture. If communities are prepared to rescue trapped people, many can be saved. Mutual aid is effective because families and neighbors are on site from the moment of the disaster, allowing them to promptly rescue those who are buried shallowly. Sometimes rescue is not so simple, though, because it requires special equipment. In those cases, local or national governments must play a role.

When the public criticizes the government for what it considers to be a poor response, the target is usually the prime minister and other facets of the central government, or local government targets such as prefectural bodies and governors. However, the central and local governments are primarily responsible for coping with political issues, institutional design, and

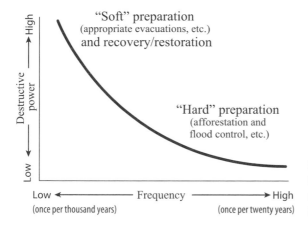

Figure 2.1. Correlation between disaster strength and frequency (countermeasures)

administrative work. When a serious situation breaks out, public officials cannot run to rescue victims from their basements.

Frontline responders—namely the police, firefighters, and members of the military—are the ones who take action at disaster sites. The coast guard, which bears responsibility for policing the waters, rescuing people stranded at sea, and firefighting along the coast, is also involved. While all these institutions maintain security, police and fire departments are generally responsible for dealing with peacetime incidents. In contrast, the core mission of the military is national defense and other emergencies. Although we are largely unaware of their existence in normal times, the military prepares for serious situations that other organizations are unable to deal with, including severe disasters. The Great Hanshin-Awaji Earthquake became an opportunity to greatly advance public recognition of the SDF's role in such situations.

In contrast, the police have in modern times been highly involved in daily civic life. Local officers in postwar Japan, compared to when they were feared in the prewar period, are increasingly approachable representatives of governmental authority, because they are a familiar sight about town. Even so, the Great Hanshin-Awaji Earthquake proved trying for the local police as well.

Police ordeals

The four-story, steel-reinforced concrete Hyōgo Prefectural Police Department collapsed, burying ten of the 28 officers who were on duty there. One died immediately, while the other nine were saved by steel desks and other furniture that intercepted the collapsing ceiling, leaving forty centimeters of airspace.

An officer who was working the switchboard that night was injured so severely he thought he would die. He called out the names of his wife, daughter, and son in turn. Another officer trapped in the rubble was trembling and thinking about how he wanted to enjoy a bath with his child just one more time. While these men could think only of their families while trapped, they spent two days and nights aiding rescue activities after they themselves were rescued, despite their wounds. No doubt they were proud of the example they were setting for their children.

Citizens' needs for assistance do not cease just because the police department has collapsed or its officers have been injured, however. As requests for assistance came in, they were added to a long list. A crimes division chief was found in the collapsed Hyōgo Prefectural Police Department with blood streaming from his head, but when his coworkers called to him, he replied, "I'm fine. Go help the others first." When the police chief arrived, he said, "We can take care of him later," and ordered the others to head out to the surrounding neighborhood. The division chief agreed to this plan. He was finally rescued several hours later when a reserve squad of police arrived and opened a hole in a wall.

Requests for assistance do not let up just because police station are busy. The above-mentioned switchboard operator related his distress at being unable to respond to the growing flood of calls for help until SDF troops and police reinforcements arrived. He said an elementary-school student arrived at the station, saying "Please help, my mother is trapped and can't get out." But no one else was at the police station, and he couldn't leave the phones. All he could do was hold her, tears streaming down his face, and say, "I am sorry. I am so very sorry."[14]

In Japan, the police are a nationwide organization that is organized in prefectural units. Hyōgo Prefectural Police Chief Takitō Kōji said that he recalled important lessons about disaster response from the 1923 Great Kantō Earthquake—namely, that wild rumors can spread quickly in disaster areas, leading to secondary disasters amid the resulting chaos. He did not want to see something like the massacre of innocent Koreans repeated. National Police Commissioner Kunimatsu Takaji, too, expressed initial apprehension about the possibility of looting.

Even though the Ministry of Home Affairs had been disbanded after World War II, the lessons of the Great Kantō Earthquake lived on in the memory of the police. Prefectural Police Chief Takitō, who had previously worked in security, said he saw suspicious-looking men on every corner of the disaster site. A fellow officer that he mentioned this to said that he felt the same way. The commissioner directed those under him to remain visible in uniform, so that residents would be highly aware of their presence, a visual sign that order would be maintained.

Unlike after the Great Kantō Earthquake, no acts of violence ultimately occurred, although some moments at the beginning did feel dangerous. Local citizens were so peaceful they received worldwide acclaim. The police distributed 10,000 radios to stricken areas to ensure that accurate information would be conveyed. Electric power was quickly restored, and the mass media did an excellent job of reporting what was happening. The nightmare of the Great Kantō Earthquake appeared to truly be a thing of the past.

An unexpected drawback to police being in uniform was that they became a target for people looking for help in assisting trapped family members. This forced them to place priority on rescue operations, even when they had other duties to attend to.

Broadly speaking, the police are a peacetime safety mechanism; they are much less equipped than the SDF or the fire department to cope with emergency situations that involve mass fatalities, because they lack the necessary equipment. In the Hanshin disaster, the fact that some three fourths of prefectural police were on the job within two hours of the earthquake, despite being victims themselves, helped make up for this lack. That same day, they were joined by 2,500 police from other prefectures, and within two days another 5,500 had arrived.[15]

The fire department rescued 1,387 people, the SDF 165, and the police 3,495. Some of these rescues were joint efforts between organizations, but this is nevertheless an impressive record for the police. Although some force members made tearful media appearances expressing regret at not having been able to do more, the record demonstrates the closeness between police and citizens.

One area that the police cited as requiring improvement in the future was traffic control: for some time after the earthquake, traffic along National Route 2 was not restricted, and as a result, ambulances, other emergency response vehicles, and utility trucks were paralyzed. Also, the fatality counts issued by the police included only those who had undergone identity verification procedures, and so in early stages underrepresented the severity of the situation.

Out-of-control fires

Fires have always been an inescapable part of earthquake disasters, but the cause of fires has changed over the years.

The main cause of conflagrations in the 1923 Great Kantō and 1948 Fukui Earthquakes was cooking fires, but Japanese lifestyles changed greatly during the period of rapid economic development in the 1960s. Major fires in the 1964 Niigata Earthquake were caused by petroleum tanks, gas appliances, and kerosene heaters.

Since the 1993 Kushirooki Earthquake, most fires have been electrical. This was the case in the 1995 Great Hanshin-Awaji Earthquake; excluding the approximately 40 percent of fires for which the cause was never determined, most fires were caused by electrical appliances, resumption of electrical service after blackouts, or gas leaks due to ruptured lines.[16]

Modern appliances are not only convenient, they have safety features that have made kitchen fires a thing of the past. A growing number of appliances automatically shut off when shaking is detected. Even so, fires still occur during earthquakes.

As mentioned above, 204 fires occurred on January 17, 1995, the day of the Great Hanshin-Awaji Earthquake, and 26 more broke out on both the 18th and the 19th. Most of the fires occurred on the morning of the earthquake. Kobe was the site of the most morning fires (138), followed by Nishinomiya (35) and Ashiya (13).

To examine how well fire departments handled the demands placed on them, let us first review what happened in Ashiya, a small city with a population of fewer than 90,000.

Nine fires occurred in Ashiya immediately after the earthquake. However, the fire department had 16 vehicles, including 5 pumpers, and 85 firefighting personnel. There was also a supporting fire brigade with over 100 members and 4 pumpers. Initial deployments were handled by the 22 on-duty personnel, who were joined by another 12 within the hour. There were more vehicles than fires, so multiple vehicles could be sent to each site. However, the city's 778 fire hydrants were nonfunctional due to damaged water lines, so 60 fire cisterns had to be used instead. Where that was insufficient, water was taken from pools or the Ashiya and Miya Rivers. Fires in the city were put out within the day, with seven buildings fully destroyed and one heavily damaged.[17]

The fire department, too, is an organization that primarily prepares for peacetime fires and accidents, and therefore does not have the resources to handle multiple simultaneous incidents. Nevertheless, Ashiya managed to

Figure 2.2. Firefighters unable to conduct firefighting activities as they wait in vain for water to arrive (January 17, 1995)

cope. Firefighting simulations have shown that a precinct with 9 pumpers can put out up to 4 simultaneous fires, but if 5 or more fires occur only 3 will be extinguished, and no more than 2 out of 9. Of course, countless variables such as wind strength and building characteristics affect the situation, but the ability of multiple fire trucks to surround a blaze is of vital importance.[18]

The situation in Nishinomiya was more dire. The Nishinomiya Fire Department was aware of 22 fires that broke out in the early morning, but in fact there were as many as 31 at the time. The fire department only had 15 pumpers to respond with. Of the 341 staff, 90 were on duty that morning, of whom 28 served as rescue personnel and 62 fought fires. Within two hours, 89 were on the scene. The Nishinomiya Fire Brigade had 729 members and 38 pumpers (note that even the Kobe Fire Brigade had only 7). This difference in numbers shows the extent to which the fire department relied on private citizens for support.

Approximately 3,800 fire hydrants could not supply water, so fire cisterns, pools, and wells were used instead. Coincidentally, the Nishinomiya Fire Department and Fire Brigade had undergone special training for firefighting during drought conditions the previous September, and therefore had extensive practice in utilizing natural water sources. This training came in handy. When the firefighters learned that the fire hydrants were unusable, 29 trucks hooked up to fire cisterns, and 19 drew water from rivers. Two pools, 4 wells, and 4 ditches were also used.[19] Of these, only the rivers did not run out of water.

Unlike Ashiya, Nishinomiya was unable to send multiple trucks to each fire. Even so, only one spread to burn an area larger than 1,000 square meters. The other fires were controlled through the joint efforts of the Nishinomiya Fire Department and the Fire Brigade, which allowed the Fire Brigade to maximize its potential, and through the flexible use of water sources as described above. Another major factor was Nishinomiya's good access, allowing 17 trucks and 67 personnel to arrive from 8 neighboring towns and cities.

The problems in Kobe were worst of all. Sixty fires had broken out within fourteen minutes of the earthquake, but there were only 49 pumpers and 292 on-duty staff (including rescue personnel), so a truck could not be sent to every fire. In addition, firefighting personnel and organizations were disaster victims themselves. Even so, 50 percent of fire department staff reported to work within 2 hours of the earthquake, and 90 percent within 5 hours—figures that demonstrate their sense of responsibility.

Three fire departments and one branch office were destroyed in the earthquake, although these events were not widely reported. The Kobe Fire Department made admirable efforts despite the severe damage. As an aside, some sectors of Japanese society demand austerity from our public institutions, and denigrate government buildings that they consider ostentatious. However, only those who are safe themselves can protect others. Social attitudes must change with regard to the importance of strengthening core institutions for protecting human lives during crises.

Little can be done when multiple fires exceed a city's firefighting capabilities. In some cases, fire trucks arrived at a blaze only to find that hydrants were dry. Fire cisterns and school pools thus became vital water resources.

The rivers along the southern Rokkō mountain range are engineered to flow straight into the sea as an erosion-prevention measure, and therefore do not form pools that can easily be used for firefighting. Sandbags were thus piled up along the Shinminato, Myōhōji, and Toga Rivers to create temporary reservoirs.

Only 32 percent of fires were extinguished at the source, and 51 percent expanded to over 1,000 square meters. Nine in particular became quite large, exceeding 33,000 square meters. Four of these were in Nagata ward.[20]

At 9:50 a.m., Kobe issued a wide-area request for firefighting assistance.

The first trucks arrived from Sanda city at 11:10 a.m., and by afternoon more were arriving from locations across western Japan. To fight the conflagration in Nagata ward, the fireboat *Tachibana* pulled into Nagata Bay and delivered seawater to six linked pumpers. A separate linkage of three fire trucks also pulled water from the bay to fight the blaze. To fight fires two kilometers north of the Japan Railways line in the Oyashiki, Mizukasa, and Matsuno areas, nine pumpers formed a relay to deliver seawater from the bay. Nearly 100 fire trucks from outside Kobe eventually managed to surround a large fire in Nagata,[21] and largely extinguished it by around 3:00 the following morning.

As mentioned above, strong winds after the Great Kantō Earthquake spread fires at a rate of up to 300 meters per hour, but the spread of fire during the Great Hanshin-Awaji Earthquake was less than one-tenth of that due to mild winds. This was fortunate, but the fact that such a large fire occurred anyway should not be overlooked. We must keep in mind that the next large earthquake—in particular, a direct hit beneath Tokyo or another large city—may come during strong winds. Such an event would no doubt exceed the capabilities of any fire department.

Kobe Fire Department Chief Kamikawa Shōjirō noted the large role that fire brigades and corporate firefighting units played.[22] He suggested that we cannot adequately prepare for the next major earthquake disaster without improving private-sector self and mutual assistance, for example by building community capacity for disaster prevention and fostering leaders' civic-disaster preparedness

As the previous chapter discussed, Edo eventually managed to control large fires by establishing local firefighting systems to supplement standing brigades. We should keep this lesson in mind. Maintaining safety and security in the twenty-first century will be impossible without building community-based disaster-prevention systems.

3. The Role of the Self-Defense Forces

Activities of the Himeji Regiment

The SDF did not immediately appear at disaster sites. By the afternoon of January 17, it was clear that the disaster had spun out of control, and many questioned their absence. Political leaders such as Deputy Chief Cabinet Secretary Ishihara Nobuo (1926–) even called the Defense Agency to yell at them for their apparent absence from the stricken areas.

The disaster caused a sudden shift in social tone regarding the SDF. It helped end the pacifist postwar ideology that saw the military running rampant, instead demanding to know what use the SDF was if it could not be deployed at a time like this.

A widespread misunderstanding exists that the SDF was slow to arrive because Kaihara Toshitami (1933–2014; in office 1986–2001), the governor of Hyōgo prefecture, was slow to request its assistance. Some suggest that the governor was hesitant to request military assistance because he was influenced by postwar antimilitary sentiments. Other arguments are that the cause was the fact that the then–prime minister, Murayama Tomiichi, was also the Chairperson of the Japan Socialist Party, which had long argued that the very existence of the SDF violated the constitution. While there is no consensus about the root cause for the apparent delay in the SDF's dispatch, as recently as 2007, Tokyo governor Ishihara Shintarō controversially claimed that the "slow response to the earthquake in Kobe led to over 2,000 needless deaths."

As a professor at Kobe University I compiled an oral history of the Great Hanshin-Awaji Earthquake, and today I work at a research institution created as a result of the disaster. I was also later President of the National Defense Academy of Japan from 2006 to 2012, so I have had the opportunity to learn about the SDF from the inside. As a scholar, I feel a duty to accurately present the facts about the organization.

The GSDF's 3rd Division (Itami), under the Middle Army (which is also headquartered in Itami), is responsible for the defense of Osaka and Kyoto and the prefectures of Hyōgo, Nara, Shiga, and Wakayama. The 36th Infantry Regiment (Itami) is responsible for disaster sites in Nishinomiya and Ashiya. The rest of Hyōgo prefecture, including Kobe, is under the jurisdiction of the 3rd Artillery Regiment in Himeji. In the event of a natural disaster, the Himeji regiment is supposed to mobilize while remaining in contact with Hyōgo prefecture and Kobe city.

In the following section, I examine the initial SDF deployment by presenting the actions of Regiment Commander Hayashi Masao.[23]

Regiment Commander Hayashi was awoken by the earthquake while in his official residence in the Himeji suburbs. Because the earthquake had occurred at the northern tip of Awaji Island and propagated toward the northeast, the shaking in Himeji, located some 50 km west of Kobe, was not particularly severe. Furniture did not fall over and the power did not go out, so the intensity was perhaps around IV. The phones were still working, and at around 7:00 a.m. Hayashi received notification from operations staff that the Itami train station and the Hyōgo police station had collapsed, and all personnel were to report for duty.

A well-functioning organization does not need to wait for its leader to issue instructions; the responsible subordinates instead move promptly to gather information according to a prescribed work procedure. Therefore, even though the commander represents the entire unit, the rapidity with which he issues commands and the speed with which his subordinates follow them is not of utmost importance if they are already doing what they are supposed to do.

At 7:30 a.m., Commander Hayashi issued orders to prepare for disaster deployment, instructing all units to be ready by around 9:30 a.m. He also sent three liaison officers in radio-equipped vehicles along different routes to Kobe—one through seaside towns, one through the northern urban area, and one along the Sanyō expressway in the northern suburbs—to determine which routes would be effective for dispatching troops. It was important to arrive quickly, to work out with the prefecture and the city to which parts of Kobe they should deploy.

Receiving reports about heavy traffic along all three routes from reconnaissance units he had sent out, the commander asked for police escorts for the regiment's move into Kobe. He also arranged for helicopters from Middle Army headquarters to allow access to otherwise unreachable areas. He furthermore ordered security officer Second Lieutenant Nakamura Hiroshi to telephone the Hyōgo prefectural government for a status update.

The prefecture's Disaster Prevention Section head Noguchi Kazuyuki first received an emergency-use radio at 8:10 a.m., and reported, "We still don't have a good grasp of the situation. We've set up a disaster response unit in a conference room on the fifth floor of the prefectural government office." He later explained that he indicated at this time that at some point there would be an official request for an SDF dispatch, but the SDF claims to have received no such notice. Possibly Noguchi intended for this message to be conveyed as subtext, but that was not clearly expressed to the SDF in a manner that they recognized. The conversation ended with an agreement to keep in touch, but no further radio communications were received after that.

At around 9:00 a.m. Hayashi told Second Lieutenant Nakamura to ask for an official request for SDF dispatch the next time he was able to contact the prefectural government. That contact came by telephone (an NTT land line, according to prefectural records) at 10:10 a.m., and when asked during that call if a dispatch was desired, Noguchi immediately answered "Yes, please." When asked where they should go, he answered "Kobe and Hokudan." It was already past 10:10 a.m., but they agreed to set the time of the request as 10:00.[24]

As instructed, by 9:30 a.m. the Himeji regiment had prepared for a dispatch. Commander Hayashi sent his second in command to the prefectural offices on a helicopter that left at 9:50 a.m., telling him to ask the governor for a dispatch request. The SDF thus sought a request via two routes, and from conversations with Hayashi, I got the impression that they were ready to move with 215 soldiers split into two battalions even without the request from the governor. However, transport required a long train of thirty-six vehicles, with two battalions of 100 soldiers each. The 1st Battalion was to go to the Nagata Police Department and the 2nd Battalion to the Hyōgo Police Department. As it was essentially two convoys, two patrol cars would be necessary, but only one had been provided. It took some time to get the second one, but the troops finally departed a little after 10:15 a.m., immediately after the agreement relating to the governor's request. In other words, from early in the morning the Himeji regiment devoted themselves to preparations and finally obtained an official request for assistance just as they were ready to go.

The three ground-based reconnaissance units that had left at 7:30 a.m. soon found themselves caught in heavy congestion, and the first to reach central Kobe arrived after 2:00 p.m. (the latest did not arrive until around 9:00 p.m.). This early notification of traffic conditions allowed Hayashi to quickly request a police escort, which greatly improved the situation. The police opened up the Himeji off-ramp on the Hanshin expressway, which had been closed after the earthquake, allowing the regiment to travel at high speed. Once off the expressway, they found that Kobe was darkened with smoke and its roads congested, but by using the highways they were able to reach the Nagata and Hyōgo police departments by 1:30 p.m.

The Himeji regiment added 200 troops to the disaster area. The transport helicopters that Commander Hayashi requested left at 2:55 p.m., heading for the Ōji stadium. Those who had lost their homes were streaming into parks, schools, and other public facilities, but the Ōji stadium was locked, preventing entry. This made it one of the only places in the city with sufficient space to use as a heliport.

In total, approximately 400 SDF troops from Himeji spread out into Kobe between 3:00 and 4:00 p.m. to aid in rescue efforts. In Nagata they teamed up with police and firefighters, and in Higashinada they established independent areas of activity. Decision-making was complicated by the

Figure 2.3. SDF vehicles and helicopters gathering at Ōji Stadium (January 18, 1995)

confusion surrounding them, and the short winter day was quickly coming to an end.

The 36th Infantry Regiment

GSDF 36th Infantry Regiment Commander Kurokawa Yuzo was sleeping alone in his military residence—an old, wooden, single-story dwelling—when a sudden shock woke him. Since he was only two kilometers from Itami Airport, north of Osaka, he thought at first that an airplane had crashed. The vertical shock was followed by horizontal ones, causing the house to wave like a fan. Furniture fell over, tableware fell from shelves, and Kurokawa found himself unable to get out of bed. These events are characteristic of an intensity VI earthquake.

Knowing that a request for dispatch would be coming, at 5:55 a.m. Kurokawa telephoned the regimental staff on duty and issued an emergency summons to seven of his staff officers. A return call at 6:10 a.m. notified him that his order had been carried out, and he immediately issued a general summons to all regiment members.[25]

On paper the regiment had 1,100 permanent personnel, but in reality the number was 850. Subtracting those who were away on training missions, etc., brought the number to around 650. Of those, 150 were administrative and logistics personnel supporting the entire regiment. That left only around 500 who could be mobilized. Over half lived off-base, so assembling them would take time.

One stroke of good luck was that the regiment had been scheduled for target practice that morning at Lake Biwa, about 60 km northeast of Osaka, so many had spent the night in the barracks. They had intended to head out before dawn, but heavy snowfall at the training site held them back. They were thus able to respond soon after the earthquake subsided.

At 6:35 a.m., the Itami police department requested SDF dispatch. The platform of the Hankyū Itami train station was on the third-floor roof of a building, but that building had collapsed, burying two police officers in a first-floor police box. At 6:50 a.m., Kurokawa sent a reconnaissance team, which confirmed that at least one of the trapped officers was still alive. A forty-two-person rescue team arrived at 7:58 a.m., and extracted a surviving officer some time before 9:00 a.m. Unfortunately, the other officer was lost.

These activities were conducted as local disaster dispatch, as stipulated in Article 83, paragraph 3 of the Self-Defense Forces Law, which can be exercised on the judgment of unit leaders at disaster sites.

At around 7:20 a.m., the 36th Regiment received several phone calls from residents of Nishinomiya requesting aid at a collapsed hospital and other sites. The city of Nishinomiya straddles the Muko River, about ten kilometers away from the base—too far for a local rescue dispatch. More to the point, Hyōgo's governor still had not requested SDF assistance. This left the regiment with a dilemma: should they sit tight and wait for an official request, or should they dispatch aid according to their own discretion? The latter was possible under a proviso to Article 83, paragraph 2 of the Self-Defense Forces Law, which says that the minister of defense and others, down to the level of division commander, can dispatch troops in particularly urgent situations that preclude waiting for a request from the governor.

Unable to contact his division commander, Kurokawa said to the deputy commander, "People are dying out there." The deputy commander agreed that they needed to help; the primary role of the SDF, after all, is protecting the lives of the people of Japan.

I asked Kurokawa whether he thought the decision to skirt formal procedures would be questioned, considering postwar attitudes regarding the military. Kurokawa, a strategist well versed in the history of warfare, answered that the situation was different from, say, that of the independent actions of the prewar Kwantung (Imperial Japanese) Army in China. "We weren't doing anything bad," he said. "We were trying to help people." When I pressed further, asking what he would have done if they had been accused of impropriety, he quietly said, "We'd accept our punishment. What else could we do?"

At 8:00 a.m., Kurokawa called one of his company commanders and ordered them to move to Nishinomiya. Forty troops who were already prepared headed out twenty minutes later, an hour and forty minutes before receiving the official request from the governor.

The situation looked very different once they crossed the Muko River, entering the hellscape of the disaster area. Kurokawa first confirmed that there was no significant damage in Osaka, his primary security responsibility, then at 11:25 a.m. dispatched two companies to Nishinomiya.

In all, 206 troops were sent to Nishinomiya that day. They rescued 6 survivors and recovered 29 bodies. Two companies comprising 118 soldiers were also dispatched to Ashiya, where they rescued 4 survivors and recovered 1 body. In both Himeji and Itami, therefore, the SDF took prompt action at the regimental level, and did all that it could. Of course, two regiments alone would not have been enough.

Failures at the strategic level

Itami is one of the core GSDF bases. It is home not only to the 36th Infantry Regiment, but also to the 3rd Division headquarters, which covers Japan's Kinki region, as well as the headquarters of the Middle Army, which also covers the Chūbu, Chūgoku, and Shikoku regions, in addition to the Kinki area, for a total of twenty-five prefectures.

Four scales of SDF emergency deployment were possible: deploying only the two regiments stationed in the two security areas of the disaster site, deploying all regiments under the 3rd Division throughout the Kinki region, deploying all regiments under command of the Middle Army, or deploying SDF regiments from throughout Japan. This was a big decision, and GSDF chief of staff Tomizawa Hikaru had to rely on the judgment of the Middle Army Commanding General on the scene, Matsushima Yūsuke.

Annoyed at the difficulties in ascertaining the extent of the damage due to being unable to contact Hyōgo prefecture or Kobe city administrators, Matsushima surveyed the situation from the sky, using a helicopter under his command at GSDF Camp Yao. An initial flight at 7:14 a.m. and a second one at 9:30 a.m. revealed that the damage was quite severe: part of the Hanshin expressway had collapsed, fires covered a broad area, buildings had toppled, and many important roads were cracked. One misleading aspect of viewing the situation from the sky, however, was that while building roofs were visible, it was not immediately obvious that lower floors had collapsed. Based on the assumption that the disaster area was limited to Kobe, the Hanshin area between Kobe and Osaka, and northern Awaji, Matsushima assumed that the 3rd Division, with some support from outside, would be able to handle the situation. However, he had misread the severity of the disaster.

The reconnaissance teams that quickly arrived at disaster sites probably could have done much to correct this misconception, but neither divisional headquarters nor Middle Army headquarters requested a status report. They seemed to think that ground reports were not needed because this was not a war; everyone should just do what they could to save as many lives as possible. But the notion that the situation was less serious than a battle—or better said, that it was not a battle—served only to delay correction of initial misjudgments.

The situation was exacerbated by extreme traffic congestion. A unit from GSDF Camp Zentsūji in Kagawa prefecture arrived at Awaji Island in the evening, but it was the only other regiment in the 3rd Division to reach the disaster area on the day of the earthquake. As table 2.1 shows, most arrived in the morning of the following day, January 18. This is highly unfortunate, because 80 percent of successful rescues occur within the first day of a disaster. And, of course, Japan is very cold in the winter, which makes rescuing people quickly all the more imperative.

The unmanageable traffic and initial underreporting of fatalities were the two main points that the police department listed as requiring significant improvement. A fatality count of 203 people released at noon on January 17 finally made Prime Minister Murayama Tomiichi recognize the severity of the situation. By 7:00 p.m., the body count had reached 1,132, leading GSDF Commanding General Matsushima to abandon the idea of relying solely on the 3rd Division. At 3:00 a.m. on the 18th, he issued orders to mobilize the 10th Division in Nagoya and the 13th Brigade in Hiroshima. Additional regiments from Hisai (Mie prefecture) and Yonago (Tottori prefecture) arrived in Kobe early morning on January 19, the third day following the earthquake.

Although they straggled in over several days, 13,000 troops had gathered in the disaster area by the evening of the 19th. On the 17th through the 20th, they rescued 32, 66, 44, and 12 people per day. In comparison, the fire department saved 1,110, 154, 92, and 16 people, while the police—the most successful organization—rescued 3,185, 245, 48, and 12 people. Notably, 91 percent of successful police rescues occurred on the first day.

The remarkably low number of successful SDF rescues on the first day is a reflection of their late arrival. It is also notable that 99 percent of rescues occurred within seventy-two hours (three days) of the earthquake; survival beyond that point was nearly miraculous. The first day was by far the most important, with approximately 86 percent of all successful rescues occurring then.

Had responsible parties assumed from the outset that an M 7–class earthquake striking a densely populated area would result in thousands of deaths, it would have been easier for the SDF to decide to mobilize its full force from the beginning. This should be a point of reflection for Japanese society as a whole.

The SDF was highly engaged in relief and recovery efforts for 100 days following the earthquake. They helped to reopen roads and remove debris, went door-to-door to ensure that all bodies were recovered, and supported social lifelines. Their thoughtful work changed their image in the eyes of the Japanese public to that of a brave and warm last line of defense for the safety of Japan and its people. Furthermore, reflection on the reasons why

TABLE 2.1 Activities of the Middle Army GSDF during the Great Hanshin-Awaji Earthquake

Main unit	Based at	Dispatched to	Arrival time
The 38th Infantry Regiment	Itami (Hyōgo)	Itami	January 17, 07:58 AM
		Nishinomiya	January 17, 10:00 AM
		Ashiya	January 17, 01:05 PM
		Amagasaki	January 18, 06:27 AM
The 3rd Artillery Regiment	Himeji (Hyōgo)	Kobe	January 17, 01:15 PM
The 3rd Anti-air Artillery Brigade	Himeji (Hyōgo)	Awajishima	January 17, 04:40 AM
The 3rd Logistic Support Regiment	Senzō (Hyōgo)	Itami, Nishinomiya, Ashiya, Kobe	January 17, 00:30 PM
The 7th Infantry Regiment	Fukuchiyama (Kyoto)	Nagata ward, Kobe	January 18, 06:00 AM
The 37th Infantry Regiment	Shinodayama (Osaka)	Kobe	January 18, 08:30 AM
The 3rd Tank Battalion	Imazu (Shiga)	Ashiya	January 18, 05:50 AM
The 15th Infantry Regiment	Zentsūji (Kagawa)	Awajishima	January 17, 05:40 PM
The 8th Anti-air Artillery Brigade	Aonohara (Hyōgo)	Suma ward, Kobe	January 18, 08:30 AM
The 8th Infantry Regiment	Yonago (Tottori)	Nada ward, Kobe	January 19, 04:30 AM
The 33rd Infantry Regiment	Hisai (Mie)	Higashinada ward, Kobe	January 19, 07:00 AM

Source: Japan Defense Agency Ground Staff Office, *Records of Actions Taken during the Dispatch for the Great Hanshin-Awaji Earthquake Disaster.*

they were slow to respond resulted in large reforms, which helped the SDF play an outstanding role after the 2011 Great East Japan Earthquake.

4. Successful Rescues in the "Belt of Destruction"

Assistance from college students

Walking ten minutes south from Fukae station in Kobe's Higashinada ward and crossing to the ocean side of National Route 43 brings you to the front gate of what was formerly the Kobe University of Mercantile Marine (now the Kobe University Faculty of Maritime Sciences following the merger of the two schools in October 2003). If you instead head northwest from Fukae station, toward National Route 2, you arrive at the university's Hakuō student dormitory building.

On the day of the Great Hanshin-Awaji Earthquake, the 250 students living in the Hakuō dormitory saved approximately 100 people trapped in collapsed homes within a two-kilometer radius. It is interesting to consider how mere college students could accomplish this, despite not having the rescue training provided to police, firefighters, and the military.

Hakuō Dormitory Student Council Chair Arita Toshiaki, who was a third-year engineering major at the time of the earthquake, said, "I don't think we did anything particularly out of the ordinary. We just did what would be expected of anyone. Our neighbors, who do so much for us, were buried alive. We just wanted to work together to help whoever we could, that's all." While his humbleness is impressive, is it really true that helping others, even neighbors, is nothing out of the ordinary?

Time is of the essence in successful rescue missions, but it can be difficult for public assistance to rapidly reach deep within a disaster area. Assistance from communities within the disaster area can therefore separate life and death.

So what is the key to realizing mutual assistance? I would like to explore this issue by examining the case of the Hakuō dormitory.[26]

One important factor is that the Hakuō dormitory was located right in the middle of the disaster site of intensity VII, but the dormitory itself was largely undamaged. Only those who are safe themselves can rescue others. Had the building or its residents not been safe, the subsequent activities of the Hakuō dormitory student council would probably have been very different. As previously described, most police and fire-department buildings in Kobe collapsed, making it difficult for their personnel to prepare for rescue missions. This was a major failure of organizations responsible for protecting society.

The Hakuō dormitory was built forty years before the earthquake, but it was a reinforced concrete structure. Despite some cracks and unevenness, it did not collapse.

Arita had gone drinking with a friend in Sannomiya, the popular downtown area of Kobe, the previous night, and did not get to bed until after 3:00 a.m. on the day of the earthquake. Second-year student Tanaka Yasuhito said that when the earthquake hit at 5:46 a.m., he thought a truck had hit the building. Arita said that a portable stereo fell on his head during the shaking, and he thought he was doomed. He made it through the tremors otherwise unharmed, but his experience reminds us that even if buildings remain sound, the furniture within them can cause significant damage. Properly securing furniture and placing beds in safe locations can prevent unnecessary tragedy.

Once the tremors subsided, Arita went out to the still-dark courtyard and confirmed that the building was intact. There he met with other officers in the student council and told them to summon all dormitory residents to the courtyard. A head count confirmed that all of the 250 residents who had been there that night were unharmed.

Immediately to the west of the Hakuō dormitory was the Sanwa market, where dormitory students would often go on various errands, making them familiar faces to those working there. As the sky brightened, the students were amazed to see that the market was gone. Buildings had fallen into the street and the arcade had collapsed, making it impossible to enter the marketplace. The area reeked of gas; had someone lit a match, a huge explosion could have occurred.

"Someone's trapped!" came a call, and some of the dormitory residents, still in pajamas, ran off to help. Arita stopped them, telling them to instead return to the dorms to fetch work clothes, winter coats, safety boots, gloves, and flashlights, and only then to head out to aid in rescue operations. He also told them not to work alone, for safety, and to provide regular status updates. Other than that, Arita was sure that since they had all practiced the details in navigation training, there was nothing more to say.[27]

These were strong young men with some equipment and training, but their task would not be easy to perform by hand. Arita sent people to standing homes to borrow tools, and in this way they obtained saws, hammers, and crowbars. While performing rescue activities, Arita climbed up on a roof and scanned the area, and saw that not just the Sanwa marketplace, but half of the wooden homes he could see had collapsed. He was stunned by the severity and extent of the damage, but the sight reinforced the need for a systematic response.

After several hours of rescue efforts, Arita returned to the dormitory, where he set up a response headquarters in the student council office and held a meeting of officers to decide on tasks and role allocations. The dormitory was a designated emergency shelter, and 460 people eventually arrived to take refuge there. Others also began coming to request aid in rescue operations. The student council dispatched teams of several students per group to help with each request. They also collected more gear, such as chainsaws and jacks from the dormitory, school, and fire department. Students tried transporting the wounded to hospitals, but the roads were so congested that they had to rely heavily on hand-pulled carts that could navigate narrow alleys.

In the interest of safety, the student council ceased all rescue efforts after the sun went down and recalled all students to the dorm. Tallying the reports from that day, they learned that they had saved over 100 people on the first day alone. Second-year student Emi Yutaka said he would never forget one sight, where a woman was calling out to her elderly parents, trapped beneath their home. "Just hang in there, Mother," he said. "I know you're hurting, but the students are on their way."

The students' response reveals how the dormitory at the Kobe University of Mercantile Marine differed from typical college dormitories, as well as from society at large. It was similar, however, to the student housing at the National Defense Academy of Japan, where I was president until 2012. There, students promptly form ranks by battalion and company to undergo inspections when called to attention by the student brigade captain. At the University of Mercantile Marine, too, young men of the sea are trained against a background of military order, with student council officers positioned below a chairman, forming an organization that allows for orderly cooperative action in times of need.

The Great Hanshin-Awaji Earthquake sent a message to Japanese society, which had long promoted modernization. Over the preceding decades, many people had moved to cities to escape the restrictions and limited opportunities of village life. This may have brought them freedom, but as the earthquake showed, the lack of ties with one's neighbors is a kind of freedom that can result in death. If cities do not work to promote close-knit social structures, then residents may have jumped from the frying pan of close but annoying community structures into the fire of freedom with no community at all.

As mentioned above, Education Director Yamada Satoru indicated that survival rates differed vastly between neighborhoods that had local festivals and those that did not. The primary precondition for community is residents who know and value each other. As the case of the Hakuō dormitory shows, however, that alone is not enough. In addition to passion, saving people requires a cool, organized response. There's a limit to how many people can be saved if rescuers are working with their bare hands; community centers and disaster-prevention centers must maintain a certain stock of tools and equipment for rescue efforts.

Most important of all are leaders, or facilitators if you prefer, who must arise from within each community, not come in from far away. In this sense, those living in the area around the Hakuō dormitory were truly blessed. I came across a similar example when speaking with residents of the Kōtōen district of Nishinomiya. They told me that an electrician living there had taken on a leadership role, calling on local residents to bring tools from their homes and cars to aid in rescuing people from their collapsed homes.

Communities need to foster leadership so that they do not depend on luck to provide them with leaders. Ideally, community training programs for disaster mitigation and rescue—not neighborhood festivals—should influences survival rates. We must recall the lessons of Edo, where major fires were largely eliminated thanks to voluntary disaster prevention organizations such as local fire brigades.

Mutual assistance accounted for 80 percent of successful rescues

Broadly speaking, everyone in the disaster area experienced personal, economic, and social losses in the Great Hanshin-Awaji Earthquake. A paper by Kyoto University Professor Kawata Yoshiaki, "Predicting Human Casualties in Large-Scale Earthquake Disasters," is frequently referenced for statistics such as the number of people who were temporarily trapped in collapsed buildings, as well as how many of those escaped by their own means and how many were rescued by others. From that paper,[28] we can make the following estimates.

TABLE 2.2 Number of persons saved and bodies recovered by various public institutions during the Great Hanshin-Awaji Earthquake

	Lives saved	Bodies recovered
Police	3,495	—
Firefighters	1,387	1,600
SDF	165	1,238
Total	5,047	2,838

Some 30,000 buildings (housing 57,000 households) collapsed immediately during the earthquake, comprising 30 percent of buildings that were structurally destroyed. At the time, there was an average of 2.87 people per household, so approximately 164,000 people were probably trapped in buildings, if only briefly. Of those, 129,000 (79 percent) were able to escape on their own, but 35,000 (21 percent) had to wait for assistance.

Police, firefighters, and SDF troops rescued a combined 7,900 people, so the remaining 27,100 were rescued by family or neighbors. In other words, 77 percent of rescues occurred through mutual assistance, and only 23 percent through public assistance. It is quite interesting that nearly 80 percent of rescues were performed by local residents despite this occurring in an urban area, where local communities are often assumed to be weaker.

Table 2.2 shows a breakdown of rescues by police, firefighters, and SDF troops, based on public statements from each organization. Note that these organizations did not always work independently, and rescues involving more than one are credited to both. There are also probably cases where fire brigades cooperated with local residents. Many people also died from their injuries after being rescued. The table lists body-recovery counts from the fire department and the SDF, but all recovered bodies were ultimately taken to the police department, which was responsible for autopsies.

There were 5,483 direct earthquake fatalities (excluding 919 of those known as *kanrenshi*, or disaster-related deaths in Hyōgo prefecture),[29] and it is believed that many of these bodies were extracted by public authorities. Disaster-related deaths, it should be pointed out, are not those who died directly in a disaster, but those whose deaths have been recognized to have been caused by the disaster in some way. Following the Great Hanshin-Awaji Earthquake, 919 people were subsequently recognized as having died as a result of the earthquake. This was the first time for this definition to be applied. This number represented 14.3 percent of the total deaths, including those who died in the disaster. The families of these victims, if recognized, received as much as five million yen in compensation from public funds. However, it is very difficult to establish causal relations, and as such, Nagaoka city, at the time of the 2004 Chūetsu Earthquake, established guidelines on the date of the death based on one week, one month, and six months following the disaster. This became known as the "Nagaoka Standard." However, there is no national standard, and there is a tendency for each municipality to decide things for itself. There have been more than 3,523 disaster-related deaths following the Great East Japan Earthquake, which represents 16.0 percent of the total, but many of those died as a result of the evacuation following the Fukushima Nuclear Accident. In the Kumamoto Earthquake, 50 people died as a direct result of the earthquake, but 175, or more than three times as many, died as a result of the disaster. Some people, afraid of staying in their homes or even in an evacuation center, chose to sleep in their vehicles, and many of those saw their health worsen and they got sick.[30]

Disassociation between faults and the "belt of destruction"

I would next like to consider the issue of the so-called "belt of destruction."

Fatalities in the Great Hanshin-Awaji Earthquake were concentrated along this belt, a narrow band stretching from the southern foothills of Mount Rokkō to Nishinomiya. The earthquake was of intensity VII in this area, which is curious since academic research suggests that there are no faults directly beneath it.

The epicenter was seventeen kilometers beneath the Akashi strait, and the earthquake ran shallowly beneath the ground surface for fifteen kilometers, southwest toward Awaji Island. It continued running east by northeast along the southern foot of Mount Rokko without reaching the ground surface. The main fault then ran approximately beneath Kobe University in Nada ward before leaving the city and entering the mountains along the Gosukebashi fault. It passed the pond of Okuike in Ashiya, entering the mountains toward Takarazuka for an unknown distance.

If the main fault ran through Okuike and the mountain range, why was central Nishinomiya, far to the southeast, so devastatingly affected? Even in Kobe, the band of intensity VII seismic activity was one to two kilometers south of the fault line running along the mountain. From Ashiya this separation widened, reaching almost ten kilometers near Nishinomiya.

Generally speaking, the intensity of shaking depends primarily on distance from the fault, and secondarily on the firmness of the ground. Perhaps in this case, however, we can explain the contradiction of the first rule by some extraordinary weakness in the ground. Earthquake researchers have not denied that possibility, but have suggested another, completely different explanation—that the large rupture was caused by a fault that ripped apart bedrock deep underground, and the "belt of destruction" was the meeting point of the two different shockwaves the rupture would make.

As shown in the upper left of the map 2.1, the resulting shockwave would have traveled through soft ground layers above the bedrock until it reached the surface. Another factor was a secondary shockwave gener-

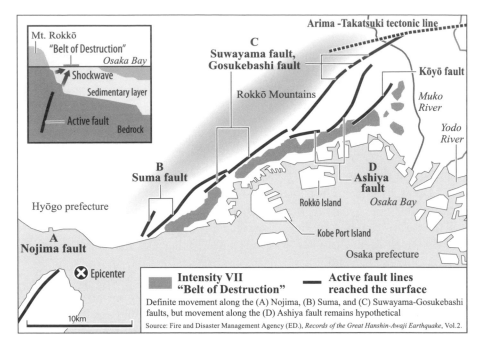

Map 2.1. Fault ruptures causing the Great Hanshin-Awaji Earthquake (A, B, C) and the "Belt of Destruction" in which intensity VII earthquakes occurred

ated in the vicinity of the boundary between sedimentary layers and the bedrock that rises to form the Rokkō mountain range, then propagated along the surface within the sedimentary layer as what is called a basin-induced surface wave. In the region one to two kilometers south of the Rokkō mountains, these two shockwaves meet, causing a synergistic effect (called a "focus effect" or "shoreline effect"), resulting in a zone of seismic intensity VII that exactly covers the busy area along the Japan Railways and Hanshin Electric Railway lines and National Route 2.

Earthquake researchers have also discovered another factor: directivity effects in rupture propagation. This earthquake started in the Akashi strait and followed the Rokkō mountain range, and as a strike-slip fault heading east-northeast it had strong directionality in its propagation, causing it to operate as a strong pulse wave. The explanation is that this resonated within the above-described region of shockwave collision, amplifying it and sending it along the belt of intensity VII stretching from eastern Kobe to Ashiya and Nishinomiya.

Most experts consider the Great Hanshin-Awaji Earthquake to be a phenomenon produced by extremely unique topographical and ground conditions and earthquake directivity. This earthquake demonstrated the need to rethink notions that the strength of tremors is a simple function of distance from the epicenter and the solidity of the underlying ground.[31]

For some unknown reason, those living in the Kansai area of Japan had developed a near-mythological belief that while the region was subject to frequent storms and floods, major earthquakes did not strike there. It is even more mind-boggling that the heads of disaster prevention in both Hyōgo prefecture and Kobe city seem to have truly believed such myths. In 1974, Kobe asked a group of earthquake researchers to investigate the possibility of a major earthquake hitting the city and was told that a movement of the fault along the southern foothills of the Rokkō mountains would result in tremors of intensity VII. This prophetic response was presented on the front page of the *Kobe Shimbun* newspaper.[32] Nonetheless, both Hyōgo and Kobe continued disaster-prevention training that assumed an intensity of V or lower.

Kobe is expected to experience an intensity V earthquake if the Yamasaki fault near Himeji moves, or if a massive earthquake occurs in the Nankai trough. The city thus ignored the possibility of a direct hit with intensity VII, and instead prepared only for an earthquake in which buildings would not collapse. This history of lackadaisical preparations made both the public and the government complacent regarding their safety.

Even in retrospect, it is unclear why such criminal neglect was allowed, but I feel that a *Kobe Shimbun* newspaper interview with the dean of the School of Engineering at Kobe University provides a hint.[33] The dean said there was no need to act as if a large earthquake would strike tomorrow, and called for a calm, reasoned response. In other words, Kobe should continue to modernize (which was called "to corporatize"), and already-limited resources should not be allocated toward an earthquake that might never come. Modernization itself would make Kobe a stronger city, including with regard to its disaster-prevention capabilities. Attitudes such as this probably led officials to downplay the possibility of an intensity VII earthquake and encouraged the public to forget that such possibilities existed throughout the region.

Known faults crisscross maps of Japan, but still represent only a fraction of those that actually exist. Even today, it is not unusual for an earthquake to reveal a previously unknown fault. There have been amazing developments in research capabilities, but while we await further results, we should concentrate on improving the safety of our own homes and communities, regardless of where we live.

Even after witnessing the oversights that led to the tragedy of Kobe,

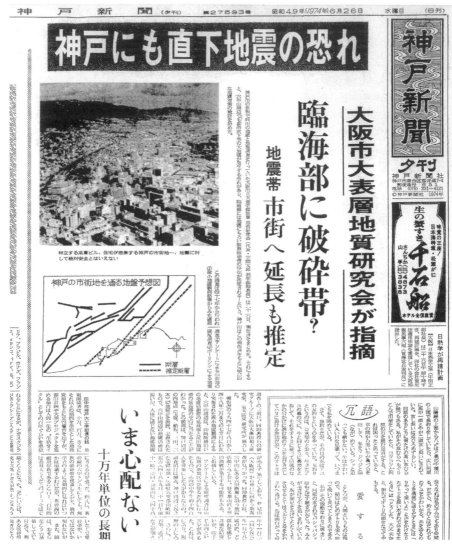

Figure 2.4. The front-page story of a local newspaper reporting the possibility of a major earthquake (© June 26, 1974, evening edition of the *Kobe Shimbun*)

people in many other parts of Japan continue to fall into the trap of thinking they are uniquely safe. We must realize that there is no place across the Japanese archipelago that is safe from earthquake disasters. Indeed, there are few safe places in the world, especially in the Ring of Fire surrounding the Pacific Ocean, it seems.

5. Initial Response by Leaders

Crisis management learned in storm and flood disasters

All the mayors of the afflicted municipalities were at home when the Great Hanshin-Awaji Earthquake struck. This is somewhat surprising considering the frequency with which they travel, but was probably the result of January being a busy period of budget-making. Although all were home, however, the amount of time it took them to reach their offices varied widely.

The first to arrive was Itami mayor Matsushita Tsutomu, who said that when the earthquake woke him, he was "being thrown about in his bed like stir-fry in a pan." When the shaking subsided, he immediately put on his clothes, jumped into his car, and arrived at the Itami city hall ten minutes later. This was unusual; as discussed in more detail below, it is common in Japan for elite politicians to be chauffeured about in government-owned vehicles. Matsushita was in fact the only civic leader in the disaster area to drive his own car to his office.

More importantly, the mayor believed he had a clear duty to reach his office as quickly as possible. Matsushita had previously served in posts such as public works director of Amagasaki city, and thus had learned crisis management in an area with frequent storm and flood disasters.

The four cities situated at the periphery of the Great Hanshin-Awaji Earthquake—Amagasaki, Itami, Kawanishi, and Inagawa—share a common fate in that each is located in the Ina drainage basin, subjecting them to the effects of torrential rain. Amagasaki, with a population just under 500,000, took a leading role in facilitating responses.

Amagasaki mayor Miyata Yoshio got a ride to his office with the daughter of his deputy mayor, who lived in the same neighborhood on the north side of the city as him. They drove down darkened, deserted streets to arrive at city hall at 6:10 a.m. Several executives had already arrived, and the general-affairs section manager had started to respond to the situation. By 6:30 a.m. they had opened an initial disaster headquarters. One-third of Amagasaki is below sea level, and so is easily subject to flooding. Miyata said that provided his city with the "sad habit" of being sensitive to natural disasters.[34] Although the Kansai area shared the region-wide mistaken assumption of being safe from earthquakes, then, this experience in dealing with storm and flood disasters served these areas well.

A typical example is Ashiya deputy mayor Gotō Tarō. As a veteran bureaucrat, which included serving as director of storm and flood response operations, Gotō was well aware of the areas within his city that were most at risk. He instinctively grasped the seriousness of the Great Hanshin-Awaji Earthquake from the moment that it tossed him up in the air. He ran down the hills of Iwazono where he lived, and arrived at city hall at 6:10 a.m. Only two night-duty staff were there, so he sent one to the home of the chair of the medical association to request medical aid, and the other to a temple to ask for a place to store bodies. When telephone service was finally restored, he ordered 100 coffins; having seen the state of the city on his way to city hall, he knew that at least that many would be needed.

Ashiya mayor Kitamura Harue was sleeping on the first floor of her two-story home in Asahigaoka, and said that when the earthquake struck, she ran out to the pitch-black yard in her pajamas. Her husband crawled outside moaning, his hip having been broken by a toppled dresser. She spread a futon on a storm door that had fallen during the shaking and laid her husband on it. As she stood there in her yard, shaking from the cold, General Affairs Section Manager Hidaka Shigeru drove up. Hidaka lived in Kusunoki town, along National Route 2, an area where many buildings had collapsed. He explained later that immediately after the earthquake he spent some time helping to pull people from the rubble in his neighborhood, then got into his car to check on relatives living to the east toward Nishinomiya. He soon had second thoughts, however, and turned back toward his office in city hall instead. This is the dilemma that public servants face: should they attend to family, relatives, and neighbors who need help, or go to work for the city as a whole?

Collapsed buildings blocked streets throughout Ashiya. Realizing that the mayor might be stuck without her driver, Hidaka headed north toward the mayor's residence. He helped the mayor take her wounded husband to the hospital, then made it to city hall after 7:00 a.m. When Deputy Mayor Gotō finally met up with her, he said, "We can expect at least one hundred fatalities. I've ordered their coffins."

This probably seemed a reasonable prognostication at the time, considering that Ashiya is a small city of fewer than 90,000, but they soon realized that it was overly optimistic. By noon, it was evident that the body count would exceed 400. Note that at the same time, the police were reporting 203 deaths throughout the entire disaster area, and even that was enough to surprise Prime Minister Murayama Tomiichi. Some local governments thus developed a more accurate understanding of the situation by observing developments around them, rather than paying attention to mistaken information circulating in society at large.[35]

Leaders awaiting their drivers

Some local leaders failed to act quickly because they did not drive, instead relying on chauffeurs to drive them in publicly owned automobiles. This caused delays because most chauffeurs and other staff were impacted by the earthquake.

Some, like the mayor of Ashiya, were fortunate to have dedicated staff able to come to their aid. Kobe mayor Sasayama Kazutoshi was stuck at his official residence in Nada ward, 5.2 kilometers from city hall, unable to contact anyone. He had gotten ready to leave, and was considering walking to his offices, when Yamashita Akihiro, a departmental director, drove up. As they headed to city hall, the mayor—who had a background in architecture and civil engineering—spoke about buildings he was concerned about, and Yamashita was surprised to see that as he had pointed out, each had collapsed or been damaged in the earthquake. They arrived at city hall at 6:35 a.m.

The roads were damaged, and some were even impassable, but still empty enough to arrive quickly after some detours. Congestion started to get serious after 7:00 a.m., however. Hyōgo prefectural governor Kaihara Toshitami was picked up after 7:30, but it took him thirty minutes to travel just three kilometers. He finally arrived at his office at 8:20 a.m.[36]

The drivers for the mayors of Takarazuka and Nishinomiya were detained due to the earthquake. The home of the driver for Takarazuka mayor Shōji Taiichirō had collapsed, but he nevertheless rode his motorcycle to city hall, where he took a public-use car to pick up the mayor. He arrived at the mayor's home in Hibarigaoka before 8:00 a.m., but due to traffic congestion they did not arrive at city hall, just five kilometers away, until 9:20 a.m. General Affairs Section Chief Sakagami Motoyuki had arrived by car within ten minutes of the earthquake and had set up a disaster-response headquarters in place of the mayor, whom he was unable to contact. The mayor first learned the seriousness of the situation from Sakagami's reports. In the end, there were twenty-seven fatalities within Takarazuka.

It must be remembered that at the time of the Great Hanshin-Awaji Earthquake, mobile phones were not commonplace. The instance of Lower House member Takami Yūichi was a rare one; he walked around the disaster area and appealed to Chief Cabinet Secretary Igarashi Kōzō (1926–2013) while talking on his mobile phone. Home and office phone lines were constantly busy, and in only rare cases did calls go through. The only lines that did work were public phones, and only when coins were used (and not prepaid telephone cards, which were more common). Only a few people realized this at the time. In any case, it was nearly impossible to make contact with one another.

Nishinomiya mayor Baba Junzō lived far from his offices, twenty-five kilometers north over the mountains in the town of Shiose. One of his directors went to pick him up, but it was 10:30 a.m. by the time they arrived at city hall. With 1,126 fatalities, Nishinomiya was second only to Kobe, and yet it took nearly five hours for the city's leader to take his post when he was most needed.

Today, there is much more resistance to leaders and others responsible for crisis management living so far from their workplaces, but it is worth considering the extent to which the absence of upper-level leadership is a substantial problem. Some say that it does not matter much. The top priority in the first hours of a disaster is saving lives and putting out fires, which are tasks for first responders such as police and firefighters, who do not need to wait for a mayor's instructions. Of course, disaster personnel in local government bodies, too, can start working without mayoral direction. Municipal tasks are typically centered in the General Affairs Section, as was the case of Takarazuka. In Nishinomiya, Education Director Yamada Satoru took charge, probably because he had previous disaster-related

TABLE 2.3 How leaders of various towns and cities made it to government office buildings after the Great Hanshin-Awaji Earthquake

Name and locale	Distance from home to office	Time from earthquake to arrival	Notes
Matsushita Tsutomu (Itami)	2.5 km	10 min	Drove by private car
Miyata Yoshio (Amagasaki)	3.5 km	25 min	Got a ride with deputy mayor living nearby
Kokubo Masao (Hokudan)	0.3 km	30 min	Walked via a circuitous route
Sasayama Kazutoshi (Kobe)	5.2 km	50 min	Picked up by city director living nearby
Kitamura Harue (Ashiya)	2.0 km	1 hr 20 min	Picked up by secretary after taking wounded husband to hospital
Kaihara Toshitami (Hyōgo prefecture)	3.0 km	2 hr 35 min	Had manager come to pick him up
Shōji Taiichirō (Takarazuka)	5.0 km	3 hr 35 min	Had driver come to pick him up in public vehicle, caught in traffic
Baba Junzō (Nishinomiya)	25.0 km	4 hr 45 min	Had city director pick him up, but delayed due to distance and traffic

experience as chief of civil engineering. He was able to set up a disaster response headquarters even as he tried to contact the absent mayor.[37]

However, emergency situations call for decisions completely unlike those made during peaceful times. Emergency shelters must be set up, the wounded must be cared for, bodies must be disposed of, and food and water must be procured. Meanwhile, assistance from outside must be requested and citizens informed. There is a veritable flood of important issues, for which there may be no rules or precedents. The attitudes of government leaders largely determine whether the response will focus on short-term measures or on compassionate rescue and recovery efforts.

Psychological pressures affect the actions and attitudes of leaders as well. Present-day social attitudes condemn elected officials who do not roll up their sleeves and get to work alongside first responders to aid victims, saying they lacked leadership and were heartless.

Initial response in Hyōgo prefecture

The actions of the Hyōgo prefectural government present an interesting example of how local governments and their leaders differ in their approaches to crisis response.

The ability of peacetime security mechanisms such as police and fire departments to handle large numbers of disaster victims and simultaneously occurring fires is limited, so governors are supposed to be able to request emergency relief from national governmental agencies and the SDF during disasters like the Great Hanshin-Awaji Earthquake. These governors are expected to negotiate with the national government on behalf of the afflicted area.

The first disaster manager to arrive at the Hyōgo prefectural government offices was Fire and Traffic Safety Section Head Noguchi Kazuyuki. Noguchi left his home in Nishi ward by car before 6:00 a.m. and arrived at around 6:40 a.m. When Noguchi arrived, the power was out and the elevators were not working, so he walked up twelve flights of stairs to his office. When he arrived, however, he was unable to get in, as toppled lockers in the office had blocked the door.

Vice Governor Ashio Chōji arrived as Noguchi stood in the hall wondering what to do. Ashio who lived in Higashinada ward, had been in charge of planning the response to a Tōkai Earthquake when he worked in Shizuoka prefecture, and therefore considered it his duty to immediately report to the prefectural offices. He got a ride from his son-in-law, who lived in the same condominiums as he did. Hearing from the guards that

Noguchi had already arrived, he followed him up the stairs to the twelfth floor. They were unable to open the door but found a section of wall that had been damaged and were able to enter the office that way. Once inside, Noguchi busied himself handling telephone calls for the hour it took for more staff to arrive.

Ashio went downstairs to the sixth-floor vice governor's office, where he tried to telephone the governor Kaihara many times before his call made it through. He notified the governor that he was forming a disaster-response headquarters in a meeting room on the fifth floor, and the governor requested that someone immediately come to pick him up.

The first disaster-response headquarters meeting was held at 8:30 a.m., ten minutes after Governor Kaihara arrived. Another three section leaders were now on site, so this first meeting was conducted by five of twenty-one staff members. This first meeting was perhaps called too early, considering that leaders had not had time to collect information and much was unknown. Electrical, gas, and water service had stopped, and they had no reliable means of communication. The windows were broken, allowing the cold winter wind to blow in.

Noguchi was asked to give a report at the meeting. He explained that the SDF (in Himeji) had telephoned at 8:10 a.m., and that he had informed them that the governor would eventually request mobilization. Although the SDF later stated it had not been told during that phone call to be ready for a request, the important point is that Noguchi reported his conversation with the SDF to prefectural leaders twenty minutes later at 8:30 at the headquarters meeting, and there was no dissent from the opinion that Noguchi was correct in informing the SDF that the governor would eventually make the request. Had that not been the case, Noguchi probably could not have assented when the second telephone call came at 10:00 a.m., during which the SDF had asked that the governor request them to dispatch. Noguchi made this decision on his own, then ran downstairs from the twelfth floor to the fifth to report to the governor on the content of the phone call. He says that the governor replied, "I suppose we have no other choice."

If the governor displayed reluctance, it was not in regard to requesting deployment of the SDF. As the early morning situation shows, everyone from the governor down to the section chiefs recognized the need to do so.

However, government ordinances specify procedures for determining areas requiring help, personnel, and equipment, based on the disaster situation. In reality, based on common procedures, local government offices and SDF leaders typically reach a consensus regarding what to do and the actual request becomes a formality. The earthquake had created an information blackout, so those in prefectural offices did not grasp the situation sufficiently to satisfy the conditions for an official request. Even the telephone worked only sporadically. As a result, the dispatch request was largely a blanket request for help, an uncomfortable situation for government bureaucrats.

Luckily, the governor's hesitation was overcome thanks to early-morning preparations by the SDF and the rapid response by on-site personnel. When I was collecting oral histories, Noguchi told me, "They called it a request from the governor, but actually it came from me," deeply impressing me with the importance of prefectural office workers, all the way down to section leaders.[38]

Governor Kaihara arrived at the prefectural offices two and a half hours after the earthquake, which some complained was "too late." While obtaining an oral history from the governor,[39] I pressed him to learn what he had been doing during that time. In particular, I wanted to know why he did not do what many seemed to expect: walk to his office, as Gotō did in Ashiya. Had he done so, he would have witnessed the horrible sight of citizens calling out from beneath piles of rubble and gained some idea of how serious the situation was, even if a full grasp was impossible. On arriving at his office, he could have quickly taken up the reins of leadership. Communications systems were largely down, but surely he could have used internal police systems to contact the chief of police, or officials in Tokyo?

In response, the governor described his reasoning. "The worst thing that can happen in an emergency is for leaders to go missing. I knew that if I remained at home, someone would contact me," he explained. Still, the governor is a larger-than-life figure, and in extreme circumstances people expect this extraordinarily charismatic figure to come to their rescue.

Telephones and other communications systems were restored before noon. The governor toured the most severely damaged areas by police car at 1:00 p.m., and the next day surveyed the disaster situation by helicopter, which finally gave him a grasp of the overall situation.[40] Following that, he exhibited strong leadership in pursuit of reconstruction.

6. Initial Response by the Prime Minister

A lack of information

Of the 5,502 deaths directly attributable to the Great Hanshin-Awaji Earthquake (excluding disaster-related deaths from the 6,434 total fatalities), the National Police Agency used autopsy reports to estimate that around 4,831 people (88 percent) were killed by compression and 550 (10 percent) by burning. It is difficult to estimate how many people died while waiting for rescue after being buried in rubble.[41] Approximately 90 percent of compression deaths are believed to have been instantaneous, and the figure for fire victims includes those whose bodies were burned after death.

One of the most pitiful scenes in a disaster is someone trapped beneath rubble who at first answers to calls from family members but then falls silent. Scenes such as this make the importance of governmental and societal preparedness painfully obvious and raise the question of what the central government was doing immediately after the earthquake.

Japan at the time was led by Prime Minister Murayama Tomiichi, who was politically supported by Chief Cabinet Secretary Igarashi Kōzō and Deputy Chief Cabinet Secretary Ishihara Nobuo. On the morning of January 17, 1995, the prime minister was in his official residence adjacent to his ministerial office, Igarashi was in his parliamentarian housing in Tokyo's Takanawa district, and Ishihara was at his private home in Kawasaki city. None of them learned of the earthquake in Kobe via emergency communications to the prime minister's office, but rather from NHK news reports at around 6:00 a.m. (Murayama and Igarashi by television, Ishihara by radio during his customary morning walk), where they heard that an earthquake of around intensity V had occurred in Kyoto. Perhaps it is not surprising in this era of twenty-four-hour cable news that mass media coverage was faster than the government's emergency-contact network, but the problem in this case is that the Japanese government's emergency-communications system was nonfunctional.

Early-morning reports suggesting that the earthquake was centered in Kyoto were due to the fact that equipment at the meteorological observatory in Kobe had been destroyed and its telephone lines cut, limiting available information. As happened in the hours and days after the atomic bomb was dropped on Hiroshima, the site of the most extensive damage in Kobe was at first treated as if it were untouched or had been unaffected. This happens when an area is so grievously harmed that it cannot even call out in pain. It becomes deadly quiet.

In a disaster, the National Land Agency's Disaster Prevention Bureau is supposed to gather information from the Meteorological Agency, the National Police Agency, the Fire Department, the Defense Agency, local governments, and other sources, and pass this information on to the prime minister's office through the government communications system. However, National Land Agency staff did not work on twenty-four-hour shifts, so the first Disaster Prevention Bureau staff to arrive in response to summons from on-duty personnel came an hour after the quake, at 6:45 a.m. Apparently, the government had no system for responding to the first moments of a crisis outside working hours.

At some point after 6:00 a.m., the Meteorological Agency sent the National Land Agency a fax stating that the intensity in Kobe was VI, but no agencies had details regarding the extent of damage. National police commissioner Kunimatsu Takaji received an early telephone call from Hyōgo Prefectural Police chief Takitō Kōji describing the situation and the state of response, and GSDF Chief of Staff Tomizawa received a similar call from the GSDF Middle Army Commander Matsushima Yūsuke. Neither, however, contacted the National Land Agency or the prime minister's office. Such is the nature of vertically organized bureaucracies, but we should ask ourselves if the prime minister should be captive to such a structure at times of crisis.

Prime Minister Murayama eventually received a telephone call from his secretary stating that the damage was probably greater than first expected, and therefore entered his offices at 8:26 a.m., an hour earlier than initially scheduled. There were still no official disaster reports, but as the darkness lifted after 7:00 a.m., television reports started showing snippets of the afflicted area from the air. After 8:00 a.m., the actual situation became clearer. Shocked by what he saw, Cabinet Secretary Igarashi strongly urged the National Land Agency to set up an emergency-response headquarters.

Deputy Chief Cabinet Secretary Ishihara, whose house was ninety minutes from the office, arrived before 9:00 a.m. and consulted with Chief Cabinet Secretary Igarashi about a conference on monthly economic reports scheduled for 9:20 a.m. that day. Because many committee members from other agencies were expected to attend, Igarashi decided to hold the meeting as scheduled. At 9:00 a.m., television news programs were reporting only a single fatality.[42]

If members of the prime minister's office had felt any need to set aside normal modes of operation to notify the government and the Japanese people of the serious situation, then surely something like a monthly economic report could have waited. More importantly, they would have urgently summoned representatives from the SDF and the fire and police departments to gather information and work out a response before the 10:00 a.m. cabinet meeting. However, neither the prime minister nor Deputy Secretary Ishihara was watching television, and considering the lack of official reports, they probably felt no need to take extraordinary measures. Thus, the prime minister and the chief cabinet secretary attended the economic meeting, while the deputy secretary left to gather information and prepare for the Cabinet meeting.

According to the Disaster Countermeasures Basic Act of 1961, local municipalities were primarily responsible for dealing with disasters, and if they were unable to handle them, the prefectures or central government would assist. However, the Great Hanshin-Awaji Earthquake and Great East Japan Earthquake showed that small municipalities and even larger prefectures were powerless in the face of a major disaster. If the country as a whole did not get involved, no one could be properly protected. Nevertheless, the central government continues to push things onto local authorities and has even failed to establish a Disaster Response Agency. There is still a reluctance to give too much power to the central government, a lingering result of occupation policies and postwar pacifism.

Television reports versus official information

Meanwhile, at around 9:00 a.m., heated discussions were underway in the office of Defense Policy Bureau director Murata Naoaki. Division chief Moriya Takemasa argued that televised reporting showed that the damage was so extensive the SDF should be deployed without waiting for an official request for assistance. Operations Director Yamazaki Shinshirō countered that there were still no credible reports, and that deploying military units would simply add to the confusion. In the end, Murata decided to tell the SDF to hurry its preparations. Here, too, those relying on television reporting battled those who trusted official information more. However, no reliable official information capturing the entirety of the situation would become available during that chaotic first day.

Participants in the 10:00 a.m. cabinet meeting decided to follow the stipulations of the Disaster Countermeasures Basic Act of 1961 and establish an disaster-response headquarters under the leadership of the director general of the National Land Agency. While this measure brought together disaster prevention officials from various ministries and agencies under one leader, it addressed only practical aspects of the problem. A political-level response would probably be needed as well, so the members of the cabinet meeting established a Ministerial Conference for Earthquake Response.

At 11:00 a.m., Prime Minister Murayama attended the Commission on Global Environment in the 21st Century, where he gave a warm address. The prime minister thus attended two routine meetings during the morning, and as a result was far less informed than the general public, who were getting a better idea of the state of crisis from their television sets. At the time, it was common practice for the prime minister to respond to reporters' questions in hallways while walking between meetings. The gap in recognition of the crisis made his responses edgy that day. When asked if he would visit the disaster site, on four separate occasions (at 9:18, 10:01, 11:03, and 11:23 a.m.) the prime minister replied he would do so "after hearing the results of the inspection by National Land Agency Director General Ozawa Kiyoshi." These repeated business-as-usual responses solidified Murayama's public image as being overly disconnected from the crisis.

It wasn't until around noon that the prime minister realized how serious things were. When passed a memo reading "203 dead," he audibly gasped. More details arrived in the form of a call to the cabinet secretary from Diet member Takami Yūichi, who was on the ground in the disaster area and had access to a mobile phone. By 12:05 Murayama was finally coming to grips with the situation, and when asked in the hallway about the departure of Diet member Yamahana Sadao from the Social Democratic Party of Japan, he snapped, "This isn't the time to discuss that." At an emergency press conference at 4:00 p.m., Murayama stated that he would like to travel to the disaster site as soon as possible and to take whatever measures were necessary. He also called the earthquake "the largest urban disaster since the Great Kantō Earthquake."

Deputy Chief Cabinet Secretary Ishihara was deluged with complaints regarding the absence of the SDF and questions about what they were doing at such a serious time. At around 2:00 p.m., he telephoned Defense Director Murata and demanded to know why the SDF was not on the scene. When Murata tried to make excuses, Ishihara cut him off, saying "I need you to tell me exactly what the SDF can do to help, and it better be every damn thing possible." Clearly, the prime minister's office was hurrying to make up for time lost during the morning.

Establishment of the Emergency Response Headquarters

On the day of the earthquake, National Land Agency Director General Ozawa flew to the disaster site to make whatever observations he could. However, the area was in such an extreme state of confusion that gaining a full picture of the situation was impossible. The secretary is no doubt a good man, but he attained his position for being able to do his job well in ordinary times; he had no passion for single-handedly resolving an extremely serious crisis. Doing so required the establishment of a central governmental framework for addressing the disaster.

Figure 2.5. (From left) Cabinet Minister Ozato Sadatoshi (special minister in charge of the Great Hanshin-Awaji Earthquake), Prime Minister Murayama Tomiichi, Chief Cabinet Secretary Igarashi Kōzō, and Construction Minister Nosaka Kōken at work. The Emergency Response Headquarters in the prime minister's office (January 21, 1995)

The prime minister first visited the disaster area on the 19th, after which a series of disaster-response systems was formed under the leadership of Deputy Chief Cabinet Secretary Ishihara. Some complained that Murayama took too long to visit the area, but nonetheless it served as an expression of the government's recognition that the situation was serious. It is difficult to find fault with the changes that came about as a result of the prime minister's visit.

The first such change was the strengthening of the above-mentioned Ministerial Conference for Earthquake Response, which was formalized as a newly established Emergency Response Headquarters. The Disaster Countermeasures Basic Act codified the establishment of this type of operational base, but it prescribes leadership by the prime minister and membership by heads of relevant ministries and agencies, and therefore is not suited to decision-making at the highest level by the prime minister and key cabinet members. The Emergency Response Headquarters was instead established with extra-legal powers as the ultimate arbiter of disaster-related policy.

The second result of the prime minister's site visit was that Cabinet

Minister Ozato Sadatoshi (1930–2016; he had previously led development agencies for Okinawa and Hokkaidō) was appointed as a full-time special minister-in-charge of the Great Hanshin-Awaji Earthquake. Murayama, Igarashi, and Ishihara all agreed to this proposal, knowing that Ozato was an extremely dedicated worker.

Interviews with Prime Minister Murayama and Ozato indicate that when Ozato visited disaster areas in Kobe on January 20, the prime minister agreed with all of his on-the-ground assessments and promised government-wide support for his decisions.[43]

The third result was that on January 22, a local-response headquarters led by National Land Agency Vice Minister Kuno Tōichirō was established in Kobe, and Ozato assigned powerful section chiefs from various ministries and agencies to staff it. This provided a framework for prioritizing on-site decisions coordinated between Hyōgo prefecture and Kobe city.

These systems connecting the regional and central governments produced their first results in the area of rubble removal. It was decided that the national government would bear the expense of clearing buildings destroyed in the disaster, including collapsed private homes. This was a wise decision, in that it allowed for a more rapid recovery. I myself was surprised at how quickly roads were cleared after this decision was made.

At noon on the day of the disaster, Governor Kaihara applied the Disaster Relief Act to ten cities and ten towns in the affected areas and specified the financial resources to be used for immediate relief. On January 24, the government officially designated the earthquake as a serious disaster, raising the level of financial support available for recovery. Under this system, central and regional governments could effectively implement emergency response and recovery measures, including the provision of temporary housing.

Incredible as it may seem, at the time of the disaster the prime minister's office had no information systems that functioned in emergency situations. This was a serious shortcoming that hampered the initial response on the morning of the earthquake. That is the image that the public remembered, but the Murayama cabinet, with the support of Chief Cabinet Secretary Igarashi and Deputy Chief Cabinet Secretary Ishihara, was able to reestablish control by the afternoon, and in the end provided a better and more efficient government response and recovery than followed either the Great Kantō or the Great East Japan Earthquake. The key to that result was empowering local governments and establishing frameworks that respected them.

7. Aspects of Recovery and Restoration

The recovery process

While individual disasters are unique, certain common patterns emerge in the response and recovery processes that follow. Even when feeling a deep sense of loss, the public is highly conscious of these governmental and societal responses.

Life-saving activities

The first phase following a disaster is emergency relief, the central concern of which is saving lives and extinguishing fires.

Large earthquakes, particularly those directly striking urban areas, cause homes to collapse, trapping and crushing those within. Many people were sleeping when the Great Hanshin-Awaji Earthquake hit, so the structural strength of their homes proved to be a fundamental factor in survival. Due to the widely held myth that the Kansai region was immune to earthquakes, self-help measures in preparation for disaster were woefully insufficient.

Saving lives is of utmost priority following a disaster, and families and society desire nothing more than live rescues. That requires mutual aid in the form of rescue efforts by family and neighbors. In this respect, too, myths regarding earthquake safety prevented sufficient preparation. A secondary priority in Japan is the rapid recovery of bodies, due to social customs calling for careful treatment of the dead.

Home collapses also unavoidably result in fires, further expanding losses of life and property. Firefighting activities are thus another high priority for first response.

Emergency aid

The next phase is the provision of life-sustaining emergency aid for survivors, in the form of food and shelter. Primary tasks include opening emergency shelters, providing lifeline support, removing rubble, and reopening roads.

Survivors who have lost their homes require emergency shelters. With water, power, and gas service stopped and convenience stores and supermarkets closed, food, water, and toilets must also be provided. At the peak of recovery following the Great Hanshin-Awaji Earthquake, over 300,000 people were housed at 1,153 emergency shelters. In Japan, opening shelters is primarily the job of town and city local government bodies. Most of the 1.38 million volunteers who garnered so much attention in the Great Hanshin-Awaji Earthquake were affiliated with these shelters.

In previous recovery efforts, it was customary for individual homeowners to be held responsible for clearing their collapsed homes. However, this is unrealistic following a large earthquake. Collapsed homes block roadways, which is a shared societal concern. In response to strong pressure from the afflicted areas, just two weeks after the earthquake the Japanese government agreed to use national funds to cover up to 95 percent of the costs of waste removal. This wise decision allowed collapsed buildings and mounds of debris to be rapidly converted to bare lots. This was the first instance ever of national funds being used to address issues on private property.

Mountains of rubble are not only a symbol of disaster, they are a symbol of delayed recovery and reconstruction. In the case of the Great Hanshin-Awaji Earthquake, the national government and the affected areas collaborated to promptly deal with this issue. In total, an estimated 14.5 million tons of rubble from homes and other sources were removed, at a cost of 265 billion yen.

Although their initial deployment was delayed, the SDF played a significant role in establishing lifelines, opening roads, removing debris, and assisting in house-to-house searches to ensure that all bodies were recovered from collapsed homes. The kindness and warmth that they showed when performing these tasks renewed the public image of the SDF.

Emergency reconstruction

The third phase of response is emergency reconstruction, primarily building temporary housing. A simultaneous concern is the recovery of infrastructure such as roads, railways, and other public facilities damaged in the disaster.

A Japanese expression says that there are no weak soldiers under a strong general, and this aptly describes Hyōgo prefecture during its recovery. Governor Kaihara did not return home for a month following the earthquake, instead setting a motivating example for his subordinates by remaining in command at the prefectural offices.

In late January, Kaihara announced plans to construct 30,000 temporary homes by the end of March. This seemed to be an impossible goal, considering that the entire prefab housing industry produced only 10,000

Figure 2.6. Temporary housing under construction at Kobe Port Island (March 1995)

units per month. Nevertheless, a little over 30,000 homes were completed by March 31, and 48,300 were completed by August. At the peak, 47,000 households were living in temporary homes. It is a great relief when families can move from shelters to the privacy of temporary homes. However, life there can be lonely and inconvenient, particularly for the elderly. The last families left these temporary homes in January 2000, three years after initial projections.

Japan Railways, including the bullet train (Shinkansen) and the Hankyū and Hanshin rail lines, all shut down following the earthquake, having sustained significant damage. The only major road that remained open was National Route 2, and the rush of people trying to travel on it resulted in paralyzing daytime traffic jams that lasted for a couple of weeks.

Recovery, however, was rapid. Rail lines provide the backbone of transportation for the area, and by January 25, Japan Railways was able to reopen the line between Osaka and Ashiya. I rode that train immediately afterward, facing forward and standing just behind the conductor. Some sections of the line between the Kōshienguchi and Ashiya stations felt unnaturally warped, to the point that I worried if the train might derail, but we traveled slowly between repair crews, and nothing happened. The line between Suma and Kobe opened on January 30, the difficult construction over the Ashiya river was completed on February 8, and Kobe and Osaka were reconnected on April 1, thus completing the Tōkaidō line. The speed of this recovery drew surprise from overseas observers.

Toward true recovery

The goal of the fourth phase is true recovery, although it occurs amid the busy activity of emergency repairs and reconstruction. Recovery plans proceed at all levels, but the construction of new housing for displaced people carries a particularly symbolic meaning.

On March 9, Hyōgo prefecture announced plans to build 125,000 homes over three years, including 79,000 units of public rental homes and apartments (over 60 percent of the total) and 46,000 private homes. Hyōgo prefecture is interesting in that it tends to base policy recommendations and medium- to long-term goals on surveys and research. Three days following the earthquake, the prefecture organized an emergency damage investigatory team in conjunction with professors from Kobe University, and spent two months on focused investigations. To estimate the number of emergency housing units needed, Hyōgo prefecture also participated in a comprehensive investigation of damaged buildings conducted by the

Association of Urban Housing Sciences. In addition, under the leadership of Urban Housing Manager Shibata Takahiro, the prefecture reviewed and confirmed all materials related to public funds applied to clearing collapsed houses. This exhaustive review covered every property in the disaster area. The prefectural government furthermore established the Hyōgo Housing Reconstruction Conference, an association of private scholars and experts, to broadly seek ideas and discussion.

Governor Kaihara had previously proposed shifting from a housing model centered on private ownership to one that prioritized rental properties, increased the importance placed on public rental housing, and established initiatives for collective housing to avoid elderly isolation. The Great Hanshin-Awaji Earthquake struck just as detailed research was beginning and served to accelerate the changes.

As mentioned above, one week after the disaster the government subsidy rate was raised for municipal governing bodies designated under the 1962 Law Concerning Special Fiscal Aid for Coping with Severe Disasters. On March 1, the national government enacted the Special Financial Assistance Act, which provided extensive financial support for municipal governments in the disaster area. These trends advanced the activities of two organizations connecting national and local government bodies: the regional headquarters led by Kuno Tōichirō and staffed by capable midlevel bureaucrats dispatched to Hyōgo prefecture, and a high-level reconstruction committee led by Shimokōbe Atsushi (1923–2016). Both played an active role in connecting the national government with local needs and plans.

Establishing funds and implementing creative reconstruction

On April 1, 1995, Hyōgo prefecture and Kobe city established the Hanshin-Awaji Earthquake Recovery Fund to manage reconstruction projects that would be difficult for the national government to handle directly. This fund, initially 600 billion yen and later expanded to 900 billion yen, was used to provide financial aid in areas such as housing, industry, livelihood recovery, and education. Support for the reconstruction of public housing, privately owned homes, and other types of housing was given particular emphasis. In addition, the Recovery Fund provided a financial base for the activities of private-sector entities, experts, volunteers, and others engaged in helping communities recover and restoring cultural properties and private schools. The fund also provided a back door for avoiding administrative barriers blocking the application of national funds to private property.

Three years later, in May 1998, this back door help make possible the Act on Support for Livelihood Recovery of Disaster Victims, which provided public funds (initially up to one million yen per case, later three million yen) to support the reconstruction of individual livelihoods and homes destroyed in the disaster.[44]

Administrative barriers to the use of public funds to reconstruct private property had faced public opposition, as well as arguments that withholding such funds from disaster victims was inhumane and a failure of the government's core responsibility to respect individuality. Hyōgo prefecture's insistence on prioritizing the rebuilding of individual lives above all else ended up being applied in future disasters.

Creative reconstruction

I close this chapter with a look at the more imaginative side of recovery following the Great Hanshin-Awaji Earthquake. Restoring basic services and infrastructure is only natural after a disaster. The Hanshin region, however, went further, pursuing creative reconstruction. As a result, some lasting contributions were made.

One of these is "HAT Kobe," a new city center built on a former Kobe Steel factory site. The center includes the Hyogo Earthquake Memorial 21st Century Research Institute think tank, the core of which is the Disaster Reduction and Human Renovation Institution and the Hyogo Institute for Traumatic Stress, along with various international organizations, hospitals, museums, reconstruction housing, etc. The intellectual resources accumulated here have global significance, and the United Nations Office for Disaster Risk Reduction refers to this model as the Hyogo Framework for Action.

A second regional contribution is the Awaji Yumebutai, a complex of beautiful parks and buildings that provides a place to enjoy nature as well as an international conference hall for international exchange, built on what was once an unsightly dig site for soil used in land-reclamation projects.

The third asset is the Hyogo Performing Arts Center in Nishinomiya, a project that was overwhelmingly supported by local residents and now greatly enriches their lives. This is a legacy of those who refused to abandon their sense of imagination and desire for great things amid extreme misery.

Kobe's initiatives aimed at becoming a center of cutting-edge medicine are also producing ongoing results.

8. The Future of Creative Reconstruction

Locally led reconstruction theory

The three major earthquake disasters that have struck modern Japan—the 1923 Great Kantō Earthquake, the 1995 Great Hanshin-Awaji Earthquake, and the 2011 Great East Japan Earthquake—were surprise attacks by nature that came at times of unstable Japanese politics. As described in the previous chapter, the Great Kantō Earthquake hit when Prime Minister Katō Tomosaburō was absent, having died of cancer. The Great Hanshin-Awaji Earthquake, too, occurred during an irregular situation, in which the Liberal Democratic Party that had ruled since 1995 finally collapsed, enabling Japan Socialist Party Chairperson Murayama Tomiichi to become prime minister after a series of unstable coalition governments. Similarly, the Great East Japan Earthquake hit just when the Cabinet of Kan Naoto (1946–), whose Democratic Party of Japan, had only recently managed to achieve a change in administration from the Liberal Democratic Party for the first time in 15 years, was weakened by an earlier defeat in the July 2010 Upper House election.

As this chapter has described, at the time of the Great Hanshin-Awaji Earthquake, the Hyōgo prefectural government was unable to grasp the extent of damage on the morning of the disaster because communication systems were almost completely down. They were not even able to contact central government offices in Tokyo. Because the central government had not constructed a crisis-time communication system, the prime minister failed to recognize the magnitude of the situation on that morning.

Both local and central governments thus performed poorly at first, but by afternoon they had regrouped and begun to cope with the situation. In the end, the recovery and reconstruction following the Great Hanshin-Awaji Earthquake was the smoothest and speediest of the three cases examined in this book. One reason was the scope and character of this disaster.

Initial conditions are of course of key importance. The other two disasters were caused by plate movements occurring over a broad area. The Great Hanshin-Awaji Earthquake in contrast was a destructive shock caused by fault movement in close proximity to a large urban area, but compound disasters were avoided due to the lack of wind and because the earthquake struck before dawn, a time when there was little road or rail activity. Fatalities were thus limited mostly to those from collapsing buildings.

A second factor contributing to speedy recovery was that the disaster only affected a portion of southern Hyōgo prefecture. The rest of Japan remained a prosperous advanced society, despite the recent collapse of its economic bubble. Around a week after the earthquake, I left the disaster area to run an errand in Osaka. Coming from a place where food, water, and newspapers were in short supply, I found myself in a completely different world. The clamorous hubbub of the big city was unchanged. The contrast with the suffering in neighboring Kobe briefly filled me with indignant anger, but I stopped to draw a breath and tell myself that this was how things should be. The unchanging cultural and economic wealth of Japanese society as a whole, I realized, would rapidly absorb the destruction in my city and allow for a smooth recovery.

A third important factor was the stability of the government. After the Great Kantō Earthquake, Gotō Shinpei launched a major reconstruction plan, but rather than being endorsed by the leading Seiyūkai and Kenseikai parties, it instead met with hostility from both, leading to its failure in just four months. After the Great East Japan Earthquake, the Kan administration was forced to engage in recovery efforts amid political difficulties caused by the fact that an opposing party controlled the Upper House of the Diet. When the Great Hanshin-Awaji Earthquake hit, a coalition between the Liberal Democratic Party, the Japan Socialist Party, and the New Party Sakigake held the majority in the Upper and Lower Houses. After that earthquake, however, the Liberal Democratic Party wanted above all else to regain power and hoped to score points with the public through a successful disaster recovery. As a result, political machinations aimed at dragging down the Japan Socialist Party prime minister did not occur.

Rumors circulated that Prime Minister Murayama was reluctant to dispatch the SDF because he was a socialist and an antimilitary pacifist, but that was not the case. As we have seen, the delayed action by the prime minister on the day of the disaster was not due to his ideology, but rather to deficiencies in the information system at the prime minister's office. The prime minister himself was highly sympathetic and felt responsibility toward the victims. When appointing Ozato Sadatoshi to lead the recovery, Murayama told him to do whatever was necessary to achieve that goal, and that Murayama himself would bear responsibility for it. He lived up to that promise.

Deputy Chief Cabinet Secretary Ishihara Nobuo displayed wisdom in coping with and directing politicians while also bringing together administrative departments within the prime minister's office. So, while the Murayama cabinet was an irregular one, it performed better than the other two governments examined in this book.

The final reason recovery proceeded so smoothly after the Great Hanshin-Awaji Earthquake was that recovery plans were coordinated not by the central government but by local leaders. Hyōgo's prefectural government proposed many recovery and reconstruction plans, and the absence of information and action on the morning of the disaster forced the central government to recognize the danger of directing operations from a distance. The wiser approach is to provide backup while leaving as much responsibility as possible to those in the disaster area. Prime Minister Murayama, Chief Cabinet Secretary Igarashi, and Deputy Chief Cabinet Secretary Ishihara were well aware of this. Furthermore, during this period a transformation in governmental practice, from one that was centralized and hierarchical to a more decentralized, regionally oriented approach, was taking place. Above all, Hyōgo prefecture itself sought greater autonomy.

My personal interest lies not in local autonomy, but in Japanese diplomacy and international relations. When I said this to Governor Kaihara some years before the earthquake, his quiet response was, "So you think that regional governance is unrelated to international relations?" Presented with this cogent argument, I began assisting Hyōgo prefecture in crafting its international strategies. Then came the earthquake, which damaged my home, sent my family seeking refuge in Hiroshima, and left me adrift writing newspaper columns and memorials for my advisee Mori Wataru.

Soon after the earthquake, I received a call from the prefectural government requesting my participation in an urban-renewal strategy roundtable made up of government and academic experts. On February 11, I thus found myself departing Itami Airport via helicopter and looking down at the blue plastic sheets that still covered damaged homes.

I was particularly surprised when we flew over Kobe. Outside the helicopter's right window, I could see Mount Rokkō, and to the left was Osaka Bay. The city itself was so narrow that I sometimes could not see it—the view of the entire city was entirely blocked by the floor of the helicopter. This made me realize that the city's shape was another factor in disaster mitigation. Had the geography been different, feats such as linking together fire trucks to draw seawater for firefighting in Nagata ward would not have been possible.

After arriving at Kobe, I attended the first roundtable meeting at the Hyōgoken Kōkan, the historic building that originally housed the prefectural government. Governor Kaihara opened the conference by thanking us for contributing to the recovery, despite our being disaster victims ourselves. Former National Land Agency administrative vice minister Shimokōbe Atsushi, who had come from Tokyo, encouraged local leadership in planning, saying "Gotō Shinpei did not create his recovery plan as a response to the Great Kantō Earthquake, he simply used that earthquake as an opportunity to realize a plan that he had already conceived. In my experience, there are few regional governments with as clear a plan for the future as Hyōgo prefecture, so I hope that 'recovery' can be replaced by implementation of those plans." That sentiment was not lip-service to those in the disaster area; Shimokōbe had already advised Prime Minister Murayama that "Disaster areas should develop their own recovery plans, and governors should oversee implementation of those plans."[45]

A leading commentator, Sakaiya Taichi (1935–2019), and Liberal Democratic Party members such as Obuchi Keizō (1937–2000) supported the establishment of a new organization along the lines of Gotō Shinpei's Reconstruction Bureau, an idea that discomfited some in the prime minister's office. This was no longer an era in which central government agencies, with a focus on a Ministry of Home Affairs, should use absolute authority for "revolution from above," they believed.

Murayama had been an influential figure in the local politics of Ōita prefecture in Kyūshū, and Igarashi had been mayor of Asahikawa in Hokkaidō. Both felt gratitude and respect toward Shimokōbe for his help and advice. This was part of the reason for Shimokōbe's being invited to lead the new Reconstruction Committee. The Murayama Cabinet was sympathetic to Shimokōbe's recovery theories that emphasized local leadership. The prime minister's office inquired of Hyōgo prefecture what form the recovery bureau modeled by Gotō would take, but the response of Hyōgo prefecture was clearly disapproving.[46]

On February 15, the Cabinet decided to establish the Hanshin-Awaji Reconstruction Committee, chaired by Shimokōbe. Residents of the disaster area were represented by Governor Kaihara and Kobe mayor Sasayama Kazutoshi, and the Kinki region financial world was represented by Kawakami Tetsurō, chair of the Kansai Economic Federation. Sakaiya Taichi and Itō Shigeru gathered ideas from pundits, while Ichibangase Yasuko presented liberal ideas. A grand old politician, Gotōda Masaharu (1914–2005), and Japan Business Federation honorary chair Hiraiwa Gaishi (1914–2007) served as advisors. With the endorsement of these advisors, Shimokōbe obtained approvals from the prime minister's office, and this small group became a central force for nimbly hammering out recovery proposals.[47]

Hyōgo prefecture hurried to prepare various task forces to handle these recovery proposals. There was a sense that the relentless pursuit of convenience in modernization had left something important behind, and now was the only opportunity for rebirth as an ideal city. What was called for was not restoration of previous conditions, but a safe, twenty-first-century urban model rooted in healthy communities. The general consensus among those with an interest in local recovery was that this should be led by the governor.

A "3-3-10" vision was presented: three months for emergency recovery, three years for strategic residential, urban, and industrial recovery, and ten years for overall recovery. On March 30, urban-renewal strategy roundtable chair Niino Kōjirō handed the governor a "Recovery Strategy Vision" laying out a detailed road map toward these goals.

The prefecture's recovery plan was presented to the government via Shimokōbe's committee and approved in July. In the end, 660 recovery projects with a combined budget of 17 trillion yen (US$148 billion) were implemented over ten years.[48]

Administrative barriers

Despite strong local support for creative reconstruction, implementation entailed many difficulties. One administrative barrier called the "Gotōda doctrine" in particular posed a tough obstacle.

National funds were allocated for restoration activities only; any efforts to make things better than they were had to be funded using local resources. From a national perspective, Kobe is a prosperous area. While the public was widely sympathetic to the city's plight, national funds could not be used in a way that might be construed as allowing Kobe to unfairly profit from disaster. Neither could special economic zones be created that operated by different rules from the rest of the country. The use of public funds for the reconstruction of collapsed private homes also raised questions of consistency with the legal system. Even with the intercession of Shimokōbe, the administrative barriers were higher than can be imagined today. The disaster area nevertheless persisted in its pursuit of creative reconstruction. The recovery process came to resemble a fierce contest of wits in devising ways to slip between barriers as they arose.

Every policy process is a product of human actions, but even more so of its institutional and sociopolitical environment. The process of recovery from a major disaster is no exception.

When an area is stricken by a major disaster, people throughout the country are shocked. They feel sympathy for those in the area and send many donations. The Great Hanshin-Awaji Earthquake became an epoch-making moment in that some 1,380,000 volunteers arrived to help.

A friend of mine who is a doctor at the Hiroshima Red Cross Hospital loaded a Red Cross vehicle with medical supplies and hurried to the disaster site, but the closer he got the worse the traffic congestion became. Hoping to save time he tried to drive between two lanes, but a rough spot caused by the earthquake caused him to lose control and hit an oncoming car. Japan is one of the strictest countries in the world with regard to traffic accidents, but on learning that my friend was hurrying to help out, the driver told him to go ahead and not to worry about the damage done to his car. Tragedies are particularly good at bringing out altruistic humanitarian behavior and strengthening community bonds that are not normally seen.

Sympathy for disaster areas also tends to strengthen criticism of the government. The public demands to know what the government is doing, and why their response is so slow. At times, authorities are condemned beyond what the facts support. When faced with unspeakable calamity, the whole of society heats up.

Yet such a heated society gradually cools, and interest shifts when the next shocking event occurs. Around two months after the Great Hanshin-Awaji Earthquake, on March 20, 1995, the Aum Shinrikyō cult launched its sarin gas attack in Tokyo, shocking the public and pushing aside news of the recovery in Hyōgo. The generous support being offered to the disaster area also rapidly slackened. Importantly, however, a framework for recovery in the Hanshin and Awaji areas had for the most part been established before the Aum attack, during the period when societal support was still strong.

The Basic Act on Reconstruction was enacted on February 22, and on February 24 the Headquarters for Reconstruction of the Hanshin-Awaji Area was established as an organization led by Prime Minister Murayama and scheduled to exist for five years. As described above, the national government's Hanshin-Awaji Reconstruction Committee (which was scheduled to function for one year), too, was established one month after the earthquake occurred. Once Japanese society has institutionalized something, implementation is generally taken seriously. So, while the country was distracted by the Aum incident, local governments and the committee led by Shimokōbe continued their work undeterred. In July, the government approved a local ten-year reconstruction plan.

Shimokōbe strongly believed that Japan should construct a memorial demonstrating to the world pride in what they had accomplished, and on October 10 the Reconstruction Committee officially proposed the creation of a comprehensive international meeting center. This center would do work in the fields of research, education, curatorship, and cultural activities, modeled on the Smithsonian Institution in Washington, D.C. Shimokōbe intended to ask Prime Minister Murayama to present this plan when he visited Kobe on the first anniversary of the earthquake, along with fifty billion yen in financial resources from the government.[49]

However, Murayama resigned as prime minister just before that first anniversary. According to his own explanation, he did this primarily in response to the reorganization of the Japan Socialist Party, and secondly ahead of the Japan–U.S. Joint Declaration on Security being prepared at the time, to circumvent blame being placed on a Japan Socialist Party prime minister for any Japanese concessions.[50] To retain power after becoming prime minister, Murayama had abandoned Socialist Party platforms related to the unconstitutionality of the SDF and the ending of the Japan–U.S. security treaty, but he was unable to bring himself to make a joint declaration for further strengthening those agreements in the twenty-first century. I spoke with Murayama at an event in Kobe commemorating the twentieth anniversary of the Great Hanshin-Awaji Earthquake, and he told me that no fifty-billion-yen plan was ever proposed.[51] Apparently, it remained nothing more than Shimokōbe's dream.

The birth of disaster-mitigation think tanks

The resignation of the Murayama Cabinet completely changed the situation surrounding earthquake recovery. The central focus of the succeeding cabinet led by Prime Minister Hashimoto Ryūtarō (1937–2006; in office 1996–98) was the issue of the consolidation and reduction of U.S. military bases in Okinawa. Financial reform was another important issue for the Hashimoto cabinet, which employed the slogan "budget reduction with no sacred cows." As illustrated by policies that cut official development assistance budgets by 10 percent three years in a row, political trends made the initiation of new projects remarkably difficult.

Shimokōbe's appointment lasted only one year, so while the original intent was for his proposal to be implemented over five years by the Headquarters for Reconstruction, in actuality it was left for national government bureaucrats, lacking any central political leadership. According to the administrative reform policy of the time, any government agency wishing to establish a new organization had to shut down an existing one, but no agency was motivated enough to make that sacrifice to create a massive organization for the disaster area. In particular, the spirit of the times did not permit the building of physical structures to demonstrate administrative achievements, as had been common in the past. The Great

Hanshin-Awaji Earthquake Memorial Association was established in 1997 to consider memorial projects, but the Japanese government refused to fund it, leaving the association to fund itself solely through contributions from local governments.

In April 1997, the Hashimoto cabinet raised the national sales tax from 3 to 5 percent. The government took financial restructuring very seriously, as evidenced by the fact that it not only failed to implement mitigation measures aimed at softening the resulting economic downturn, but also increased the real tax burden. The economy faltered as a result, and in conjunction with the simultaneously occurring East Asian Economic Crisis, Japan faced a financial crisis. As a result, the Liberal Democratic Party lost in upper-house elections the following year, and the entire Hashimoto Cabinet resigned.

The succeeding Obuchi Keizō cabinet broke the economic crisis by naming former prime minister Miyazawa Kiichi (1919–2007) as finance minister. The accumulated national budget deficit was large, but the new government decided to set that aside for the moment, instead placing priority on economic recovery. Grasping for immediate solutions, the government established a large supplementary budget with the goal of fiscal stimulus to rejuvenate the economies of Japan and Asia. Economic Planning Agency director general Sakaiya Taichi asked Hyōgo prefecture if it had any good projects. The political climate indeed frequently changes. While there was a sense that the change from the Murayama to the Hashimoto Cabinet may have frozen funding, the financial collapse instead instigated a sudden wind of aggressive fiscal policy, leaving us wondering whether the earthquake memorial project will be revived at some point in the future.

In the wake of the Great Hanshin-Awaji Earthquake, it is crucial that we not merely accomplish full recovery in the disaster area, but also build a foundation for an advanced twenty-first-century society. Doing so is both a true form of mourning for the victims, and a boon to the country and the world. It should therefore be supported by the country as a whole. This was the conviction that drove Governor Kaihara's actions. Great Hanshin-Awaji Earthquake Memorial Association Chairman Ishihara Nobuo, however cautioned against overly ambitious projects and focusing on the tasks that the country needed to accomplish, in order to gain broad public support.

Ultimately, Saitō Tomio spearheaded a proposal for an International Disaster Prevention Safety Organization, and the Great Hanshin-Awaji Earthquake Memorial Center was planned following the advice of Ishihara to display and transmit information related to the disaster, conduct research, foster human-resource development, and support disaster-prevention efforts across a wide area. This constitutes the intellectual foundation for protecting people from future disasters. The central government at first opposed these initiatives as too expensive, but political progress was eventually made. The Kōmeitō party, which became the ruling party by joining together with Prime Minister Obuchi Keizō (in office 1998–2000), was particularly active on disaster-prevention issues.

In 1999, large earthquakes occurred in Turkey in August and in Taiwan in September, provoking renewed recognition that earthquake disasters pose a continuing threat. Hyōgo prefecture dispatched teams to both locales, and their activities received extensive media coverage. Staff with a favorable attitude toward the memorial center concept eventually gained influence in the government's reconstruction headquarters, and the National Land Agency's Disaster Management Bureau requested budgeting for it.

It was chief cabinet secretary of the Obuchi Cabinet (and later, secretary general of the Liberal Democratic Party) Nonaka Hiromu (1925–2018) who decided on the matter. He was sympathetic to Hyōgo prefecture's proactiveness, and decided that the national government should cover half the costs of construction and operations. The project was renamed the Disaster Reduction and Human Renovation Institution, which was finally established in April 2002 under the leadership of Kyoto University professor Kawata Yoshiaki. Thus was born Japan's only think tank that applies scientific earthquake research to disaster mitigation to improve public safety. That this organization, which I currently head, was established despite the rapidly changing political climate strikes me as quite an accomplishment.[52]

THREE

The Great East Japan Earthquake (1)

Ground Zero

1. An Offshore Earthquake and an Enormous Tsunami

A monster from the sea

Among the various types of natural disasters, violent earthquakes are particularly terrifying. This is because the shaking of the earth betrays our belief in its solidity. The movement of the ground becomes fluid, confusing horizontal and vertical as it flattens towns. Black fissures open, swallowing people. The very earth, the source of the bounty that provides the four seasons and the life that supports us, becomes a force for destruction.

I experienced this firsthand in the 1995 Great Hanshin-Awaji Earthquake, in which just twenty seconds of shaking felt like several minutes of hell. My life feels as if it is divided into two eras, one before and one after that earthquake.

The 2011 Great East Japan Earthquake was an unprecedented M 9 earthquake that shook for five minutes, but that was not all. This earth devil was joined by a sea monster, an enormous tsunami that slammed against Japan's northeastern coast thirty minutes after the earthquake. According to autopsy reports, over 90 percent of deaths in this disaster were caused by drowning in the tsunami.[1] Later statistics that included disaster-related deaths tallied 19,418 fatalities and 2,592 missing, for a total of 22,010 lost lives.[2]

Figures 3.1. The incoming tsunami, swallowing houses in Miyagi prefecture (March 11, 2011)

Furthermore, a tertiary disaster occurred when a fifteen-meter tsunami hit the Fukushima Daiichi (First) Nuclear Power Plant, causing total loss of power. Power was also lost at the Daini (Second) Nuclear Power Plant farther south in the same prefecture, but operators there were able to restore power. Unfortunately, at the Daiichi plant they were unable to restore cooling systems, leading to meltdowns in three units. This led to hydrogen explosions that released radioactive material into the atmosphere. As will be described in more detail later, there was no explosion in a second unit, not because there was no meltdown, but because an external window called a blowout panel was accidentally destroyed, releasing more radioactive material. The plant was cooled down using water from helicopters and ground vehicles, but this event came within a hair's breadth of making all of eastern Japan, including Tokyo, uninhabitable.

While the Great East Japan Earthquake was a large compound disaster, I will first focus on the tsunami, which caused the most fatalities.

The earthquake epicenter was 130 kilometers east-southeast offshore from the Oshika Peninsula in Miyagi prefecture, around 24 kilometers underneath the surface. In part of that area (an asperity), a land-side plate is dragged and moves together with the Pacific Plate, which plunges below the Japanese archipelago at a rate of nearly ten centimeters per year. At times the pressure builds, and the land-side plate violently jerks upward. The area around the epicenter is said to have moved 24 meters eastward and 5 meters upward during the earthquake. In addition, sediment from the continental plate near the Japan Trench, 200 kilometers east of the epicenter, collapsed toward the trench, moving more seawater and making the tsunami even larger.[3] In all, the earth moved over an undersea area stretching 500 kilometers north-south and 200 kilometers east-west, causing a tsunami of a scale unprecedented in Japan's recorded history.

The earthquake began at 2:46 p.m., and the Japan Meteorological Agency issued a tsunami alert three minutes later, warning of a wave potentially reaching six meters in Miyagi prefecture and three meters in Iwate and Fukushima prefectures. This optimistic prediction was based on initial data, which underestimated the magnitude of the earthquake as only M 7.9. But fault movements continued for several minutes and had not yet ended when the warning was issued.

Rapid issuance of warnings is of course important. Emergency alerts delivered by television and cell-phone networks warned those on the coast that a large earthquake would soon arrive, but they were issued so close to the actual event that people had no time to prepare. One benefit of the emergency warning system was that it allowed time for the ten Shinkansen trains traveling up and down the three prefectures most affected by the earthquake to safely stop. However, premature warnings of a three- to six-meter tsunami unfortunately led many to believe that they were protected by seawalls, and that they would be safe if they remained in their homes.

The Japan Meteorological Agency released a second warning at 3:14 p.m., twenty-eight minutes after the earthquake, approximately doubling its previous estimate to a tsunami reaching ten meters in Miyagi prefecture and six meters in Iwate and Fukushima prefectures. Amid the confusion and blackouts caused by the earthquake, however, not many people heard this still-optimistic revision. Even if they had heard it, they probably wouldn't have had enough time to run for safety, since the first tsunami hit the Sanriku coast just four minutes later.

The epicenter was offshore from Miyagi prefecture, so tsunami warnings focused on that area, but the tsunami unexpectedly reached the cities of Ōfunato and Kamaishi in Iwate prefecture first. There is some ambiguity between the initial tide-level fluctuations and full-fledged arrival of a tsunami, but generally speaking the tsunami struck Ōfunato thirty-two minutes after the earthquake, then Kamaishi and Miyako at the thirty-five- and forty-minute marks, respectively.

Tsunami do not travel at equal speed in all directions from the epicenter. Complex asymmetries occur due to factors such as the manner in which the seafloor rises and the submarine terrain over which the tsunami passes. The tsunami arrived at Iwate prefecture first because faults initially spread northward. It did not hit the geographically closest location on the Japanese coastline—Ayukawa on the Oshika Peninsula in Ishinomaki, Miyagi prefecture—until forty minutes after the earthquake, just as it hit Miyako in Iwate.

Another large fault pointed southward, toward Fukushima prefecture. An initial 4-meter wave arrived at the Fukushima Daiichi Power Plant 41 minutes after the earthquake, followed by a 15-meter wave 8 minutes later that resulted in serious damage. The tsunami hit Iwaki city in Fukushima prefecture at the 53-minute mark. A 9.3-meter wave arrived at Sōma city in Fukushima at 65 minutes, and the tsunami finally arrived at the Yuriage district in Natori, Miyagi, at 3:52 p.m., 66 minutes after the earthquake. The last location to be hit was the Sendai plains.

The tsunami thus hit Iwate with an upper arm and Fukushima with a lower arm, finally closing in on the Sendai plains in between.[4]

In terms of run-up height (the highest ground elevation that the tsunami reaches, a combined result of tsunami height and local geography), the tsunami was highest along Iwate prefecture's Sanriku coast at Aneyoshi, a hamlet in Miyako (40.4 m), and the Shirahama in the Ryōri Bay of Ōfunato (26.7 m), followed by Port Onagawa (18.4 m), Rikuzentakata (18.0 m), Minamisanriku (15.9 m), and the Fukushima Daiichi Power Plant (15.0 m).

It is impossible to record the height of a wave without tide-measuring equipment, but we can measure the maximum elevation at which water damage in a particular area occurred by observing buildings. It reached 18.3 m at Ryōishi Bay in northern Kamaishi city, 16.7 m at Ryōri Bay, 16.5 m at Okirai Bay in Ōfunato city, 15.9 m at Tarō in Miyako city and Sanriku in Miyagi prefecture, 15.8 m at Rikuzentakata, 15.5 m at Ogatsu in Ishinomaki city, and 14.8 m at Onagawa Bay.[5]

In a comparison of the 1896 Meiji Sanriku Tsunami and the 1933 Shōwa Sanriku Tsunami, a 1934 field survey of traces of the Meiji Sanriku Tsunami indicated the following relations between the earthquake and tsunami:

1. The tsunami was higher in bays that directly faced the open sea, and lower within larger, deeper bays.
2. The tsunami rose higher in V-shaped bays than in U-shaped bays.

3. The tsunami heights were suppressed along shallow coastlines with no deformations due to bays or other features.

This closely matches experiential knowledge, and relation 1 is highly applicable to the Great East Japan Earthquake. However, in that event the entire open sea rose so high that it overcame relations 2 and 3, which is why it caused such extensive devastation.[6]

Thirty or forty minutes is not a long time. Those who had already started righting fallen furniture and cleaning up after the earthquake were caught by the tsunami. Those who went to pick children up from school did not have time to evacuate to safer ground. People in places like the Sendai plains had over an hour to escape and should have had sufficient time to get away. However, history has shown that it is personal recognition of danger and disaster preparedness, more than time, that separates life from death.

In Ōfunato, where the tsunami arrived first, 417 people were killed and 79 remain missing, but these figures are actually lower than in some towns.[7] The land at the deep end of the bay is flat, but it is surrounded by steep slopes with houses on them, so the water only inundated limited areas of the city, despite destruction of the breakwaters at the bay entrance.

Even so, thirty minutes was a short evacuation window, particularly for the elderly. One elderly care home was located one kilometer inland from the innermost part of Okirai Bay, on sloping ground in the northern part of the city, and 59 of the 91 residents at this home died. The tsunami arrived, pushing before it a wall of debris, just as seven residents were being loaded into a van for evacuation. The car washed up on a riverbank one hundred meters away, but two of its occupants had already drowned. At an adjacent specialty care center for the disabled and elderly, ten staff members did their best to push sixty-seven residents to higher ground in wheelchairs, but the tsunami soon caught up with them, and fifty-three elderly persons died.[8] Those thirty minutes surely felt cruelly short to the caretakers. The Great East Japan Earthquake powerfully demonstrated the importance of locating hospitals and facilities for the elderly and disabled on high ground.

The case of Okirai Elementary School in Ofunato presents a contrasting example. While this school was completely destroyed, all seventy-three pupils and thirteen faculty remained safe. This was possible thanks to the existence of an emergency escape route, a bridge over Prefectural Highway 9 connecting the second floor of the school with a hill on the other side. This bridge had been completed just the year before, after city-council member Hirata Takeshi warned that elementary schools below bluffs were dangerous in the event of a tsunami, and the municipality allocated funds accordingly. The pupils crossed this bridge and took refuge in the plaza in front of the Sanriku train station. There, they heard warnings of a large tsunami on a disaster radio, so faculty led the children to a community center on higher ground. From that vantage point, they watched as the tsunami washed away automobiles and homes, reaching up to the third floor of their school. The school had practiced evacuation drills twice each year, using the slogan "evacuate higher and faster"—a principle they effectively put into practice during the actual disaster.[9]

Struggles of the fishermen

Even in a global context, the Sanriku coast is an extremely bountiful rias shoreline area, and the key tool for obtaining that bounty is fishing boats. Some 1,400 boats operated out of the Ōfunato Bay at the time of the Great East Japan Earthquake.

Fishermen are professional sea workers, so tsunamis are not completely unexpected events for them. Most of the fishermen who were at sea that day—and the older ones in particular—knew that a large earthquake was likely to be followed by a tsunami. We can learn much from these fishermen and the wisdom they have passed on to each other.

The most widely shared lesson is that boats should take refuge from a tsunami offshore. It is considered best to be in waters at least 100 meters deep, 200 if possible. A tsunami is nothing more than a gentle swelling in the deep sea, but as it advances through shallow waters toward the coast it rises up to become a wall.

Even with that knowledge, few fishing boats actually made it to open waters. Between 80 and 90 percent capsized within the bay or were pushed up on shore to unexpected locations. This happened because thirty minutes or even an hour is not enough time to reach the boats, prepare for departure, and escape from the bay. Doing so is nearly impossible for large boats in particular, unless they happen to already be prepared to start a voyage. For a Russian freighter in Ōfunato, it can take up to fifteen to thirty minutes just to start the engines. Even assuming that departure would take ten minutes after the shaking stopped, it would take over twenty minutes to leave the bay and reach waters 100 meters deep. Most would probably meet with a wall of water before they could get that far.

Fishermen also pass on lessons regarding sailing during disasters. One lesson is to "sail away from faraway storms, straight into nearby ones," and this also holds true for tsunami. When a wall-like wave approaches, you don't want it to hit a boat from the rear or from the sides; the only way to prevent a capsize is to sail straight into and over it.

Shida Keiyō, a sixty-three-year-old fisherman from Ōfunato, remembered, "If a tsunami comes, you have to give up on your house and save your boat. If you have the boat, you'll be able to build another house." Shida was in a dinghy attending to his oyster rafts when he noticed the earthquake. He quickly boarded his larger fishing boat, the *Shiwa-maru*, and skillfully traversed six kilometers of narrow waterways to depart the Ōfunato Bay for the open sea.

About ten kilometers outside of the bay mouth, he joined around 60 other boats that had gathered and were exchanging information by radio. While 60 may seem like a lot, this represented only a small portion of the approximately 1,400 boats operating out of Ōfunato Bay. Someone on the radio said, "Look north!" When he did so, Shida saw white spray rising up in the air as the tsunami crashed into the tip of the cape in Ryōri, the tsunami's first landfall. Floating 100 meters above the ocean floor, the boats just gently rocked.

Tsuma Takao, a seventy-five-year-old fisherman who was at home when the earthquake struck, and thus took longer to reach his small boat, was halfway across the bay when he saw the wall of water press against the breakwaters at the bay mouth. The mouth is particularly narrow, causing the water to rise almost vertically, and Tsuma saw it lift one boat straight up. Someone in another boat shouted on the radio, "Don't come out! Get back!" and another said, "Here we go!" as his boat was swallowed by the tsunami.

Knowing that it was too dangerous to try to head out to open sea, Tsuma decided to do battle with the constantly changing push and pull of the waves in the bay by taking shelter behind Sangoshima Island in its center.[10]

Taiheiyō Cement has a plant in Ōfunato, making it one of the few industrial cities on the Sanriku coast. The 5,000-ton cement cargo vessel *Kenkai-maru* berthed there and had just finished loading when the earthquake struck. Fifteen minutes later, the tide suddenly receded, a precursor to the approaching tsunami, causing the *Kenkai-maru*'s mooring rope to slip and detach the ship from its pier. The tsunami destroyed the breakwaters at the bay entrance and formed a large whirlpool while rushing into the back of the bay at a height of about ten meters. *Kenkai-maru* captain Kawasaki Naoki, fifty-four, and other experienced crew knew these waters well, and so moved the ship to the center of the bay and dropped anchor to prevent the ship from being washed away. They also engaged the engines to drive against incoming waves and opened them up at full power to fight the rapidly receding tide. The ship had two anchors, but they lowered only one; had both been down the chains could have become tangled during violent shifting back and forth, limiting the crew's ability to pilot the ship.

The crew of the Russian freighter *Khrizolitovyy* was unfamiliar with such anti-tsunami measures and dropped anchor near the shore. They were pushed up onto shore by incoming waves, then violently yanked back out by receding ones. They dropped their second anchor to prevent being tossed about so much, which only worsened the situation; the anchors became entangled, nearly capsizing the ship. The Russian ship requested assistance from the nearby *Kenkai-maru*, and its fifteen crewmembers took refuge on that boat. An injured Russian chief engineer was transported to a hospital in a fire department rapid-response helicopter.

Tsuma remained aboard his small fishing boat overnight to fight the debris-filled tsunami waves that entered the bay. The outgoing waves were rougher than the incoming ones. The narrow geography of the bay caused torrential currents that pulled other boats under the water. As Shida was slowly piloting the *Shiwa-maru* home, careful not to lose its propeller to floating debris, he passed close by Tsuma. Surprised that a man even older than him in such a small boat could have managed such a feat, he called out, "Have you been here all night?" "I guess you haven't eaten," he added, and pulled up alongside to give Tsuma some snacks and drinks. Tsuma was delighted by this act of kindness from a stranger. Having successfully protected his boat, as was his code, Shida found himself crying tears of relief after advancing far enough to see that his house was still standing.

Shida later chaired the Marine Mutual Relief Association, which erected a memorial on a hill overlooking the bay to honor the fishermen who lost their lives in its waters, along with another one for the sunken ships. As chair, he delivered a speech at the dedication ceremony, in which he said, "I strongly feel that meeting with tsunami is our destiny as fishermen. However, even if tsunami are our destiny, disaster is something different. Disaster is something that we overcome."

At the fishing port of Ishihama, located on a cape in the northern part of Minamisanriku in Miyagi prefecture, fishermen often say that being in water fifty meters deep is enough to stay safe, and indeed ships that were one kilometer offshore (a depth of seventy meters) felt no swells.

In Fukushima prefecture, however, the 100 or so ships that had headed out from the fishing port at Matsukawaura in Sōma thought that being four kilometers offshore would be safe, and yet were hit by seven- to eight-meter high triangular waves. The sailors decided to take the wave head-on,

Figure 3.2. Fishing boats affected in the tsunami, now grounded onshore (left), along with those that returned safely and moored together (March 13, 2011)

running up it with engines at full power, then cutting the engines at the top (because they could burn out if the propeller left the water under full power) to glide down. Each time they thought they were safe after making it over a surge, they were met by another wall-like wave. After repeating this six or seven times, they found themselves fifteen kilometers offshore.[11]

There is a ferry with a capacity of seventy-two called the *Whale* that connects Kinkazan Island with the fishing port Ayukawa near the tip of the Oshika Peninsula in Miyagi prefecture. When the earthquake struck, it was moored at the Kinkazan dock, waiting for its scheduled 3:00 p.m. departure. Two passengers rushed aboard, and five minutes later the tide rose ominously. Chief engineer Suzuki Takashi, sixty-three, who had the helm because the captain was absent, immediately detached the boat from the wharf. He received a radio transmission from Endō Tokuya, seventy, the president of the ferry company who was at the Ayukawa Port, saying "Get any passengers on board and head out to sea for safety." Not that Suzuki could have returned; the wharf was already starting to sink. He headed off for deeper water, calling over his loudspeaker to those on shore to evacuate to higher ground.

They proceeded on, with Aji Island on their right and Kinkazan Island on their left. After a time, they saw a 500-meter-wide wall of water rushing toward them from the left, smashing against Kinkazan as if pursuing the *Whale*. When they looked back after traveling five kilometers from shore, there was a receding wave so large it exposed the seabed between Kinkazan and the Oshika Peninsula.[12]

Most boats were not so lucky, having never made it offshore in the first place. Approximately 20,000 fishing boats were lost across the entire disaster area, and when pleasure boats, freighters, and other craft are included, the tally reaches 36,000.[13]

Perhaps the fishermen and captains I have focused on here are not representative of the majority. But even if that is the case, I am sure that there were many equally dedicated individuals with the courage to overcome their destiny of facing a tsunami.

2. Tsunamis along the Sanriku Coast

The Meiji Sanriku Tsunami

Seismologist Imamura Akitsune, who issued stern warnings regarding the arrival of the 1923 Great Kantō Earthquake and in 1929 became the first chair of the Seismological Society of Japan, once described the Sanriku coast as "the area most frequently hit by tsunami, not only in Japan but in the entire world." In addition to promoting academic earthquake research, Imamura worked hard to improve societal disaster prevention.

Previous research has suggested that tsunamis hit this area "nearly every forty years"[14] or "at thirty-five-year cycles"[15] or "repeatedly in cycles of one to several decades,"[16] an inconceivable rate in other places.[17]

Perceptions by both individuals and society are dominated by recent experience. For example, earthquake preparedness changed markedly after the 1611 Keichō Great Tsunami, which caused extensive damage from the Sanriku coast to the Sendai plains. Between that event and the end of the Edo Era in 1868, however, massive life-destroying disasters did not occur along the Sanriku coast, despite the continued periodic onslaught of tsunamis described above. Residents became used to this seeming safety, and their complacency made the destruction of the 1896 Meiji Sanriku Tsunami seem all the more enormous.

That disaster struck in the year following the end of the First Sino-Japanese War, on June 15, which was the day of Japan's Boy's Festival by the old calendar. There were lively celebrations throughout the region,

Figure 3.3 Kamaishi (Iwate prefecture) saw the worst of the destruction in the Meiji Sanriku Tsunami (1896)

despite the rain that had been falling since morning, but at 7:32 p.m.—the height of the festivities—a small earthquake of intensity II to III shook the ground for around five minutes. This was not enough to cause anyone to cease their celebrations, but thirty minutes later they heard heavy booms coming from the ocean, as if from exploding artillery shells. Those who stepped outside to see what was going on saw a wall of water higher than their houses, and few had time to escape.

The Meiji Sanriku Tsunami was a massive wave, reaching a height of 38.2 meters as measured at Shirahama in the Ryōri Bay. In the village of Ryōri, 1,269 people (56 percent of the village's population) were swallowed by the wave. To the south of Kamaishi, a 16.7-meter wave hit the village of Tōni, killing 66.4 percent (1,684) of its residents. Kamaishi itself had a population of around 7,000, making it the largest town on the Sanriku coast, and lost 3,765 (54 percent). These figures are difficult to conceive of, especially considering that not everyone in this area lived along the coastline—there were also inland villages—and indicate that towns near the coast were completely wiped out. There were 18,158 fatalities in Iwate prefecture, 3,452 in Miyagi prefecture, 343 in Aomori prefecture, and 6 in Hokkaidō. The total was nearly 22,000 victims, making the Meiji Sanriku

Tsunami an even deadlier disaster than the Great East Japan Earthquake of 2011.

One reason for the large number of deaths was the length of time since the last major tsunami, which as mentioned above made residents complacent, but more importantly, no one took refuge because the intensity of the earthquake was so low. While some few recognized the possibility of a tsunami due to the long duration of the weak earthquake of intensity II to III, they were the exception.

It is interesting to consider the mechanism by which such a weak earthquake could result in such a massive wave, which recent research has elucidated. The Meiji Sanriku Tsunami occurred approximately 200 kilometers offshore near the Japan Trench, where the Pacific Plate slides beneath a continental plate. The region of contact between these two plates is not hard and rocky, so slippage between them tends to be long and slow, not sudden and jolting. However, the Japan Trench plunges to depths of eight to ten kilometers, and its landward side is covered with accumulated sediment. Due to shaking by the earthquake and ground heat from the seabed, this sediment collapsed into the deep trench, moving more seawater. These factors resulted in a tsunami that was far out of proportion to the ground motion resulting from the earthquake.[18]

Turning to the question of how society reacted to this disaster, we must first keep in mind that in the middle of the Meiji Period, the Sanriku coast was still an isolated region. It was well populated, thanks to the rich bounty of its seas, but the Japanese National Railways' Tōhoku line had only reached the area in 1891, just five years before, and no railways or automobile roads extended all the way to the coast; there were only mountain paths just wide enough for rickshaws to pass. When the Meiji Sanriku Tsunami occurred, it took Home Minister Itagaki Taisuke (1837–1919) three days to travel by rickshaw from Morioka to Miyako to survey the damage. Iwate prefecture sent rice and other provisions from Morioka, but doing so required transport far south to Ishinomaki at the mouth of the Kitakami River, then transferring goods to steamboats that shipped them north again to the Sanriku inlet.

Some telegraphs in Miyagi prefecture were still usable, so aid came relatively quickly from Sendai, but all communications to disaster areas in Iwate prefecture had been cut, leaving people there isolated and unattended to. The hardest-hit villages were left with very few people capable of performing rescue operations, and adjacent villages could provide little help, since they too had been destroyed.

In the evening of the day after the tsunami, the governor of the Kamihei district and the police chief of Tōno, a district located slightly inland, led seven patrolmen and over eighty firefighters to Kamaishi to do what they could there. As things turned out, Tōno would again support coastal disaster areas in 2011.

As news of the disaster spread, the government and military responded to the prefecture's calls for aid by sending medical and material support, and many donations were collected. The prefecture and the central government provided disaster victims with generous daily rice allocations for thirty days, along with funds to construct emergency housing. Those who lost homes were given ten yen as compensation, rather generous support for the times, made possible due to the previous year's victory in the First Sino-Japanese War. Six weeks later, additional public funds were provided to aid in reconstruction of the local fishing industry.

Things looked quite grim for a time, but one year later fish catches had recovered, and as had occurred after many disasters in the past, homes were being rapidly rebuilt. However, while one might take pride in this spirit of recovery, rebuilding in the same location from which one's home was washed away would seem to invite repeated disaster. There were no nationally funded projects for building safer towns, but the horrors of the Meiji Sanriku Tsunami prompted quite a few areas to consider relocating to higher ground. Niinuma Buemon, mayor of Yoshihama in the Kesen district, rebuilt local roads higher up in the mountains, prompting residents to move there. The Kirikiri and Namiita districts in Ōtsuchi and the Funakoshi district in Yamada also relocated.[19]

Relocations in the Meiji Period

The Home Ministry report[20] describes ten cases of attempts at safer town planning in Miyagi and Iwate prefectures following the Meiji Sanriku Tsunami, including successful, partially successful, and unsuccessful cases. The report presents five successful cases.

One was Ōsawa in the Karakuwa district of Miyagi prefecture, which was hit by a 6.5-meter tsunami in the Meiji Period that caused extensive damage. In the Shōwa Period, after the changes were implemented, it was hit by a 3.9-meter wave, but this event resulted in the deaths of just 5 of its 806 residents. The village of Ōtani lost 241 residents in the Meiji Period, but after the village relocated, no one was killed in the Shōwa wave. The Hakozaki district in Unozumai, Iwate prefecture, was hit by an 8.5-meter tsunami that nearly destroyed it. Residents spontaneously rebuilt on higher ground, and when a 4.4-meter tsunami hit during the Shōwa

Period the town experienced almost no damage. In the village of Funako-shi, both the Yamada Bay to the north and the Funakoshi Bay to the south are subject to tsunamis, and the village experienced serious damage when a 6.5-meter wave hit in the Meiji Period. The Funakoshi region overall experienced 1,250 fatalities. Residents there, too, spontaneously relocated to higher ground and improved their roads. As a result, they experienced only 4 deaths in the Shōwa Sanriku Tsunami.

In contrast, the Tadakoshi region in Karakuwa, Miyagi prefecture, presents a case of failure. The area was hit by an 8.3-meter tsunami in the Meiji Period, resulting in 241 deaths. Residents initiated land-development projects with the aim of relocating to higher ground, but they hit bedrock. This increased construction costs, so in the end they decided to only create a ninety-centimeter-wide emergency road. The region was then hit by a 6.6-meter tsunami in the Shōwa Period, which killed twenty-four people who were unable to escape.

A similar case is that of the Sakihama district in Okirai, Iwate prefecture, which was seriously damaged by an 11.6-meter tsunami in the Meiji Period. In response, the village did not relocate to higher ground, but instead only raised the land slightly, simply rebuilding the town right where it had been. Most of the town was again washed away when a 7.8-meter wave struck in the Shōwa Period, killing fifty people.

The Ogatsu region of Jūgohama, too, tried to improve the safety of settlements near the sea by raising the ground 1.3 meters, but a wave twice that size hit in the Shōwa Period, demonstrating that insufficient safety measures are no better than none at all.

The Hongō region of Yoshihama partially relocated to higher ground after being hit by a 26.2-meter tsunami in the Meiji Period, and the community constructed an 8.2-meter seawall around shoreline settlements and planted a ten-meter-wide protective forest on the inland side. However, a 14.3-meter wave in the Shōwa Period swept away the protective forest. Clearly, protective plantings must be of sufficient strength to be of any help.

The Koshirahama district in Tōni suffered a particularly curious fate. The area was almost completely destroyed by the Meiji Sanriku Tsunami, which took several hundred lives. Afterward, residents used donated funds to purchase fields on higher ground and relocate. However, their work required access to the ocean, which was made difficult by poor roads, so one by one families ended up moving back to the seaside. The hills were also subject to fires, which burned down highland settlements with limited access to water, causing more families to return. As a result, 108 of the 158 houses in the town were washed away when an 11.6-meter wave hit in the Shōwa Period.

The Meiji Sanriku Tsunami came at the very beginning of Japan's early modern period, so national assistance for reconstruction was almost nonexistent. Instead, various trial-and-error social experiments were carried out at the village, neighborhood, and individual levels. Many such experiments ended disastrously, but one fortunate result was that after the Shōwa Sanriku Tsunami, the Ministry of Home Affairs was able to attempt meaningful tsunami countermeasures based on lessons learned from this and the previous Sanriku Tsunamis. The most important lessons were that absolute safety from tsunamis can be achieved only by relocating to higher ground, and that when rebuilding in seaside areas there is no substitute for large, strong seawalls. Having gained these insights, the government was better able to respond.

After the Meiji Sanriku Tsunami, a north-south railway connecting the Sanriku coast with other regions was proposed as a reconstruction measure, but this plan was not realized until 1984. Construction began on a railroad to connect the Sanriku coast with Morioka and other inland locations, but it was not completed in the early Shōwa Period.

The Shōwa Sanriku Tsunami

The 1933 Shōwa Sanriku Tsunami occurred thirty-seven years after the Meiji Sanriku Tsunami. The memory of that earlier disaster was still fresh in the minds of local residents; someone who had been ten years old at the time of the Meiji Sanriku Tsunami would have been just forty-seven years old during the Shōwa event. There had furthermore been frequent noticeable earthquakes starting several years earlier, so the people in the region were alert to natural events.

A intensity V earthquake shook the Sanriku region at 2:31 a.m. on March 3, the day of the Girl's Day festival. Yamashita Fumio, author of *Sad Stories of Sanriku Tsunami*,[21] was a fourth-grader in Ryōri at the time, and recalls items falling from the family shrine and the house groaning as if it would be ripped apart. The ten members of his family awoke with shouts, and Yamashita clung to his father. While the Meiji Sanriku Tsunami struck without warning, the Shōwa Sanriku Tsunami came after repeated clear forewarnings. The Shōwa Sanriku Tsunami was also less forceful than the Meiji one, but still reached 28.7 meters at Ryōri and took the lives of 178 people, 6.7 percent of the town's total population. Tōni was hit by an 8.3-meter wave that took 360 lives, or 10.7 percent of its population.

The Shōwa Sanriku Earthquake was an M 8.1 fault earthquake that occurred within the Pacific Plate on the outer side of the Japan Trench. It caused 3,064 deaths, less than one-seventh the number of fatalities in the larger, more powerful Meiji Sanriku Tsunami. Even so, waves reached over ten meters high in many inlets, and if people in the area had not known that they should run away from the shore, losses might have been comparable to those in the Meiji Period.

This is illustrated by the fact that in the Meiji Sanriku Tsunami, 984 houses were washed away in Miyagi prefecture and 5,446 in Iwate, for a total of 6,430. The numbers were only slightly lower in the Shōwa Sanriku Tsunami: 1,241 in Miyagi and 4,962 in Iwate, for a total of 6,203.[22] Despite this, fatalities were far lower in the second event. This disparity was the result of the previous painful lesson and the fact that tremors were stronger in the Shōwa Sanriku Tsunami, which was sufficient to convince most people to head for higher ground despite the late hour and the −10°C temperatures. Such "soft" factors related to human perceptions were thus as much a determining factor for safety as were physical conditions.

Ten years earlier, the Ministry of Home Affairs had gained valuable experience in urban reconstruction following the Great Kantō Earthquake. Following the Shōwa Sanriku Tsunami, the Ministry of Home Affairs made plans for relocating approximately 3,000 homes to higher ground, with the enthusiastic help of seismologist Imamura Akitsune. Within the Ministry of Home Affairs, postdisaster reconstruction planning and residential land-development projects fell under the jurisdiction of the minister's office. As of January 1934, the year after the earthquake, specific achievements were as follows: in Miyagi prefecture, 801 homes from 15 towns and 60 settlements were moved to higher ground. Eleven villages were totally relocated, and a number of individual homes in 49 villages were moved, depending on their location. Among them, Ogatsu of Jūgohama district, in which 226 homes were moved, was the biggest.

In Iwate prefecture, 2,199 homes from 18 towns and villages and 38 hamlets were relocated. The largest mass relocation was of 500 homes from Tarō village, but the scope of land to be redeveloped for that project was not clearly delineated; it long remained in a state of "planned for construction in the near future," but the plans were never implemented. Construction for other relocations (other than Tarō) had already been started, and much of it was already implemented.[23] So while there were some exceptions among the 3,000 homes in both prefectures slated for relocation—in particular the 500 homes in Tarō—nearly all had in fact relocated to higher ground within a few years after the Shōwa Sanriku Tsunami.

These relocations were funded with low-interest loans of 540,000 yen to cover land preparation costs, with the interest paid for through assistance from the national treasury. In another program, the national treasury provided seven towns and villages in Iwate prefecture with 85,000 yen to help cover road-rebuilding projects, with a total budget of 100,000 yen.

Considering that almost no nationally supported town-redevelopment projects occurred following the Meiji Sanriku Tsunami, efforts by the Ministry of Home Affairs after the Shōwa Sanriku Tsunami—particularly the relocation of 2,500 homes—were a landmark achievement. Even so, these efforts were selective and did not cover all villages at risk from tsunamis. Furthermore, assistance came only in the form of low-interest loans and assistance with interest payments. While this may have been considered whole-hearted support at the time, it is hard to avoid comparison with the total financial support from the national treasury following the Great East Japan Earthquake. Note that 27.5 percent of land redevelopment costs in Miyagi prefecture following the Meiji Sanriku Tsunami were obtained through charitable donations.[24]

Rural villages in the Tōhoku region experienced economic hardship during the Shōwa Depression (1929–31), as evidenced by accounts of families selling daughters. The Ministry of Agriculture and Forestry was sensitive to the problems farmers faced, and after the tsunami worked to improve livelihoods through industry associations and other social organizations. Looking to the example of the Great Kantō Earthquake, some residents in the disaster area considered it their natural right to receive reconstruction assistance from the country. The experience of the Great Kantō Earthquake, which came during the period of Taishō democracy, thus significantly shifted both public opinion and government views regarding disaster response.[25]

The Tarō breakwater

Among the tsunamis that struck the Sanriku coast in the Meiji, Shōwa, and Heisei Periods, the Meiji wave caused the most fatalities. Such absolute numbers are particularly startling when one considers the overall populations of the Tōhoku region and Japan at the time; the fatality rates as a percentage of population are truly astounding.

Among the villages destroyed, the devastation of Tarō in particular stands out. The town's ocean-facing bay exposed it to the full force of the tsunami. In the Meiji disaster it was hit by a 14.6-meter wave that swallowed nearly all of the 345 homes and killed 1,867 people, 83 percent of its population. The only survivors were 60 fishermen who had gone out to sea and 36 nonfishermen. Those arriving at Tarō the following day were met with a hellish scene. Where the town had once stood was only sand, broken here and there by partially exposed limbs and heads. One investigator tried to chase away wild dogs who were feeding on the dead and was in turn attacked himself.[26]

Even so, the town was rebuilt. The sea is bountiful in that area, and the natural beauty makes it a wonderful place to live. A three-part recovery plan was drawn up emphasizing relocation to higher ground, the building of a seawall, and land preparation in the foothills, all to be funded largely through donations. However, calls to address the poverty of residents led to abandonment of the plan's first two aspects, both of which are fundamental for building a safer town. Tarō was thus rebuilt in more or less the same location, advancing short-term revitalization but inviting a repeat of what had just occurred.

Sure enough, in the Shōwa Sanriku Tsunami, Tarō was again the town that experienced the worst destruction. Since the earthquake struck at 2:31 a.m. on a cold night, many took refuge in the hills, but when no sign of a tsunami appeared, some were quick to return to their warm beds. However, a 10.1-meter wave struck at 3:00 a.m., washing away 500 of the 558 homes in the town and killing 901 residents, some 32.5 percent of the population. The wave sank 990 fishing boats, every one that wasn't out to sea.

Despite this grievous second blow, Tarō implemented an aggressive recovery plan under the strong leadership of its mayor, Sekiguchi Matsutarō. Rather than relocation funded by the Ministry of Home Affairs, Sekiguchi—who felt Tarō did not have enough high land for relocation—adopted a program for in-place redevelopment that emphasized the construction of a seawall, comprehensive reorganization of roads, and expanded emergency escape routes. With funding from the national government, a 960-meter-long, 10-meter-high seawall was completed seven years later. It was designed to deflect waves in the manner of a boat's hull and to mitigate any tsunami large enough to crest it. Incidentally, this wall was highly praised for successfully blocking the tsunami resulting from the 1960 Valdivia (Chile) Earthquake.

After World War II, however, Tarō's Otobe district and others spread beyond the protection of this first wall, prompting the construction of a second wall following the coastline. When it was completed in 1979, it formed an X-shape safeguarding the town. This second wall was destroyed by a 19.5-meter tsunami in the 2011 Great East Japan Earthquake, which swept away homes and residents in eastern Otobe district. The force of this

Figure 3.4. A massive seawall was built at Tarō following the 1933 Shōwa Sanriku Tsunami, but it was insufficient to stop the tsunami caused by the 2011 Great East Japan Earthquake.

wave focused at the center of the X, not only destroying the second wall but pushing the wave over the first and inundating western Tarō as a result. The embankments held, however, so while the older inner sections of the town experienced relatively extensive flooding, fatalities were limited to around one-tenth those in the Meiji Sanriku Tsunami, with most occurring in the town's eastern districts.

I visited Tarō in April 2015 to see what the town looks like today, after surviving three devastating disasters. I was guided by Yamamoto Masanori, mayor of Miyako, the city to which Tarō now belongs. Yamamoto holds a deep fondness for Tarō. His rejection of the historical notion that Tarō doesn't have enough high ground for relocation was particularly impressive. Today, the hills north of the Otobe district are the site of massive construction for what is called the Sannō housing development, which will result in 285 homes being relocated to higher ground.

The ten-meter-high seawall that has long protected the western side of Tarō still exists, and inland areas from National Highway 45 toward the hills are being raised to form safer residential and commercial districts. The previous X-shaped design has been improved with a new 14.5-meter-high coastal seawall, adding a second layer of defense. In the eastern parts of the town that were destroyed in the Great East Japan Earthquake and Tsunami, buildings other than fishing-related facilities, offices, and the Tarō Kankō Hotel—the remains of which are preserved as a memorial—have been relocated. From all appearances, Tarō today is a much safer town than it ever was in the past.

3. Fire Brigades Battle to Survive

Fire brigades and citizens

I visited the Tōhoku region one month after the Great East Japan Earthquake, and what I saw shocked me. The sight of Rikuzentakata in Iwate prefecture was particularly disturbing. At the center of this city on the Sanriku coastline is a district called Takata. That district is blessed with relatively wide stretches of flat ground for that area, but when I visited, I saw nothing except ruins. The homes, train station, shopping arcade, and what had been a pine grove were all stripped away, leaving behind only a field of debris. It was a dead zone, with no people in sight, only the occasional truck weaving along an emergency route cleared by Self-Defense Forces (SDF) personnel.

The city center was further inland on the plains, and in the middle of it, a splendid three-story city hall still remained. I went to speak with Mayor Toba Futoshi about his experience during the tsunami. He told me that he had taken refuge atop city hall. From there he watched the waves climb higher and higher, eventually reaching him on top of the building. Had some younger people not pulled him up onto a partial fourth floor on the roof, he probably would have died.

Considering that the waves had crested the roof of a three-story building, it is no surprise that the town below was reduced to rubble. Takata had suffered only nineteen fatalities in the Meiji Sanriku Tsunami and three in the Shōwa Sanriku Tsunami. Those statistics led to a widespread belief that tsunamis hardly reached Takata, which extends well inland from the large Hirota Bay, so residents were taken unawares. This raises the question of what the town's residents were doing after the earthquake.

In Japan, citizen fire brigades work alongside fire departments to help save as many people as possible during extreme disasters. Fire-brigade members wear distinctive *haori* overcoats that at a glance make them appear to be professional firefighters, but they are in fact just ordinary citizens. Ōsaka Jun, fifty-four, chief of the Takata fire brigade at the time of the Great East Japan Earthquake, owned a photo shop in the shopping arcade near the train station, and another brigade member named Kumagai Sakaki, forty-four, had quit his office job to open a pub.

Despite being simply civilians, these brigade members were at least as conscious of their civic duty as any public official. They wholly engaged in firefighting activities without regard for their own safety. Chief Ōsaka left his home immediately after the earthquake, telling his wife to grab any cash they had and run to her parents' home on higher ground. Kumagai, too, immediately left his home, telling his wife he had to go to the fire station.[27]

There was a common assumption that a tsunami would reach the town twenty-five minutes after an earthquake. It was the fire brigade's job to close floodgates before that time, so Kumagai rode in a fire truck to ensure that the gates in his district were taken care of. Chief Ōsaka headed to the fire department, where he learned that tremors had damaged some coastal floodgates, preventing their closure. Knowing that this situation could lead to the deaths of fire-brigade members, Ōsaka drove through the town telling members to immediately evacuate along with other residents.

A small number of firefighters did die while trying to close floodgates. The tsunami first hit land at Ōfunato thirty-two minutes after the earthquake, and reached the Sendai plains an hour after, so in most cases fire departments and fire brigades were able to safely complete their tasks. However, the tsunami easily washed over closed gates, limiting their effectiveness. Another problem was that many fire-brigade members returned to their communities to encourage remaining residents to evacuate, only to be swallowed up by the tsunami themselves. While 30 police and 27 fire department personnel died or went missing in the course of their duties during the Great East Japan Earthquake, 254 fire-brigade members were lost.[28]

Fire brigades play a particularly important role in communities like those lining inlets of the Sanriku coast, where official fire departments have few staff. One might expect that as community members themselves, fire-brigade members would be particularly focused on helping their neighbors, and reluctant to leave a single person behind. Chief Osaka's cool-headed and wise order for brigade members to immediately flee, however, contradicts this expectation. In recent years, we have seen a similar phenomenon in airplane captains ordering flight crew to take their seats when encountering turbulence, placing safety over service. Considering that only those who are safe themselves can work for the safety of others, this is as it should be.

Despite his wise orders, Chief Ōsaka himself was nearly unable to escape from the tsunami. The wave was catching up with him as he tried to drive to higher ground. Before the castle park, he got stuck at a T junction at the train station. Turning right or left would have been of no use, but he happened to remember a narrow alley that he had frequently played in as a child. He got out of his car and ran through that alley and up a hill. The waves reached the hill and battered him from all sides but had lost enough of their force that he, while wet, miraculously was able to stand his ground.

Knowing that Kumagai's fire truck was behind him, Ōsaka figured that he and those with him were lost. Most of the town, after all, now lay fifteen meters below water. As it turned out, however, Kumagai's group managed to make it to safety. Upon realizing that the wave was approaching too quickly to allow escape to the hills, a brigade member riding on the back of the fire truck shouted, "We aren't going to make it! Head for the supermarket!" They ran for the parking lot, then up an emergency stairway. Looking back from a landing, they saw their fire truck being swallowed by the wave. They continued up, chased by rising waters that stopped just short of the roof, leaving them stranded in a black sea. Like Ōsaka, Kumagai assumed that his friend was lost along with the town.

The four fire brigade members were left to spend the night atop the supermarket, along with ten other residents. While there, they watched helplessly as someone floating on a board shouted for help, first pushed toward them then pulled away again by the waves.

Hard lessons for a soft society

The Takata district formed the center of Rikuzentakata, and 1,100 of its 7,600 residents were killed. For whatever reason, they had been unable to evacuate immediately after the earthquake. Among those were the wives of both Ōsaka and Kumagai, the fire brigade members who had themselves only barely escaped with their lives in pursuit of their duties.

Nonetheless, society should not depend too much on the self-sacrificing impulses of those such as fire-brigade members who are so dedicated to community safety that they disregard their own safety. Instead, we must prepare manuals for relief activities that can ensure the safety of those who follow them.

A story from the Yuriage distinct in Natori city, Miyagi prefecture presents an extreme example of how important disaster preparation can be. Neighbors were urging an elderly woman to evacuate with them, but she refused, saying that she would rather die where she was than be separated from the home where she had lived for so long. Her neighbors persisted, but she only softened after a close friend joined them. She asked to bring this and that with her, and to use the bathroom before leaving, while her neighbors waited for her. By the time they left, thirty minutes had passed in trying to persuade her. It took thirty more minutes for the tsunami to hit their neighborhood, but even so it caught them while they were still driving to safety, and all but one of the group were killed.[29]

I suspect that in a similar situation in the West, the elderly woman's wishes would have been respected and she would have been left behind with a "Good luck." Instead, the Japanese sense of kindness and cloying all-for-one principle led to many lost lives. Frequent training for disaster evacuation can prevent the need for thirty minutes of persuasion that separate life from death.

The experience of the Great Hanshin-Awaji Earthquake resulted in organizational reforms among first-responder groups such as firefighters, police, and the SDF. These included measures such as increasing stocks of emergency supplies and equipment, but the most important reforms were related to building mutual support systems at a national scale. Fire-fighting is fundamentally conducted at the local level, but a national emergency firefighting-support team was founded in June 1995, the same year as the Great Hanshin-Awaji Earthquake, and the nationwide authority of the Fire and Disaster Management Agency was established in June 2003. These changes proved effective after the Great East Japan Earthquake, when firefighting helicopters and vehicles rushed to the affected areas from across the country.

As in the case of Rikuzentakata, the town of Minamisanriku was located on plains and thus completely inundated. Hearing that emergency fire-fighting support teams from Kyoto, Hyōgo, and Tottori were on their way, Fire Chief Obata Masatoshi headed to the city entrance early in the morning on March 13, to greet them. When he saw a train of fifty firetrucks entering the town, shaking the ground, he found himself unable to hold back his tears.[30]

4. Police Response Capabilities

Earthquake and tsunami disasters

As described in the previous chapter, the police had by far the best record among first responders for saving lives in the Great Hanshin-Awaji Earthquake. Even keeping in mind that the statistics include cooperative operations, the police saved 3,495 people, the fire department 1,387, and the SDF 165. Of those, 86 percent were saved on the day of the earthquake, and 99 percent by the third day. While the first seventy-two hours after an earthquake are considered to be the critical lifesaving period, clearly the first twenty-four are of particular importance. Voices calling for help from beneath a collapsed house can fall silent hour by hour. It was thus the high density of police amid the population that allowed them to save so many people. In contrast, the physical distance between the disaster and the SDF troops is what led to their low number of rescues. In the Great East Japan Earthquake, too, the police saved approximately 3,750 people,[31] but the method of saving them was different in the two disasters.

In the Great Hanshin-Awaji Earthquake, many of those trapped beneath rubble were actually rescued by family and neighbors. Those who could not be so easily dug out were saved by public entities. As described in the previous chapter, the ratio between the two forms of rescue was 4:1, rescue by family/neighbors vs. rescue by police/fire men.

After the Great East Japan Earthquake and Tsunami, however, most people responded by trying to escape to higher ground. Some of those who were caught by the tsunami swam until they could grab onto a tree or a telephone pole and were later saved by members of public institutions such as the police, the fire department, or the SDF. In other words, those who were unsuccessful at self-assistance sank beneath the waves, beyond the possibility of rescue. Those capable of self-assistance only to the point of preserving their lives were left stranded and shivering, to be saved later by helicopters or other emergency vehicles and transported to safety. (An untold number, of course, probably died of hypothermia waiting to be rescued.) While there were many variations in this scenario, escaping on one's own and being saved later by public servants or others was the primary form of rescue in the Great East Japan Earthquake.

Wondering whether his own family was safe as he attended to the disaster site, Iwakihigashi Police Department patrolman Uyama Hiroshi recalled a question he was asked when interviewing for his job: "The difference between police officers and other public servants is that we must put our lives on the line to protect others. At times, you will be called upon to prioritize the safety of strangers above that of your own family. Can you do that?"[32]

Similarly, SDF troops take a pledge to "pursue their duties without regard to themselves," and other first responders such as the fire brigades discussed above share the same spirit.

Thirty police officers lost their lives in the Great East Japan Earth-

Figure 3.5. Shinchi station on the Japan Railways Jōban line, destroyed by the tsunami (March 17, 2011)

quake. They headed to seaside towns with loudspeakers to warn residents to take refuge from the approaching tsunami, sometimes stopping to help those falling behind or hindered by handicaps or old age, and in many cases were swallowed by a wave far larger than anything they had imagined. One policeman in Fukushima prefecture whose police car was washed away escaped by breaking his window from the inside, then climbing on top of his police car and up a tree, from which he was later rescued.[33]

A train on the Japan Railways Jōban line was stopped at the Shinchi station in Fukushima prefecture when the earthquake hit. The tremors were so strong that it was impossible to remain standing, and the station itself warped like jelly. Among the forty passengers were two young officers who had just completed their training at the police academy. They did what they had learned, making sure everyone was safe and assisting the wounded. Splitting up, one headed forward and the other back to confirm the safety of everyone on board, and after reporting to the train's conductor they received warnings of a large tsunami via their cellphones. Shinchi station is on flat ground, just 500 meters from the sea. Normally they may have hesitated from fear of inconveniencing the passengers, but in light of the predicted scale of the tsunami, they decided to evacuate everyone.

The officers formed passengers into a column and led them toward an inland municipal office atop a hill. The officer at the end of the line, Saitō Kei, was slower than the rest because he was assisting an elderly woman who had trouble walking. After they had walked for around fifteen minutes, he heard a loud rumbling, and turned around to see a wall of water rushing toward them. He was sure they were doomed, but just then a light truck passed by. He hailed it and loaded the woman and several other people onboard, thus narrowly escaping. The waters ended up rising to just below the municipal office, and the wave mangled the train at Shinchi station beyond recognition, leaving parts of it pointing straight up toward the sky.[34]

Wide-area support and disaster brigades

Disasters bring about police reforms, and in particular there have been two major improvements since the Great Hanshin-Awaji Earthquake: wide-area support systems and the establishment of disaster brigades.

In June 1995, after the emergency response to the Great Hanshin-Awaji Earthquake had somewhat settled, the National Police Agency established a system of wide-area emergency support brigades. Altogether these brigades comprised 2,500 police for rescue operations and 1,500 traffic-management officers to prevent the extreme congestion seen in the Great Hanshin-Awaji Earthquake. The aim of the system is to focus resources from across the country on afflicted areas, improving emergency response. The commissioner general of the National Police Agency leads the system. Later, a special rescue unit of 200 officers equipped with disaster-countermeasure equipment was added in April 2005, following the 2004 Chūetsu Earthquake.

After the Great East Japan Earthuake, the emergency disaster brigades were augmented with a wide-area police air team in helicopters, a new mobile police team using the latest communication technologies, and district special-response teams, making it possible to support disaster areas with up to 10,000 rapid-response personnel. The three prefectures primarily affected by the Great East Japan Earthquake have a total of 8,000 police during peacetime, and after the earthquake up to 4,800 wide-area support police arrived in the three prefectures each day. This system thus proved to be a significant reform that overcame the traditional prefecture-based territoriality of police organizations to effectively realize a dynamic and integrated emergency-response framework. During the Great Hanshin-Awaji Earthquake I had the impression that while the police were present in large numbers compared with the fire department and the SDF, they had more primitive equipment—although this impression may have been due to personal bias. The situation is very different today. In addition to the newly established special rescue brigades described above, there are also now all-female teams dedicated to community safety. It is thus now possible to bring all the latest equipment and methodologies to bear in disaster areas.

The first ground-based wide-area response brigades arrived in the early morning of the day following the earthquake. Approximately 100 police arrived in Sendai city, which was flooded and covered in debris, and set off in columns to rescue those still trapped in isolated areas.

For example, the 2011 Great East Japan Tsunami inundated the area around the Yuriage bridge over the Natori River, but the bridge itself and a walkway spanning the river remained exposed, and people waited there for rescue. A police helicopter manned by special response forces arrived on the day of the disaster and rescued six of the stranded victims, including a mother and her baby.

Wide-area response units contributed to a near-miraculous rescue on the evening of March 20, nine days after the earthquake, when a young boy and his grandmother were pulled from beneath their collapsed home in Ishinomaki, Miyagi. They were transported to a hospital by a police helicopter provided by the Kagoshima prefecture police.

In the three prefectures, the tsunami washed away 58 police stations and 247 substations. Japan is proud of its *kōban* police substations, but so long as there are seaside towns and villages, the *kōban* within them will share their vulnerability. Police departments must therefore take great care not to become disaster victims themselves. The same is true for fire departments, SDF bases, city halls, and prefectural government buildings. Those entrusted with protecting others must keep in mind something that I have emphasized throughout this book: only those who are safe themselves can help others.

The tsunami destroyed seventy-one police cars, three ships, and two helicopters in the three most affected prefectures. However, police departments from across the country supplied the disaster area with far more mobility than they previously possessed, starting with 1,000 police cars.

All areas in Japan are subject to natural disaster, but none have the resources required to respond to an extraordinary event alone. Indeed, police budgets allow for little more than what is required to cope with everyday events and accidents. Establishing mobile forces that can be deployed anywhere in the country during emergencies is therefore entirely logical.

This holds not only for historically significant events; Japan's need for agile defensive capabilities over broad regions is only likely to rise in the future in the era of decreasing population. Social structures have evolved through coping with the successive Great Hanshin-Awaji, Chūetsu, Chūetsu oki, and Great East Japan Earthquakes, and the historical significance of this evolution goes beyond disaster-time capabilities.[35]

5. The Mission of the SDF

"I will pursue my duties without regard to myself"

When I became president of the National Defense Academy in 2006, I received my official appointment from the director general of the Defense Agency. Reading the boilerplate words of the oath of appointment, I was struck by one line: "I will pursue my duties without regard to myself." It made me realize that not only uniformed soldiers, but Defense Agency staff in suits took the same oath.

I wondered if this was to be taken literally, or if it was only rhetorical posturing. When Mori Tsutomu, Chief of Staff of the Ground Self-Defense Forces (GSDF), visited the Academy, he gave a speech to the cadets in which he said about himself, "There is nothing to dying. The question is whether I accomplish my mission." I was deeply impressed with how easily he could assert that. It made me realize how many in the SDF, from top to bottom, had the will to be so selfless.

However, the value of this attitude does have limits. A good leader cares for those beneath him and will not allow them to waste their lives. While military leaders expect indomitable bravery, they also know the limits of those under their command and should issue orders that protect the unit and its members within those boundaries. Organizational logic calls for maintenance of fighting strength. Working to the point of collapse should not be viewed as heroic. One must take rational measures for recovery of fighting potential.

For SDF forces, the hardest part of the Great East Japan Earthquake was not self-sacrifice. That was part of the job, and many continued to perform altruistic rescue activities without complaint. Not a few worked for three days straight, with little sleep or rest.

The problem was not disregarding their own needs, but rather those of their families. Local troops certainly wanted to save their spouses and children, or at least confirm their safety. They were forced to bury such desires from the moment the earthquake hit and instead focus on organizational rescue activities. It is hard to imagine the pain of abandoning one's family to save another, not to mention the agony felt when recovering the body of a child of a similar age to one's own.

Defense of the six prefectures in the Tōhoku region is the responsibility of the 6th Division (located in Higashine of Yamagata prefecture) and the 9th Division (Aomori) of the Japan Ground Self-Defense Force, Northeastern Army (Sendai). Along with the Air Self-Defense Forces' Matsushima Air Base, the base for the 22nd Infantry Regiment under the 6th Division in Tagajō city, Miyagi prefecture, was closest to the disaster site. So close, in fact, that half of Camp Tagajō was inundated and became a disaster area itself, despite not being originally included in area disaster maps as a flood zone. The tsunami swallowed the homes of soldiers living near the seaside, so one wonders how they were able to handle the conflict between the desire to fulfill their public duty and to ensure the safety of their families.

One soldier whose home was next to the river, and thus almost certain to be hit by the tsunami, worried about his child and pregnant wife. He said nothing, but his superior officer knew he must be concerned, and so in the evening told him to go home to check on them. Relieved from his night shift, he waded through water, alone in the dark, but on arriving home he found it empty and filled with water. He says he does not even remember how he got back to base.

The wife of another soldier was caught by the tsunami while driving to pick up their son. She managed to escape, and phoned her husband, wet and shaking from the cold, to ask for his help. His first inclination was to run straight to her, but he and his comrades had trained long and hard to protect the public, and the time to do so had come. The lives of his wife and son were on the line, and more than anything he wanted to be with them. Just as he was considering desertion, he got a second call from his wife: "We're safe. You go on and help others." Finally, able to focus on his duties, he wholeheartedly engaged in rescue activities. "I must express my gratitude to my wife and son," he wrote. "Thank you, truly."[36]

Of course, top-level responses to an emergency play a key role in determining outcomes. Immediately after the earthquake, Kunitomo Akira, commander of the Tagajō regiment, was able to communicate via cellphone with his commanding officer, 6th Division Commander Kunō Yūji. "We're heading out," Kunitomo said, to which Kunō responded, "Good." That was all. Neither hailed from the Tōhoku region, but both had developed a deep love for the area of their command and were proud to lead soldiers dedicated to the protection of their homeland.

Land, sea, and air units from across Japan gathered as part of a joint task force, established on March 14, and led by Commander of the Northeastern Army Kimizuka Eiji (1952–2015). General Kimizuka had the serene appearance of a scholar, but also an excellent ability to see the big picture, and both Japanese and U.S. forces who watched his precise handling of situational updates—briefings held at 8:00 a.m. and 8:00 p.m. each day—were highly impressed.

Before his troops headed out into the disaster area, General Kimizuka shared the following words with them: "If we were any other organization, the SDF would have our backs, and we could leave everything up to them. But we are the SDF, and no one has our backs. We're last at bat. There are people out there counting on us. Should a disaster victim offer you a hot meal, saying they have extra, refuse it. There will be time for comfort later, after the last victim is taken care of." Troops followed this last bit of advice, forgoing warm meals for Meal, Ready-to-Eat eaten in the back of trucks. Kimizuka closed with a final admonition: "Treat the deceased carefully, as if they might still be alive, and as if they were your own family members."[37]

Japan and its people rely on the vital altruistic service that SDF troops provide. While it is fine for troops to fulfill their oath by fighting day and night without rest, I cannot help but think that it would be worthwhile to devote resources to confirming the safety of soldiers' families when required. Society as a whole would no doubt support me in saying that such a function is important in maintaining the effectiveness of our military.

The chief of staff takes the initiative

When the earthquake struck, Ministry of Defense (the Defense Agency had become by this point a full ministry in 2007) leaders were in a meeting on the eleventh floor of Ministry of Defense headquarters in Ichigaya, Tokyo. Established rules called for a general summons in the event of an earthquake of intensity V Upper. As soon as the shaking started, the meeting was halted, and a television turned on. The news was reporting a large earthquake with its epicenter offshore from Miyagi prefecture.

Knowing that this was a major event, GSDF Chief of Staff Hibako Yoshifumi headed downstairs, considering as he did so whether troops should be mobilized nationwide. He had a plan in mind by the time he reached his office on the fourth floor.

As in battle, a speedy concentration of force was called for. Hibako first telephoned Commanding General Kimizuka. "We've been hit hard," Kimizuka said. "Our office is a mess. There's a cloud of dust rising from the new government building next to us. The power is out, so we can't turn on a television." Hibako told him that while official orders would eventually come from the minister of defense or chief of the Joint Staff, he should deploy immediately rather than wait. He furthermore assured Kimizuka that reinforcements would be arriving from across the country. He next telephoned the GSDF Western Army (Kumamoto), and ordered deployment of the 4th Division (Kasuga in Fukuoka prefecture) and the 5th Engineer Brigade (Ogōri in Fukuoka prefecture). He ordered that the 8th Division (Kumamoto) and 15th Brigade (Naha) be withheld, however, to maintain the security of East China Sea regions. Hibako then called the remaining five armies in Japan and delivered similar instructions.[38]

When I asked Chief of Staff Hibako if his quick orders were delivered according to some preexisting SDF plan for emergency situations, he said that was not the case.[39] The Northeastern Army had plans and training for typical earthquakes and tsunami occurring offshore of Miyagi prefecture, but there were no nationwide mobilization plans for handling an enormous earthquake, so he had given those orders based on his own judgment. It surprised me that he was willing to risk making such a decision on his own. But Hibako told me he sensed that doing so was the appropriate response given the seriousness of the situation.

A Defense Ministry response conference was held at 3:30 p.m. on that day, and Hibako's immediate actions, which some might have considered overreach, were acknowledged and formalized. At the beginning of the meeting, Defense Minister Kitazawa Toshimi announced that Prime Minister Kan Naoto (in office 2010–11) had requested the quickest-possible response from the SDF, to which the GSDF chief of staff replied that arrangements had already been made. The minister did not congratulate him for his initiative, but neither did he reprimand him, thus giving implicit government approval for his actions.

While no plans were in place for nationwide deployment in a situation like the Great East Japan Earthquake, neither was there a complete lack of consideration of what to do in such an event. In the event of an earthquake striking directly beneath Tokyo, plans called for deployment of 120,000 to 130,000 troops, including those already based in Tokyo, or approximately half of all SDF troops—the most that the SDF could safely muster. In any event, two categories of units could not be moved: units charged with protecting vital locations such as Tokyo, Osaka, and Sapporo, and frontline troops for national defense. The chief of staff used this view of the SDF's role in natural disasters as a basis for forming a specific plan of action.[40]

Major SDF reforms

The SDF's slow initial response following the Great Hanshin-Awaji Earthquake resulted in thorough reforms. For one, the GSDF adopted a rotation that would allow immediate deployment of one platoon (approximately thirty soldiers) in every camp throughout Japan at any time, twenty-four hours a day, as soon as a disaster strikes. This was later named "Fast Force." When an earthquake of intensity V Upper strikes, a camera-equipped helicopter is dispatched to allow command centers to view live video of the situation. Equipment stores, too, have been greatly expanded, including trucks equipped with a suite of lifesaving gear. In addition to the already excellent capabilities of engineering and supply corps, this greatly expanded SDF capabilities for dealing with major disasters.

Two major systemic reforms unrelated to disaster prevention also indirectly improved disaster-response capabilities. In 2006, the ground, sea, and air SDF adopted an integrated operations system that streamlined effective use and concentration of forces. In addition, the Central Readiness Force was formed in 2007, and later aided in the response to the Fukushima nuclear disaster. While SDF budgets and personnel levels shrank during the sixteen-year period between the Great Hanshin-Awaji and Great East Japan Earthquakes, it was also a period of many reforms related to the SDF's new roles, both domestic and overseas.

Leadership at the Defense Ministry during the time of the Great East Japan Earthquake were actively engaged in this type of structural reform. A major motivation was the determination to not repeat previous mistakes that led to slow, understaffed emergency deployments. GSDF Chief of Staff Hibako's immediate response to the Great East Japan Earthquake serves as a prime example. Commander in Chief of the Self Defense Fleet Kuramoto Kenichi immediately ordered all deployable ships to head to the Sanriku coast, and Yokosuka Area Commander Takashima Hiromi put that order into action.[41]

After confirming Prime Minister Kan's desire for maximal engagement, Defense Minister Kitazawa and Oriki Ryōichi, chief of staff, Joint Staff, ordered the largest deployment of troops in the SDF's history—107,000, including SDF reservists and ready-reserve personnel. As a result, in stark contrast to its performance in the Great Hanshin-Awaji Earthquake, the SDF was able to assist in the rescue of approximately 20,000 people, accounting for 72 percent of all successful rescue operations.

6. Hands-on Response

The other first responders

While at many central ministries the primary tasks amount to desk work, the Ministry of Land, Infrastructure, and Transport (MLIT) was highly active, playing a major role in emergency response to the Great East Japan Earthquake. When the earthquake hit, Tokuyama Hideo, head of the MLIT's Tōhoku Regional Bureau, was in the Sendai bureau chief's office. Lockers toppled, cracks appeared in walls, and the power went out, but a few seconds later the building's backup generator kicked in and the lights came back on. Tokuyama moved to the disaster-response office, thirty meters away on the same floor, while the building was still swaying. Disaster Prevention Section Head Kumagai Junko proposed an "unmanned" flight of the MLIT disaster-response helicopter in Sendai Airport, meaning a flight by aviation company staff with no accompanying MLIT representatives. Tokuyama immediately agreed. Thankfully the helicopter had not been swallowed by the tsunami, and so was able to provide live video feeds of Sendai Airport and towns along the coast.

At 10:00 p.m., the Sendai Bureau held a teleconference with the central MLIT offices in Tokyo, in which MLIT Minister Ōhata Akihiro gave two clear instructions based on lessons learned in the Great Hanshin-Awaji Earthquake: to prioritize lifesaving operations above all else, and to give Tokuyama the authority to do whatever he deemed necessary on behalf of the ministry and the country. Ōhata stated that normal ministerial structures could be ignored, and that he would bear responsibility for any related pushback. This teleconference was open to all MLIT organizations throughout the country, allowing Tokuyama to obtain support throughout the ministry.

Tokuyama first concentrated on reopening roads in the disaster area to reconnect it with Tokyo. The Tōhoku Expressway had suffered cracks and potholes in some stretches, so it was closed. Initial emergency repairs were completed within the day, clearing at least a single lane so that SDF vehicles could pass through. Police manned expressway entrances, warning rescue vehicles that they would have to proceed at their own risk, but with the Shinkansen rail line down, the Tōhoku Expressway was the main artery connecting the region to the rest of the country.

The emphasis then shifted to opening the fifteen roads branching off from the north-south Tōhoku Expressway. Four hundred local construction companies aided in that effort, starting work late on the night of the 11th. They were told to not worry about making roads pretty, just to open lanes as quickly as possible so that rescue vehicles could arrive while victims were still alive. Amazingly, eleven roads were opened by March 12, the day after the earthquake, and all routes were available by the 15th.

Drainage pumps were gathered from across the country and used to drain Sendai Airport. Support from the U.S. armed forces came in the form of Operation Tomodachi, described later, and the airport was surveyed on March 10 by representatives of the U.S. military, the runways cleared of cars and debris by local contractors and the U.S. military, and the first military aircraft landed on the 18th. The airport itself was partially reopened on April 13 to chartered commercial aircraft, and the grand reopening came a half-year later.

Recovery support by land and air arrived with surprising speed. After the roads were opened, Tokuyama focused on supporting local governments in disaster-affected areas. Taking advantage of the fact that MLIT communications systems remained active, local leaders were able to notify others of problems and needs, allowing rapid supply of everything from food and tents to coffins and sanitary napkins, delivered from across the country in MLIT vehicles. MLIT "TEC Force" disaster emergency-response groups coordinated with regional mayors to provide assistance. Private-sector firms from the construction and transport industries also cooperated, effectively developing site-focused activities very unlike what might be expected from government-led projects, making the MLIT itself something like a primary-response organization.[42]

Medical support from DMAT

An estimated 160,000 people were instantly trapped beneath collapsed homes when the Great Hanshin-Awaji Earthquake hit. There were 6,434 dead (including disaster-related deaths) and 43,792 injured, of whom 10,684 were seriously wounded. Many of the latter eventually died, in part because the hospitals they would normally have been taken to and the staff that would have cared for them were themselves victims of the earthquake. When a powerful earthquake cuts regional lifelines, it can become impossible to provide the care that would save lives in normal circumstances. Volunteer medical workers arriving from across the country were shocked at what they saw. The phrase "preventable disaster deaths" arose all too frequently.

Both the medical community and Japanese society as a whole realized the need for change. The initial response was to establish disaster-response hospitals throughout the country. Medical teams gained further experience in the 2004 Chūetsu Earthquake, and in April 2005 the Ministry of Health, Labor and Welfare established a National Disaster Medical Assistance Team (DMAT) system under its jurisdiction. This system created a registry of hospitals with the capacity and mobility to accept patients in the most acute phases of a disaster (generally the first forty-eight hours), and trained teams for deployment to disaster areas wherever they might occur. To prevent burdening disaster areas, DMATs brought their own food, water, and sleeping bags, aiming to provide self-contained medical support.

As will be described in more detail below, at 3:37 p.m.—just fifty-two minutes after the Great East Japan Earthquake struck—the prime minister's office held the first meeting of the Emergency Response Headquarters and established a policy with five core tenets, including deployment of police, firefighters, the SDF, and the Coast Guard, as well as medical support from DMATs. While DMATs were first spontaneously formed by compassionate doctors, by the time of the Great East Japan Earthquake they were being run as a public organization managed at the national level.

Between March 11 and 22, 380 DMATs comprising 1,800 members from across the country gathered in the disaster area to support local hospitals and doctors by providing triage and emergency medical care, and to transport patients to hospitals within and outside of the disaster area, depending on their condition.

Considering that medical institutions in a disaster area are often heavily damaged, residents truly appreciate the presence of DMATs. Positioning DMATs as a national system ensures that all regions of Japan can receive their support when called for, which is truly lifesaving in this land of disasters. I hope that they continue to grow.

However, DMATs arriving at disaster sites after the Great East Japan Earthquake were perplexed. While in the Great Hanshin-Awaji Earthquake there were nearly seven times as many wounded as dead, in the Great East Japan Earthquake there were only 6,114 wounded and nearly 20,000 dead. There was much less demand than anticipated for surgical care, and many more patients needing internal care such as dialysis. In this way, earthquake and tsunami disasters take very different forms.

In response, over the following week internal medicine teams rapidly replaced surgical teams. Learning from this experience, Japan will doubtless enhance its comprehensive capabilities for medical response to disasters.

In this respect, few organizations had a better grasp of what to expect after a tsunami disaster than the Japanese Red Cross Kumamoto Hospital, a front-runner in disaster medical care. That hospital had provided on-site medical assistance in Sumatra after the 2004 Indian Ocean Tsunami. On receiving reports of the Great East Japan Earthquake, staff imagined a wave like they had seen in Sumatra—one that swept away everything standing—and decided that large disaster-rescue vehicles capable of providing assistance within 72 hours would be needed.

The first team left at 9:00 p.m., and by midnight the hospital had deployed six rescue vehicles, including two or three "disaster rescue" buses with capabilities equivalent to those of a small hospital. The following day they chartered five ten-ton trucks from private companies to supply the area with ninety tons of supplies. These vehicles left Kumamoto for the Japanese Red Cross Ishinomaki Hospital, arriving forty hours later. By the end of May, the Kumamoto Hospital had deployed 231 doctors and staff.[43]

Japanese society has long viewed doctors as elite, and sometimes aloof, scholarly types, rather than as medical staff serving on the ground. The activities of medical groups in the Great Hanshin-Awaji and Great East Japan Earthquakes, however, changed that perception to one of idealists with a strong sense of responsibility and deep caring for those in need of help. Extraordinary misery reveals aspects of character that are hard to see on a daily basis.

Schools and teachers

The earthquake was particularly trying for schools and teachers entrusted with the care and education of the next generation. In addition to teaching children, schools served as emergency shelters, and many teachers supported shelter operations.

Educational institutions, including elementary and junior high schools in the disaster area, suffered major damage. Some schools, such as Ōkawa Elementary School in Ishinomaki in Miyagi prefecture, were completely swallowed by the wave, along with their teachers and students. At Naka-hama Elementary School in Yamamoto in Miyagi prefecture, the water rose to the second-floor ceiling, but ninety-two staff and students were able to take refuge in an attic room, where they ended up spending the night waiting for rescue.

Five hundred and ninety students from kindergarten through college lost their lives in the three primary disaster prefectures, along with thirty-six teachers. In the 1896 Meiji Sanriku Tsunami, elementary school students alone (there were only elementary schools in the region at the time) accounted for some 6,000 fatalities, so in that regard there has been tremendous progress. Even so, 590 casualties are far too many.

There were 6,484 public schools in the stricken area, among which the Ministry of Education classified 202 schools as having experienced a Category I (most serious) disaster. Students and faculty at some schools, such as those in Unozumai of Kamaishi city and Okirai of Ōfunato city, were able to evacuate to higher ground, but the school buildings themselves were swallowed by the wave, making them unusable.

Most schools that were not inundated became shelters for local residents. Schools in Japan frequently host disaster-prevention activities, sports, festivals, and the like, but during disasters they become shelters that can save lives and even serve as temporary homes for those who have lost their own. Indeed, 523 schools in the three prefectures (64 in Iwate, 310 in Miyagi, and 149 in Fukushima) had been converted to shelters as of March 17, 2011. Conversely, school teachers and staff who had themselves suffered greatly were called on not only to resume educational services, but to provide special support for local residents.

Many provided self-sacrificing service to their communities. According to Ministry of Education surveys, the full faculty at 47.2 percent of schools along the coast in the disaster area and at least half of the faculty at 21.5 percent of schools helped to operate disaster shelters. Watching television three months after the tsunami, I saw images of a graduation ceremony in an auditorium, half of which was still being used as an emergency shelter, where several refugees were sitting on futon, a scene that symbolized the affected communities.

Twenty-first-century Japan is an aging society, where low birth rates are leading to the consolidation and closure of rural schools nationwide. The Great East Japan Earthquake served only to accelerate that trend. The closure of the schools in some cases also means the unavailability of shelters in the future.

In the three most affected prefectures, 104 schools were forced to start the new school year in April by holding classes in other schools. There were 1,987 elementary and junior high schools in the three prefectures at the time of the earthquake, but three years later 160 (68 in Iwate, 47 in Miyagi, and 45 in Fukushima) had been closed. This disaster came at a particularly difficult time of pullback, consolidation, and reorganization. It is thus all the more important to remember how hard schools and teachers fought not only for the children they taught, but for all residents of disaster areas.[44]

7. Wide-Area Support between Local Governments

The "counterpart method" of the Union of Kansai Governments

The Great Hanshin-Awaji Earthquake triggered what was called the "year of the volunteer" or the "volunteer revolution" in Japan, an outpouring of nearly 1.38 million volunteers who came to assist in recovery efforts. It also led to establishment of the Law Concerning the Promotion of Specific Non-Profit Organization (NPO) Activities (the "NPO Law"), further promoting the development of civil society in Japan.

In turn, one social phenomenon resulting from the Great East Japan Earthquake was a focus on the activities of organized, specific-purpose NPOs. Organized support activities by companies also matured, and cooperation and support through social media emerged. However, the most important new phenomenon was wide-area support among local governments. Against the backdrop of a hierarchical Japanese national structure, many prefectural and town governments throughout the country have developed horizontal relationships for sustainable wide-area support of disaster-affected municipalities.

Before the Great East Japan Earthquake, there were reportedly some one hundred mutual-support agreements between municipalities for disaster-related assistance. Of these, approximately twenty were between municipalities in neighboring prefectures, and so could prove ineffective in the case of a large-scale event like the Great East Japan Earthquake that affected both partners. Real support can best be provided between distant partners that both have resources such as usable airports and oil reserves.[45]

Another approach was the "counterpart" activities undertaken by the Union of Kansai Governments (UKG), which became a major engine for lateral support among municipalities. The UKG is a special local public entity established in 2010 with the aim of promoting decentralization and regional administration in the Kansai region. It was the first wide-area union of local governments in Japan, originally comprising the five prefectures in the Kinki region and the prefectures of Tottori (Chūgoku region) and Tokushima (Shikoku region), later joined by Nara in 2015. The first union leader was Hyōgo prefectural governor Ido Toshizō.

One characteristic of the UKG is that each prefecture has a separate role. For example, Kyoto handles tourism and culture, Osaka industry, Wakayama agricultural water, and Shiga the environment, in a horizontal structure that allows each prefecture to lead in a field according to its strength. Hyōgo prefecture's lead area of disaster prevention became most active after several disasters occurred, raising concerns about an earthquake and tsunami originating from the Nankai trough.

Then came the Great East Japan Earthquake. Two days later, on March 13, 2011, a UKG commission urgently met in Kobe, bringing together member governors. UKG President Ido proposed a "counterpart" approach to aiding the affected prefectures, providing them with support based on lessons learned through the Kansai region's experience in the Great Hanshin-Awaji Earthquake. There were also proposals for assistance to all six prefectures in the Tōhoku region, but in the end, it was decided that multiple Kansai prefectures would double up to focus efforts on the three most severely hit Tōhoku prefectures. Kyoto and Shiga were assigned to Fukushima, Osaka and Wakayama to Iwate, and Hyōgo, Tottori, and Tokushima to Miyagi.

From their own disaster experiences, UKG members knew it was difficult for the worst-hit areas to even request aid. They therefore decided to preemptively send goods they felt would be needed without waiting for official requests. It is important not to hold back out of fear of waste due to mismatched donations. While there are arguments for not overloading disaster areas with relief supplies by "pushing" too much, the new thinking is that it is better to have more than they need than to not have enough.

Postwar Japan has preferred that the bureaucracy get involved only after the responsible official on the ground has made a request. Assistance abroad (such as ODA, etc.) tends to also be based on local requests. However, during a crisis such as a large disaster, waiting to react based on a local request is the same as abandoning the victims. Hyōgo prefecture, for example, based on its experience during the 1995 Great Hanshin-Awaji Earthquake, pushed relief supplies and personnel to the Tōhoku disaster area.

The UKG set up local offices in their assigned locales and set out to provide a wide range of needed goods, including food, warm clothing, portable toilets, tarpaulins, baby products, hygienic items, and disposable diapers. The Kansai region also sheltered approximately 5,000 people for one year following the earthquake. Furthermore, the UKG provided a nationwide evacuee communications system developed from the bitter experience of evacuees in Hyōgo being unable to obtain information.

Most important, however, was the dispatch of staff to the disaster area. The team departing from Kyoto and Shiga first went to Niigata to obtain information related to the nuclear power plants, then on March 16 set up liaison offices in government buildings in Aizuwakamatsu and Fukushima. On March 14, the team dispatched to Iwate from Osaka and Wakayama similarly set up liaison offices in the Iwate prefectural government complex, as well as an office in Tōno city to provide a rearward support base for afflicted coastal areas. Later, in November, they established another office in the city hall at Kamaishi. The team dispatched to Miyagi from Hyōgo, Tottori, and Tokushima established their liaison office in the Miyagi prefectural offices on March 14 and established local support offices in Kesennuma, Minamisanriku, and Ishinomaki on the 23rd.

These teams worked as advance units to assess local situations, and later helped build pathways and bases for support activities. Through these activities, the number of supporters from UKG prefectures and cities swelled to over 60,000 in the first year alone. In the four years up to January 2015, the total number of staff dispatches from Hyōgo prefecture and its cities exceeded 230,000.[46]

Generally speaking, early missions to disaster sites lasted for up to one week. No hotels were operating in the disaster site, and spending longer than that sleeping in conference rooms and buses would be an undue hardship. Staff dispatched from prefectural offices generally performed "soft" duties, such as managing support activities, summarizing and reporting local needs, and performing tasks related to material supply and shelter maintenance.

In contrast, staff from cities and towns served as replacements for local staff lost in the disaster, thanks to their expertise at everyday clerical tasks such as regenerating family registries, processing disaster loss claims, filing death certificates, handling national pension paperwork, and addressing taxation issues. After a few months, they also took on tasks related to temporary housing and donation allocations, and after a year, specialists conversant in home reconstruction, agricultural engineering, and town planning were also needed. Acting on their own disaster experience, the Kansai region supplied not only general medical teams but also specialists who could provide psychological counseling services, as well as inspectors capable of determining the degree of structural damage to buildings.

As the focus gradually shifted to rebuilding towns and workplaces, more specialized personnel became necessary. As a result, town planners and engineers were dispatched for one-year deployments. Prefectures in the Kansai region and beyond started hiring new staff for one-year periods, renewable for up to three years, specifically for dispatch to disaster areas. Some retired staff with particular expertise and competencies were rehired, financed by national-level programs that covered the costs of these hires to promote intermunicipal support.[47]

"Scrum support" by Suginami ward, Tokyo

Of course, the UKG was not the only intergovernmental body providing support. The Ministry of Internal Affairs and Communications' *Status of Prefectural Support for Disaster-Affected Prefectures (March 21, 2012)*,[48] a collection of reports gathered from prefectural websites, shows that most prefectures sent support teams along with emergency firefighting and medical teams. For example, Shizuoka prefecture—which had for many years been preparing for a disaster of its own—sent large medical and regional support teams to the towns of Yamada and Ōtsuchi in Iwate prefecture on March 19, and continued to supplement both.

Support was not limited to the prefectural level. From a relationship developed through Little League baseball, Tokyo's Suginami ward had established a mutual disaster-support agreement with Minamisōma city in Fukushima prefecture. Suginami ward chief Tanaka Ryō also contacted Higashiagatsuma in Gunma prefecture, Ojiya in Niigata, and Nayoro in Hokkaidō—all local governments with which Suginami had some form of cooperative relationship—and invited them to establish a "Municipal Government Scrum Support Conference" in support of Minamisoma.

Some residents in these locales expressed dissenting opinions regarding spending local tax money in support of a distant disaster area. Even so, an ordinance was passed to allow support of other local governments, and Suginami ward supplemented financial support from the national government by raising over 500 million yen in donations. Suginami's quick decision-making and actions helped launch a new phase in inter-municipality disaster support, bringing about an era of multifaceted, multilayered approaches to wide-area disaster prevention.[49]

The formation of support networks between municipalities nationwide has great significance, and in recent years the independence of municipal governments has been both legally and socially fortified. Even so, municipal governments remain overly vulnerable to major disasters. In Ōtsuchi, for instance, one in four city employees—including the mayor himself—died in the Great East Japan Earthquake. It is difficult for the nation and its people to compensate for such losses, but the best strategy for doing so is through the support of other municipal governments, which are themselves engaged in similar activities. Recovery ultimately depends on the initiative of the afflicted government, but the support of friends from afar is a vital resource nonetheless.

In retrospect, horizontal intermunicipal support was a crucial supplement to national-level support. However, the lack of overall coordination by the central government deserves criticism. The Japanese government never stops involving itself in regional affairs during peacetime, but it has been incapable of planning responses for major disasters or providing sufficient leadership in times of crisis. Regional governments cannot do these things on their own, and therefore the central government's efforts should be strengthened to cope with big disasters.

A new stage in corporate support

At a meeting in Tokyo in autumn of 2011, Mitsubishi Corporation chair Kojima Yorihiko told me that his company was supporting the recovery by continuously sending employees to volunteer in the afflicted areas. This seemed to be a different level of corporate support than I had witnessed in the past, so I asked him why this was happening. He told me that employees changed through their time in the disaster area—that young employees who had previously awaited instructions from above learned to proactively make suggestions themselves, thus benefitting the company. This felt like something new.

A study by Fujisawa Retsu[50] describes how Mitsubishi Corporation carries out large-scale support activities through its various subordinate companies. By the end of 2014, for example, 3,529 Mitsubishi employees had conducted volunteer activities in the Tōhoku region. Furthermore, the company established a ten-billion-yen recovery fund immediately after the Great East Japan Earthquake, and in the following year established the Mitsubishi Corporation Disaster Relief Foundation as a vehicle for performing various relief activities. Over three years, the company provided 3,695 college and graduate school students in the disaster area with a 100,000-yen monthly scholarship. It has also worked with nonprofit organizations in the disaster area to assist in the development of 425 projects and has invested in or financed 44 businesses there. In other words, Mitsubishi is supporting disaster-area reconstruction by cooperating—primarily by providing financial support—with various actors engaged on the ground.

The Foundation has also formed an agreement with Kōriyama city aimed at industrial revitalization and recovery of the fruit industry in Fukushima prefecture. In October 2015, the Foundation completed construction of a winery, an attempt at wine and liqueur production to create demand for wine grapes. These activities are not only helping Fukushima overcome the damage done to its reputation for food safety due to the nuclear disaster, they are giving the region the capacity to build its own facilities.

The courier company Yamato Transport also carried out unique initiatives. Five of the company's employees lost their lives in the Great East Japan Earthquake, and many others spontaneously volunteered to transport materials without waiting for orders from above. In response, the company organized a relief transport delivery brigade comprising some 1,000 employees from across the country, which enabled Yamato to resume local delivery services in the disaster zone.

The company also donated ten yen to disaster recovery for each package it delivered. Yamato carries about 1.3 billion parcels each year, and so became one of the largest corporate donors, contributing some 14.2 billion yen (around 40 percent of profits) over a year. They directed these funds to the Yamato Welfare Foundation, which supports the fishing, tourism, medical care, and childcare fields. For example, in Minamisanriku the foundation set up a temporary seafood market, which after 300 million yen in investment was able to hold its first auction in October 2011, seven months after the earthquake.

Since 2015, Yamato Transport has furthermore been cooperating with Northern Iwate Transportation, Inc., in a project where packages for home delivery are loaded onto the backs of buses, thereby providing transport of both people and goods between Miyako, Morioka, and other cities. This is a mutually beneficial arrangement for bus companies and goods-transport systems in an aging society where use of public transportation is down due to declining population.

The project that best demonstrates Yamato's policy of close regional ties, however, is its "Heartful Deliveries." This is a shopping-support service through which Yamato delivers products from local stores, ordered from catalogs distributed to the elderly by social-welfare councils. Drivers furthermore inquire into the health and well-being of elderly customers. Eldercare is generally considered the responsibility of local welfare commissioners, but sufficient care can be difficult to maintain since Japan's elderly population is growing dramatically. The arrival of a package can cheer up elderly people who are lonely or have become withdrawn. The delivery person can share information about any noticeable changes to regional welfare commissions to help them keep track of the condition of the elderly in the area. Today, the program has spread beyond the Tōhoku region and is being deployed in depopulated regions throughout the country.

Many companies besides Mitsubishi and Yamato have contributed to disaster area recovery, including the Kirin Company, Recruit Career, and Globis. Given that private company theoretically exist to make profits, it is interesting to consider why they might wish to be so deeply involved in supporting disaster recovery.

"Corporate social responsibility"—the concept that profits should be partially returned to society through activities promoting social betterment—became a keyword in the 1980s. This trend subsided somewhat during the "lost two decades" following the bursting of Japan's economic bubble, but at the same time we witnessed the appearance of 1.38 million volunteers following the Great Hanshin-Awaji Earthquake, and the establishment of the NPO law a few years later. Furthermore, the Great East Japan Earthquake hit at a time of social awareness regarding the need for private support of the social good. Certain prosperous companies and ambitious organizations became involved in the Tōhoku disaster areas, and the capital and organizational strength that they brought had a major impact.

Participation in the public sphere might be considered a common ideal among these companies, but as the previously-mentioned paper by Fujisawa[51] points out, the concept of "creating shared value" proposed by Harvard University's Michael Porter is also important. New value is created when companies work in coordination with other actors to resolve social issues. This increases employee morale and pride, as well as enhances corporate image.

While Yamato Transport's profitability fell after it directed 40 percent of its annual profits to disaster relief, the company recovered rapidly in the following year, demonstrating how creating close bonds with the people of a region can provide a powerful competitive advantage. While not necessarily offering new services that boost corporate profits, innovative activities aimed at meeting public needs also enhance corporate competitiveness.

During disaster recovery, it is interesting to see that a businesslike sense of profitability and sustainability can work toward creating new social value. Successful examples of corporate support demonstrate that important factors for success include not only a company's financial and management abilities, but also partnerships with local governments and NGOs. Private-sector activity in the Great Hanshin-Awaji Earthquake was predominantly amateurish volunteerism, but sixteen years later, after the Great East Japan Earthquake, we saw the establishment of NGOs and other specialized organizations that proved themselves to be irreplaceable elements of Japanese society, a truly amazing development.

The miracle of Tōno city

If someone asked me which regional government played the greatest role in supporting disaster areas after the Great East Japan Earthquake, without hesitation I would say Tōno city, located slightly inland from the coast of Iwate prefecture. The examples described above of the UKG's "counterpart" method for wide-area support and the "scrum support" approach of Tokyo's Suginami ward were also important, but Tōno's contributions went far beyond both.

The city's own disaster preparations must first be noted. Knowing that an earthquake would eventually strike offshore from Miyagi prefecture, Tōno mayor Honda Toshiaki had constantly worked toward improving awareness among public servants of the need for disaster preparedness and mitigation through training programs. A peak of these programs was the 2008 Tōhoku emergency drill called "Michinoku Alert," which gathered twenty-five regional governments from cities and towns on the Tōhoku coast, along with police, firefighters, the SDF, and private-sector organizations. GSDF Northern Army Commander Munakata Hisao was a vocal supporter and ensured the active involvement of the Northern Army.

Training focused on response to a predicted M 8 earthquake occurring offshore of Miyagi prefecture, but what actually hit three years later was a much larger M 9 quake. In this sense preparations were insufficient, but even so they provided the foundation for a core response, as the testimonies of many survivors showed. Compared to the Kansai region, where the myth of safety among both local officials and other residents hindered any real preparation, schools and leaders in the Tōhoku region to a certain extent acknowledged, trained for, and prepared for a major earthquake.

Tōno's second contribution was to become an inland base for initial response. Tōno sits behind several cities along the Sanriku coast. Kamaishi and Ōtsuchi are the closest, about thirty kilometers away. Approximately forty kilometers to the south are Ōfunato and Rikuzentakata, and sixty kilometers to the north is Miyako. All are connected by roads spreading out from Tōno like a fan.

Tōno's city hall was damaged in the earthquake, but it was sufficiently inland to be safe from the tsunami. The SDF and others thus used an athletic park there as a gathering point, and the park became a focal point for support activities. Tōno welcomed its role as host for these activities and became a de facto command post for gathering information related to coastal disaster areas. Those who wished to volunteer but had no specific goals in mind would head to Tōno, where they could find a site in need of help. In addition to city officials, NGOs and other organizations with specialized skills gathered in Tōno to direct activities.

Indeed, the city of Tōno itself served as a volunteer organization, from Mayor Honda on down. Tōno took on tasks that the prefectural government would normally perform but were difficult for such a large organization to address. The city's disaster preparations, ability to manage the initial crisis response, and strong leader all situated it to play this remarkable role.[52]

FOUR

The Great East Japan Earthquake (2)

Response by Japanese Society and the Government

1. Initial Response by the Japanese Government

A completely new system for initial response

As described in chapter 2, the prime minister's office had no information-gathering system during the Great Hanshin-Awaji Earthquake. Sixteen years later, the situation was starkly different.

Previously, the National Land Agency's Disaster Prevention Bureau received information from ministries and regional governments, which it reported to the prime minister's office. The National Land Agency did not operate in twenty-four-hour shifts, however, and so was not functioning when the Great Hanshin-Awaji Earthquake hit at 5:46 a.m. As a result, the prime minister remained unaware of the seriousness of the event until around noon.

By the time the Great East Japan Earthquake hit on March 11, 2011, a new crisis-management center had been constructed underground beneath the prime minister's office. An appointed crisis-management supervisor—former Metropolitan Police Chief Itō Tetsurō at the time—served a central role in the event of disaster, gathering information, convening ministry and agency directors to prepare response plans, and assisting the chief cabinet secretary and vice secretary. The system was designed such that key members would immediately convene in the event of an earthquake of

161

intensity V Upper in metropolitan Tokyo (VI Lower in other locales), and therefore was triggered in the Great East Japan Earthquake.

In the Diet, when the earthquake hit, the Upper House financial committee was discussing a scandal related to Prime Minister Kan Naoto's acceptance of foreign political donations. The chandelier overhead shook so much that some feared it would fall, leaving attendees transfixed in their seats. The committee chair recessed the meeting and instructed everyone to take shelter under their desks.

Crisis-management supervisor Itō was in his office on the fourth floor of the prime minister's office, and as soon as the shaking started, he issued orders to assemble the emergency team. He then walked downstairs to the crisis-management center to set up an official response headquarters in an executive meeting room. A large adjacent room was equipped with ten large monitors, allowing up to 200 personnel from different ministries to gather. Deputy Chief Cabinet Secretary Fukuyama Tetsurō soon arrived, followed by Chief Cabinet Secretary Edano Yukio, and the emergency response team started its first discussion at 3:00 p.m., just fourteen minutes after the earthquake hit. Itō proposed creating an Extreme Disaster Management Headquarters, to which Edano agreed. Prime Minister Kan arrived from the Diet at 3:07 and immediately approved the plan.

Disaster regulations stipulate that a Major Disaster Management Headquarters headed by the Disaster Prevention Minister should be established in the case of a major disaster, but that in an abnormally severe disaster, a cabinet decision can establish an Extreme Disaster Management Response Headquarters with the prime minister as its leader instead. Itō proposed doing so, and the headquarters was established at 3:14, even before the tsunami hit. This provides evidence that officials recognized the seriousness of the situation from the start.

The emergency response team that met at 3:00 p.m. furthermore established a policy of prioritizing lifesaving activities above all others, entrusting this task to firefighters, the police, the SDF, the Coast Guard, and DMATs. This was formalized at the first Extreme Disaster Management Response Headquarters meeting, held at 3:37 p.m., then announced as the government's basic official response policies. As this timeline shows, a pre-established disaster-response-policy protocol, prepared by the crisis-management supervisor and the cabinet, made possible a prompt response.[1]

Defense Minister Kitazawa Toshimi also joined the underground conference, knowing that an SDF response would be essential. Inability to connect to the outside by phone proved too inconvenient, however, and he soon returned to the Ministry of Defense. He presided over a meet-

Figure 4.1. Prime Minister Kan Naoto at a combined meeting of the ruling and opposition parties, asking for cooperation in the Great East Japan Earthquake (March 11, 2011)

ing there at 3:30 p.m., where he announced that the prime minister had instructed the SDF to make maximal efforts. In response, GSDF Chief of Staff Hibako Yoshifumi informed Kitazawa that he had already issued deployment orders to the five armies. Kitazawa did not praise him for his quick—possibly too quick—response, but neither did he scold Hibako for his preemptive actions. This demonstrates that those present shared a common sense of urgency.[2]

The actions taken during this first hour could hardly be more different from those the government took after the Great Hanshin-Awaji Earthquake. Clearly, the prime minister's office and the SDF had learned much from their failures sixteen years before.

The nuclear disaster

However, this was no ordinary disaster. While the prime minister's office grasped the seriousness of the event from the beginning, its true nature was far beyond what anyone could imagine.

At 3:42 p.m., an announcement came over the intercom in the underground crisis-management center announcing that the power supply from Unit 1 of the Fukushima Daiichi Nuclear Power Plant had been fully lost. Those without extensive knowledge of nuclear power plants did not understand the implications of this, but Deputy Chief Cabinet Secretary Fukuyama later recalled that this announcement marked a definite shift in the mood among those present.[3] While Japanese society is remarkably resilient to fleeting disasters, the power loss was the first hint of this earthquake's true destructive potential.

The government announced a nuclear emergency at 7:03 p.m. and established a Nuclear Emergency Response Headquarters headed by the prime minister. According to Article 10 of the 2000 Nuclear Disaster Response Special Measures Law, it is necessary to report unusual occurrences, such as when radiation leaks outside. In more serious cases, according to Article 15, the prime minister must declare a nuclear emergency. When that was in fact declared at 7:03 p.m. on March 11, 2011, it meant that the situation had become serious enough to warrant the Japanese government to take the necessary measures to protect the public from radiation from the reactor.

Kan had decided to leave the earthquake and tsunami response to those in the first group so he could focus on responding to the out-of-control nuclear power plants. The crisis-management center was fully occupied with coordinating a response to the tsunami, so after some back-and-forth regarding the nuclear disaster, the prime minister moved his base of operations to his fifth-floor chambers.

Kan was originally a civil activist, and after he became a politician and served as Minister of Health and Welfare, he had clashed with bureaucrats over their attempts to cover up a HIV/AIDS scandal about tainted blood. As a result, he came to believe that it was more necessary to limit the influence of bureaucrats when making decisions, rather than making use of them.

A lack of accurate information and expert knowledge made it difficult for the prime minister's office to cope with the nuclear disaster. Information from the Tokyo Electric Power Company (TEPCO), which manages the Fukushima nuclear power plant, was unclear and difficult to understand. The chair and president of TEPCO were unfortunately both travelling separately on the day of the event, possibly worsening the situation, but there was little improvement when the president returned to Tokyo the following day. Most TEPCO executives were not nuclear engineers, making it difficult for them to accurately comprehend and evaluate reports coming from the disaster site for transmission to the prime minister's office.

This frustrated the prime minister, who called for experts capable of better explaining the fragmentary information that arrived as the situation rapidly evolved. However, officials from the Nuclear and Industrial Safety

Agency and the Nuclear Safety Commission also failed to provide satisfactory explanations. There were simply no experts in the prime minister's office who could describe what was happening or what would happen next based on a deep understanding of nuclear power plants in general and familiarity with this site in particular. It is thus understandable that the prime minister would become irritated, but as anger began to tinge his statements the mood among those there to advise and assist him also darkened.

Prime Minister Kan did not have a particular talent for moving governmental organizations toward resolving problems. Rather, he had a strong tendency to attempt to solve problems on his own. In the initial stages of coping with the nuclear disaster, Kan took two actions that typified this approach: his visit to the accident site on March 12, and his visit to TEPCO's headquarters on the 15th. In both cases, Kan later received harsh criticism that his behavior lacked composure and he failed to demonstrate the wisdom that top leaders should have at times like this. Visiting the disaster site the day after the disaster was not only dangerous to the prime minister himself, it disturbed the efforts of those on the ground who were fully occupied coping with the situation. From Kan's perspective, however, remaining in the prime minister's office with no accurate information amounted to abandoning his duties.

Had TEPCO been able to competently cope with the situation on its own, Kan could have left it to do so. Instead, the company seemed to have only dubious prospects for regaining control, and the situation was worsening due to the culture's lack of responsibility and transparency. At such a time, it seems that without an immediate visit by a government official (the prime minister or anyone else) to obtain a more accurate grasp of the situation, there could be no hope of working out a solution. At a minimum, this visit served to show Kan that Fukushima Daiichi Plant Manager Yoshida Masao (1955–2013) was doing all he could to lead recovery efforts at the site, and Yoshida's mobile phone number was obtained so that key personnel in the prime minister's office could contact him directly. This was unusual but probably necessary.

2. On the Ground at Fukushima

Power loss due to the tsunami

At 2:46 p.m. on March 11, the Great East Japan Earthquake struck the Fukushima Nuclear Power Plant with an intensity VI Upper, causing the ground to rumble loudly. Approximately 750 TEPCO employees led by Plant Manager Yoshida worked at the Fukushima Daiichi Plant, along with 5,650 staff from affiliated companies. Units 1–3 of six were operating at the time (Units 4–6 were shut down for scheduled maintenance), but the violent shaking caused them to perform emergency shutdowns, ceasing power production. However, nuclear fuel rods continue to emit heat even after power is stopped. Moreover, the system used to cool them requires electricity. Since all external power supplies had been cut off, the plant switched to emergency diesel generators.

Yoshida confirmed the safety of the plant staff and thought the worst was over, even after hearing reports of a three-meter tsunami approaching Fukushima. After all, the plant was built at ten meters above sea level. Nevertheless, Yoshida and the other management staff established a crisis-management headquarters in an earthquake-resistant building that had been built the previous year thirty-five meters above sea level. This enclosed command center was considered the safest location at the plant but did not allow views of the outside.

Approximately fifty minutes after the earthquake, the emergency generators stopped for a reason as yet unknown to those in the crisis headquarters, cutting all power. The reactor cooling systems in Units 1–5 shut down one after another. For a brief time, those in the crisis headquarters remained ignorant of what was happening.

Those on the outside watched an unbelievable scene unfold. The first wave arrived at 3:27 p.m., a ten-meter tsunami that smashed against the seawall, sending up a sheet of spray. After that came a receding wave so extreme it revealed the sea floor. A second, fifteen-meter wave arrived at 3:35, reaching the plant buildings. The emergency diesel generators for Units 1–4 at the Daiichi plant had unfortunately been installed beneath those buildings due to the American designs of the plant, making them the worst place for a tsunami to hit. Two engineers who had entered Unit 4 to inspect equipment immediately after the earthquake were caught by the tsunami and drowned. Unit 2 employed a reactor-core-isolation cooling system that propelled coolant via pumps powered by steam from the reactor, and engineers were able to restart this system immediately after the earthquake.

At 3:42 p.m., Yoshida held a video conference with TEPCO headquarters in Tokyo. The plant had lost all power, he reported, and they were in a "station blackout" state in which no instruments could be read. Article 10 of the Act on Special Measures Concerning Nuclear Emergency Preparedness stipulates that the national government must be immediately notified in such an event. Yoshida's report was relayed from TEPCO headquarters to the underground crisis-management center at the prime minister's office, where as described above it was received with shock. As mentioned earlier, this law came into being in 2000 following the 1999 criticality accident at Tōkaimura. When the nuclear-reactor accident happened following the Great East Japan Earthquake, this law was used to respond, but its shortcomings quickly became apparent. Since then, there have been some major overhauls of the Act.

Ten minutes later, it became impossible to inject water into the core coolant system, which heightened the emergency to "Article 15" status according to Japan's Special Law of Nuclear Emergency Preparedness. In Yoshida's words, it was like they were "flying an airplane whose engines had stopped and instruments were unreadable." The plant could no longer be run by normal means. At 5:12 p.m., Yoshida tried reopening coolant lines by using the fire-extinguishing system to force-inject water. To do so, a team had to be sent into the darkened unit to manually operate a valve that normally could be opened with the press of a button. However, the fire-extinguishing system had been destroyed in the tsunami and produced no water. Yoshida next tried using fire trucks in a desperate attempt to supply water by any means, primitive though they may be, to buy time until the power could be restored and the cooling system restarted.

A suicide squad heads for the vents

Over the eight nighttime hours during which the reactor lost cooling, radiation doses near Unit 1 increased, and pressure within the containment vessel exceeded its rating limits. There was no longer any way to deny that the plant was facing the worst possible scenario, a nuclear meltdown.

At 12:06 a.m. on March 12, Yoshida ordered preparations to open containment vessel vents, an emergency procedure to release steam outside the unit. Venting through water in a so-called "wet vent" would reduce the amount of radiation, but the system for doing so could not be easily repaired. A "dry vent" would release a great deal of radiation, polluting the surrounding area, but would decrease the risk of a massive Chernobyl-like reactor explosion. The reactor could not be controlled remotely and was too hot for humans to approach; venting would require a team entering the highly irradiated building to manually open the vents.

Izawa Ikuo, fifty-two, chief controller of Units 1 and 2, called his staff together and said, "I hate to even ask, but is anyone willing to go in?" He continued in a solemn voice, saying, "I can't send anyone young, so I'll be going myself." Several voices broke the silence, volunteering and saying that Izawa needed to stay behind to lead the control room.[4]

At 7:11 a.m. on the 12th, an AS332 Super Puma helicopter arrived on the Daiichi Reactor grounds with Prime Minister Kan aboard. He was met by TEPCO Vice President Mutō Sakae, of whom he immediately demanded, "Why haven't you opened the vents yet?" Those on site had relayed the idea of doing so to the prime minister's office via TEPCO headquarters for approval, which he had granted at 1:30 a.m. Kan was apparently annoyed that this plan had not yet been acted on. Vice President Mutō—the TEPCO executive with the deepest knowledge of nuclear-power generation, who had just arrived the night before—found himself at a loss for words when faced with such hostility. The prime minister was creating an atmosphere that made cooperation difficult even among those able to provide it.

At around 7:30 a.m., Kan similarly questioned plant manager Yoshida and others in the second-floor conference room within the earthquake-resistant building. Yoshida calmly explained the situation by showing plant schematics and explaining how the task would have to be performed in a high-radiation environment. Yoshida then looked the prime minister in the eye and said, "We'll open the vents, even if we have to form a suicide squad to do so."

This caused Kan to reevaluate his opinion of the plant manager. After Kan left, Yoshida issued orders to open the vents by 9:00 a.m. The first team to enter the building successfully opened the valve, but the second team met radiation so high as to push dosimeter needles off the scale. Two of that team gave up and turned back, becoming the first victims to receive a cumulative radiation dose exceeding 100 millisieverts, which at the time was the exposure limit for workers in emergency situations. They were ordered to leave the plant site. Opening the vent was thus delayed, but a second team sent into Unit 1 was apparently successful at around 2:30 p.m.

The meltdown

At 3:36 p.m. on March 12—twenty-four hours after the first tsunami struck—a hydrogen explosion occurred in the Unit 1 reactor building, suggesting that fuel rods in the pressure vessel had been exposed from their water bath, leading to a meltdown. If the fuel rods were not again immersed, a great deal of radiation would be released, making the situation far worse. Water had to be injected to cool the reactor at all costs. At 7:04 p.m., three fire trucks were brought to the scene and connected by hoses to pump seawater into Unit 1.

Figure 4.2. A hydrogen explosion occurred in the Unit 1 reactor building of the Fukushima Daiichi Nuclear Power Plant (March 12, 2011. Broadcasted by Fukushima Central Television)

At around 7:20 p.m., TEPCO Fellow and representative to the prime minister's office Takekuro Ichirō called Yoshida and told him to cease seawater injection, because the prime minister had not yet given his approval. Kan was not necessarily opposed to the idea, but since cooling the reactors through the injecting of seawater would take some time, he said at a 6:00 p.m. meeting that the situation be monitored to see if any problems emerged. Afraid of potentially angering the irritable Kan, Takekuro instead prematurely ordered the operation to stop. Thinking this order strange, Yoshida made sure his subordinates understood that he was going to simply act out a role and that they were to ignore his upcoming order to cease pumping seawater. He then turned on the video conferencing system to issue the order as demanded by the prime minister's office. This incident later resulted in criticism from the Liberal Democratic Party's Abe Shinzō, who claimed that the prime minister had inappropriately applied pressure that caused a nuclear crisis, but in actuality the accident site was never under Kan's control.

Unit 3, too, fell into a state of crisis when a second hydrogen explosion—much larger than the one at Unit 1—occurred at 11:01 a.m. on the 14th, injuring seven TEPCO staff and four SDF members. Considering the resulting falling down of upper parts of the building, it is a miracle that no fatalities occurred.

This second explosion increased worries of an explosion in Unit 2. As described above, the cooling system in Unit 2 had remained functional, but it failed at 1:25 p.m. on the 14th, and pressure within the pressure vessel started to climb. On the side of the building was a blue door that could be used as a blow-out panel to relieve pressure, but at around 1:45 p.m. Yoshida had reported to the TEPCO head office that it had some-how become broken and left open.[5] This meant that radiation was being constantly released into the air, but ironically, the situation had averted an explosion. Workers managed to connect a battery at 6:00 p.m., allowing them to open a safety release valve from which they could pump seawater and reduce pressure within the reactor. In another twist of events, however, the fire trucks ran out of fuel and so could no longer pump water.

The fuel rods in Unit 2 are believed to have been exposed at around 6:22 p.m. (though Daiichi Plant engineers estimate the time as 7:22 p.m.) on the 14th. A total meltdown occurred two hours later, and the rods were expected to melt through the pressure vessel floor approximately two hours after that. "That was when I first thought I would die on the site," Yoshida later said. Even as he steeled himself for his own death, he remained deter-mined to do everything he could before that happened. "Around ten col-leagues would be willing to die with me." However, he wanted all non-essential personnel to escape. He telephoned prime ministerial advisor Hosono Gōshi to inform him of his decision, then started preparations for the evacuation of these personnel to the Daini Plant.[6]

Why the situation got so bad

The situation at the Fukushima Daiichi Nuclear Power Plant rose to a Level 7 incident on the International Nuclear Event Scale, the same level as the Chernobyl disaster. Even so, workers managed to achieve a cold shutdown without a single fatality after the initial drownings due to the tsunami. On June 29, 2015, I visited the plant to find out how that was accomplished, as well as how the situation got so bad in the first place.

When entering the site, I was instructed to keep a radiation dosimeter in my chest pocket. It read 0.01 millisieverts after a nearly two-hour visit, less than what one would experience from an X-ray. Some personnel were wearing special masks and lead-lined vests, but many were dressed in ordi-nary attire like those in my group.

I expected the site of a decommissioned nuclear reactor to be a lonely place, but 7,000 personnel were working there, more than the 5,000 who would have been present when the plant was functioning. The most outstanding feature was the myriad contaminated-water storage tanks, evidence of the most challenging issue at that time.

Of the four units that suffered serious accidents, it felt strange that only Unit 2 was still in its original state. Masuda Naohiro, manager of the Fukushima Daini plant at the time of the earthquake (and president of the company in charge of decommissioning the Daiichi plant at the time of this writing) met with us, and kindly provided frank answers to our questions.

I first asked why the accident became so severe. Units 1–3 automatically stopped as soon as the earthquake hit, and on-site diesel generators automatically kicked in, allowing the reactor cooling system to continue functioning despite the loss of external power. I learned that this loss was not due to a general blackout caused by the earthquake, but rather to mudslides that knocked out high-voltage transmission lines connecting the Daiichi plant to a substation.

Next came the tsunami. At the Daiichi plant, Units 1–4 were built at ten meters above sea level, and Units 5 and 6 were at thirteen meters. The tsunami that hit the plant was fifteen meters high, high enough to inundate all six units. The backup generators in Units 1–4 had been installed underground beneath the turbine buildings and were therefore flooded. The power supply was thus completely cut, including backup power. All plant operations were normally conducted by pressing buttons from three central control rooms, which controlled two units each. The power loss meant that controls were inoperable, and meters could not be read.

In a reactor that has lost its cooling system, intense heat from the nuclear fuel rods evaporates the water they are immersed in, eventually exposing them and causing a meltdown, which releases large amounts of radioactive material. Restoring power was key to preventing such a disaster, but that would take time. In the interval, a meltdown could be avoided only by continually pumping water into each reactor's pressure vessel. In the event of a meltdown, if the collapsing nuclear fuel rods are not immersed in water, they will melt through the bottom of the pressure vessel and become debris so radioactive that no human can come near. There is also danger of a so-called "recriticality" event, in which nuclear fission resumes. In any case, the only way to cope with the situation was to keep injecting water into the system while waiting for power to be restored.

Radiation released from exposed nuclear material first accumulated in the reactor vessels, then throughout their enclosing buildings. As described earlier, the most expedient means of preventing an explosion that would release a large amount of radiation into the atmosphere is to vent air to the outside, reducing pressure. Doing so still releases radioactivity into the atmosphere and endangers people in the area, but an explosion would release far more radiation and make the reactor forever inoperable, a far worse situation. The decision to evacuate local residents and vent the reactors was thus made.

However, hydrogen explosions occurred in Unit 1 of the Fukushima Daiichi Plant at 3:36 p.m. on March 12 and in Unit 3 at 11:01 a.m. on the 14th, blowing out the upper portions of those buildings. Various attempts at cooling and venting were subsequently made, some even using suicide teams, but despite early indications that these were having an effect, more explosions occurred. If an explosion at Unit 2 had occurred as well, the situation could have spiraled further out of control.

However, Unit 2 did not explode. Its reactor core isolation cooling system, an automated system that does not require electricity, continued functioning for the first three days after the tsunami. Also, as previously mentioned, the large blowout panel on the side of the building was damaged for some unknown reason, allowing pressure to escape. These factors prevented an explosion, to the great benefit of those present. Eventually, staff evacuated to the Daini Plant were called back.

Hard work and luck

While Japan is today well on its way to recovering from the Great East Japan Earthquake, we got here only through a combination of dedicated workers on the ground and sheer luck.

Units 5 and 6 at Fukushima Daiichi were the latest-model nuclear power plants, capable of producing 1.1 million kilowatts of power. (For comparison, Unit 1 produced 460,000 kilowatts.) Both were inundated in the tsunami, but because the backup diesel power generators for these units were located in a two-story warehouse next to Unit 6 rather than underground (reportedly not as a tsunami countermeasure but strictly due to geographical considerations), they continued to function and cooling systems were not lost.

The four units at the Daini plant several kilometers away, also of the latest high-output type, were inundated by the tsunami and suffered extensive damage. Unlike at the Daiichi plant, however, one of the four power lines leading to an external power plant was salvageable. Employees rushed to restore the connection, completing the task with unbelievable speed.

Motors to replace those destroyed by flooding were flown to Fukushima from the Japan Air Self-Defense Forces (ASDF) Komaki Airbase in Aichi prefecture, but traffic congestion delayed their arrival. "Had they been just a few hours later," plant manager Masuda said, "we might have shared the Daiichi plant's fate."

There was one further threat at Daiichi, in the form of spent fuel rods immersed in pools in the reactor buildings. The pool in Unit 4 in particular contained 1,535 rods and posed a heightened risk. Should the water in that pool evaporate, the rods could catch fire. On March 16, in a hearing of the U.S. House of Representatives, U.S. Nuclear Regulatory Commission Chair Gregory Jaczko discussed the danger that Unit 4 posed: should such a large number of fuel rods lose their bath and catch fire, all of eastern Japan—including Tokyo—could become unlivable.

Following the hydrogen explosions at Units 1 and 3, another hydrogen explosion occurred at the nonoperating Unit 4 shortly after 6:00 a.m. on March 15, apparently because hydrogen from Unit 3 leaked there via ductwork. The openings created by the loss of the roofs resulting from these explosions allowed water to be poured into the spent fuel pools in Units 1, 3, and 4.

After visual inspections by aerial reconnaissance confirmed the existence of water in the Unit 4 pool, the SDF started conducting helicopter missions to fill the Unit 3 pool at 9:48 a.m. on March 17. While the amounts added were far from enough, these missions sent a powerful message that the Japanese state was not giving up the fight to contain the nuclear disaster. Knowing that the SDF had no helicopters capable of blocking radiation, the U.S. military saw with its own eyes Japan's willpower and efforts to overcome the crisis, leading to a renewed desire on the U.S. side to contribute to Operation Tomodachi. Meanwhile, the SDF and the fire and police departments continued efforts to fill the Unit 3 and 4 spent fuel pools from the ground. The fire department's high-rise pumper called "the Giraffe" was particularly effective. In the end, the safety of all the spent-fuel pools was retained.

Television reporting featured extensive coverage of the efforts to supply water but cooling the reactors themselves and restoring power was at least as important.

Through heroic efforts by TEPCO staff, external power was reconnected to Unit 2 on March 20. The central control room for Units 3 and 4 was restored on the 22nd, and controls for Units 1 and 2 were restored the following day. Many people were forced to abandon their homes due to the large amounts of radioactive materials released, but the worst-case scenario—huge explosions in the three units experiencing meltdowns, blasting apart their pressure vessels and containment structures—was avoided, and the plants were eventually cooled to the point where they could be stabilized.

It was a near-miracle that this nuclear disaster produced no direct fatalities. Had the second "suicide team" that entered Unit 1 on March 12 not turned back after noticing the amount of radiation they were absorbing, they might have died from radiation poisoning. Eleven TEPCO staff and SDF soldiers were near Unit 3 when it violently exploded. The pieces thrown into the air were large enough to destroy a car, but those in the area escaped alive.[7]

3. Operation Tomodachi

Operation Tomodachi was a U.S. military program to provide support following the Great East Japan Earthquake. Yet while the name—which means "operation friendship"—remains fresh in the minds of many Japanese, surprisingly few know what that operation entailed or how significant it was.

Images of the massive tsunami that struck the Tōhoku coast thirty minutes after the earthquake were broadcast worldwide, shocking all who viewed them. The U.S. government responded immediately; U.S. President Barack Obama (1961–; in office 2009–17) made a statement within the day and phoned his condolences to Prime Minister Kan, promising to stand beside Japan and provide any necessary support. The Japanese government responded quickly to this offer: at 8:25 p.m. that evening, Minister of Foreign Affairs Matsumoto Takeaki telephoned U.S. Ambassador John Roos (1955–; in office 2009–13) to officially request whatever assistance the U.S. military could provide.

International disaster support

Providing disaster support by donating money or supplies is common practice in the international community. Japan made a large, heartfelt contribution to the United States following the 1906 San Francisco Earthquake, greatly impressing residents there. The United States compensated with an even larger contribution to Japan after the 1923 Great Kantō Earthquake. Cyrus Woods (1861–1938; in office 1923–24), American ambassador at the time, went so far as to suggest that this would resolve the discord between the two governments. However, while the money and goods were much appreciated, troops aboard the warship that pulled into port were not allowed to disembark, with Japanese forces instead handling all unloading and transport.[8] Furthermore, the warm sentiments arising from disaster relief were insufficient to significantly affect bilateral relations. Indeed, the following year the U.S. Congress passed the Immigration Act of 1924, which included the Japanese Exclusion Act, significantly worsening relations.[9]

Following its defeat in World War II, Japan was occupied by the Allied Powers, particularly the U.S. Army, and the Imperial Army and Navy were disbanded. Occupying forces were tasked not only with national defense, but with disaster response. Indeed, U.S. and Australian forces carried out the primary response to the 1946 Shōwa Nankai Earthquake and Tsunami, and the flooding due to Typhoon Judith in August 1949.

U.S. forces remained stationed in Japan after the occupation ended in 1952, but the responsibility for disaster response reverted to domestic first responders such as police, firefighters, and the SDF; U.S. military forces were mobilized only on request by the Japanese government. Following the unprecedented flooding caused by Typhoon Vera in 1959, which claimed some 5,000 lives, the governor of Aichi prefecture requested aid from the SDF, then the U.S. military. The result was a U.S.-Japan joint operation involving twenty-three U.S. helicopters. This effort rescued 16,500 people from flooded areas.[10]

The SDF had emphasized its role in protecting Japanese citizens from disaster since its earlier incarnation as the National Police Reserve, a stance furthered by Prime Minister Yoshida Shigeru (1878–1967; in office 1946–47, 1948–54) immediately after the war ended. The Japan Disaster Relief Team was established in 1987 to provide international disaster aid, and the 1992 "Act on Cooperation for United Nations Peacekeeping Operations" authorized the SDF to assist overseas disaster-relief operations as well as peace-keeping operations. The SDF was first dispatched overseas for disaster relief in 1998 to aid Honduras after a hurricane. This was followed by support operations after the huge earthquake off Sumatra in 2006, an earthquake in Haiti (2010), a hurricane in the Philippines (2013), and an earthquake in Nepal (2015), demonstrating Japan's motivation and ability to provide both military and civilian international disaster relief.

Providing and receiving support

Following the 1995 Great Hanshin-Awaji Earthquake, the U.S. government offered to dispatch U.S. warships to Kobe and make them available to use for housing, but the Japanese government did not accept the offer. During this age of intense postwar pacifism, Kobe had in essence forbidden the docking of warships. Besides the United States, two international organizations and seventy-one nations from around the world offered to supply emergency assistance, but Japan wanted to demonstrate its self-sufficiency and was not eager to accept foreign personnel. While the country did accept donations of cash and materials, and reluctantly admitted units accompanying rescue dogs and some relief organizations, that was the extent of the aid it permitted. Japan's eagerness to provide aid but not to receive it was identified as a problem, so three years after the Great Hanshin-Awaji Earthquake the government established policies for receiving aid at various ministries.

After the end of the Cold War, the U.S. military expanded its activities to nonmilitary tasks such as rebuilding after disasters and conflicts, primarily performing dangerous humanitarian assistance and disaster-relief tasks that are in the civilian sphere but can best be performed by the military at a particular juncture. The U.S. military provided frequent disaster-rescue support in Asia, aiding in as many as eleven incidents in the six years between the December 2004 Sumatra Tsunami and the Great East Japan Earthquake. This was also reflected in a broadened and deepened Japan-U.S. alliance. The two countries agreed that they would assist one another when responding to disasters abroad in the 1997 revisions to the Guidelines for Japan-U.S. Defense Cooperation, a revised Acquisition and Cross-Servicing Agreement in 2004, and the Japan-U.S. Security Consultative Committee by ministers of both foreign affairs and defense in 2005.[11]

The U.S. government follows three principles when dispatching troops overseas for disaster aid: whether there is a request from the affected country, whether the disaster exceeds the country's ability to recover, and U.S. national interest. These are quite reasonable standards, and many nations, including Japan, probably follow similar guidelines. While common policies exist for providing support, however, the same does not hold regarding policies for accepting support. For example, developed countries such as the U.S. and Japan are proud and confident of their abilities, and so may be hesitant to accept assistance—military support in particular—even in major disasters that exceed their ability to respond. Through reflection on its actions after the Great Hanshin-Awaji Earthquake and a deepened Japan-U.S. alliance, Japan was able to overcome such hesitance after the Great East Japan Earthquake.

As mentioned above, Japan and the U.S. rapidly reached a consensus on military disaster support. More interesting, however, is the fact that as soon as reports of the earthquake arrived—and even before receiving official instructions based on bilateral agreements—the U.S. military from the uppermost ranks of the Pentagon down to the 31st Marine Expeditionary Unit (MEU) in Okinawa began preparing for assistance, considering aid to a close ally to be only natural. Within the day of the earthquake, the 31st MEU began gathering at U.S. air stations in Iwakuni and Yokota. The *Wasp*-class amphibious assault ship USS *Essex* left its assignment in Southeast Asia to head for Japan. Furthermore, the aircraft carrier USS *Ronald Reagan* left the U.S.–Korean military exercises it was assigned to and arrived on the morning of March 13 at the Sanriku coast, where along with the Maritime SDF carrier JDS *Hyūga* it engaged in air-support activities.

An unprecedented level of U.S. support

One of the biggest problems in the Great East Japan Earthquake was the Fukushima nuclear disaster. A hydrogen explosion occurred in Unit 1 of the plant at 3:36 p.m. on March 12, the day after the tsunami, and a second explosion destroyed Unit 3 at 11:00 a.m. on the 14th. In neither case was plant owner TEPCO or the Japanese government able to adequately respond, or even fully grasp what was happening. The U.S. government became irritated at this state of affairs and demanded that Japan address the situation by all possible means. While the U.S. dispatched nuclear-power experts, radiation levels exceeded U.S. Navy safety standards, forcing carriers offshore along the Sanriku coast and at Yokosuka to pull back and prompting the evacuation of the families of U.S. military personnel to return to their home country. These concerns were not without merit; had the response been delayed more than it ultimately was, the result could have been a series of explosions in the spent fuel pool of Unit 4 and in Units 2, 5, and 6, possibly making all of eastern Japan uninhabitable.[12]

Had the SDF attempts on the 17th to supply water by helicopter and other means failed, and the nuclear disaster thus spread farther, U.S. military forces deployed for the relief operations probably would have fully pulled out of eastern Japan. Such an outcome was thankfully averted, allowing Operation Tomodachi to proceed in earnest.

Operation Tomodachi was a troop dispatch of unprecedented scale. In addition to the USS *Ronald Reagan*, the U.S. military provided 24 warships, 189 aircraft, and, at the peak of operations, some 24,500 Army, Navy, Air Force, and Marine Corps personnel. The extent of this operation exceeded the command capabilities of the Yokota headquarters, led by Lt. General Burton Field, so from March 24 to April 12, Pacific Fleet Commander

Rear Admiral Patrick Walsh took command. Japanese and U.S. armed forces furthermore set up bilateral coordination cells at the Ministry of Defense in Ichigaya, at U.S. Forces Japan headquarters in Yokota, and at the GSDF North Eastern Army headquarters in Sendai, to make the joint operations go more smoothly.

The U.S. military has a very high capacity for mobilization and transport, and so first engaged in air transport of food and supplies. Large Marine Corps KC-130 transport planes carried gasoline tankers and other refueling equipment to Yamagata Airport. Related agencies from both Japan and the U.S. worked hard to reopen Sendai Airport, which had been inundated by the tsunami. U.S. military planes were able to land on a repaired runway on March 17, just six days after the earthquake. Under normal circumstances recovery would have taken at least six months, but chartered commercial flights resumed as early as April 13, one month after the disaster. This rapid recovery of the airport was highly symbolic, showing that support would ultimately arrive even to the most remote parts of the disaster area.

The U.S. Marine Corps makes up for the largest part of the 40,000–50,000 U.S. military forces stationed in Japan, and as scenes from Iōtō Island during the Pacific War suggest, they are known for their fierce frontal and amphibious assaults. At the same time, however, they are also utility forces who play a central role in humanitarian assistance and disaster-relief efforts. The Marines arrived at disaster sites hoping to aid in reconstruction and recovery efforts, and while distributing materials to various sites turned their attention to Ōshima on late March, an island in the Kesennuma Bay that had been completely cut off. The Marines were given permission to land there through coordination with the Japanese government and local leaders on the island.

Before dawn on April 1, 177 troops boarded USS *Essex*, which by then was anchored twenty kilometers offshore. The ship plowed through a debris-laden sea to Tanakahama on the eastern side of Ōshima. The disembarking troops conducted operations to restore lifelines such as reopening roads, rebuilding the port, and restoring power, which was accomplished over the following week using vehicles and heavy equipment that were brought in along with another 300 or so workers. The Marines surprised residents by marching to Uranohama, the main town on the other side of the island, where they formed ranks and held a moment of silence for the disaster victims. Such respect for disaster victims was highly symbolic of the spirit of Operation Tomodachi and set the mood for the week to come.[13]

This combination of state-of-the-art military capabilities and heartfelt

Figure 4.3. U.S. Marines conducting a moment of silence before beginning cleanup operations at Ōshima's Uranohama port (April 1, 2011. Photo courtesy of U.S. Marines)

friendship activities gave Operation Tomodachi a unique nuance. "A friend in need is a friend indeed," as they say, and through efforts far exceeding what the alliance demanded, the U.S. military did much to provide hope to those in the disaster area, and all of Japan. I would be amiss to not also mention the assistance provided by Australia, which kept transport aircraft flying at full capacity.

Regarding the development of Operation Tomodachi, I should also mention the efforts of Robert Eldridge, who did much to bridge gaps between the U.S. and Japan. After graduating from university in the United States, Eldridge participated in the Japan Exchange and Teaching Program, through which he served for two years as an English teaching assistant in a small town in Hyogo prefecture. Following that he attended graduate school at Kobe University, where his doctoral thesis became the basis for *The Origins of the Bilateral Okinawa Problem: Okinawa in Postwar US-Japan Relations, 1945–1952* (Routledge, 2003), the Japanese edition of which received the Suntory Prize for Social Sciences and Humanities and was a runner-up for the Asian Affairs Research Council's Asia Pacific Award. He experienced the Great Hanshin-Awaji Earthquake while a graduate student at Kobe University, and while working as an associate professor at Osaka University in 2006, he proposed specific policies for the use of U.S. forces in Japan during a large-scale natural disaster in a manner similar to what became Operation Tomodachi. In 2009, he was appointed deputy assistant chief of staff for government and external affairs at the Marine Corps Installations Pacific in Okinawa. While some military executives supported his plan, the U.S. military did not actively promote it or his push for cooperation in disaster preparedness ahead of time with likely-to-be affected communities. Following the Great East Japan Earthquake, however, the Marines sent him to work under North Eastern Army Commander Kimizuka to facilitate Japan-U.S. joint operations. Eldridge had not only proposed the reopening of Sendai Airport and led the initial coordination, he established a home-stay program in Okinawa for the children from Kesennuma city's Ōshima Island following the disaster, and helped plan for future Marine assistance to various coastal prefectures in the event of a future earthquake at the Nankai trough or Tōkai earthquake, as well as in Okinawa itself.[14]

Operation Tomodachi and security

Operation Tomodachi was significant for another reason as well. When the SDF dispatches more than 100,000 of its 250,000 troops (or 70,000 of the 140,000 GSDF troops), it must be careful not to leave national borders or other strategic points undefended. This is easier said than done, however, so in many cases it was impossible to avoid leaving some bases and camps nearly empty—an undesirable situation should an enemy attack. Pacific-region U.S. military activities are largely centered around aircraft carriers, as seen by the participation of the USS *Ronald Reagan* in the Tōhoku relief operations, which provide more than enough of a military presence to make up for any such gaps.

Prime Minister Hatoyama Yukio (1947–; in office 2009–10), who came to power when the Democratic Party of Japan took control of the government in September 2009, dreamed of forming an East Asian Community to seek equalization in relations with the U.S. However, he carelessly handled problems related to Marine Corps Air Station Futenma in Okinawa, darkening the Japan-U.S. alliance. Besides this discord with the United States, Japan was having diplomatic problems with neighboring countries related to issues such as sovereignty over the Senkaku and Kuril Islands. The Great East Japan Earthquake thus struck at a time of serious political weakness, so unprecedented U.S. support in the form of Operation Tomodachi served well to enhance the importance of the Japan-U.S. alliance.

4. The Reconstruction Design Council in Response to the Great East Japan Earthquake

A phone call from the prime minister

I was president of the National Defense Academy of Japan when the Great

East Japan Earthquake struck. The academy's 55th graduation ceremony was to take place nine days later, on March 20. This was an important ceremony for supplementing the SDF with fresh officers, since graduates receive their commissions on this day, and it could not be cancelled. We thus decided to hold a small, modest ceremony despite the crisis, even if there would be no special visitors.

To my surprise, we received word that Prime Minister Kan Naoto would attend. When his helicopter arrived, I impertinently asked him if this was really where he should be at such a time, in the midst of a nuclear disaster. He told me that he had come to express his thanks for everything the SDF had done.[15]

The prime minister's office began formulating reconstruction plans in the final week of March, as the national crisis of the nuclear disaster was coming under control.[16] No official, comprehensive reconstruction plan had ever been formulated before reconstruction began in any of Japan's many past disasters. However, the Great East Japan Earthquake was unique in terms of its extent, complexity, and intensity. The disaster spanned multiple prefectures and the response involved numerous ministries and agencies, each acting on a location-by-location basis, making it difficult to obtain a clear overall picture of what needed to happen.

Given the unprecedented nature of the disaster, it is no surprise that the government's response was criticized on a daily basis for being slow and insufficient. One can only assume that the timeline of the response was being compared to that of the Great Hanshin-Awaji Earthquake. Just one month after that event, a recovery committee—headed by former National Land Agency administrative vice-minister Shimokōbe Atsushi and including the governor of Hyōgo prefecture and the mayor of Kobe—had already been established, thereby providing a steady stream of accurate and timely recommendations to support a rapid recovery. The prime minister's office therefore decided to establish the Reconstruction Design Council within one month of the Great East Japan Earthquake.

Initial plans for the Council were drafted by Deputy Chief Cabinet Secretary Takino Kinya, and called for participation by around ten members, including the governors of the three hardest-hit prefectures. The small size was an attempt to emphasize flexibility, avoiding "too many chefs in the kitchen" who might hinder progress. The ruling Democratic Party of Japan had a strong aversion to bureaucratic rule, however, and rather than unquestioningly accept a proposal from the prime minister's office instead submitted the draft to political colleagues for a second opinion. Based on recommendations from the prime minister's office and ruling party leadership, participation expanded to include well-known figures from the Tōhoku region and experts from various disaster-related fields, eventually swelling to over thirty members. Worried about whether such a large group could actually make any decisions, Takino restructured it into two tiers, an upper main conference and a lower-level group primarily comprising younger experts.

Prime Minister Kan suddenly called me on the night of April 5. My initial reaction was to wonder how the prime minister had gotten hold of my cellphone number. Kan asked me to serve not as a member of the Reconstruction Design Council, but as its chair. I put him off, citing how busy my work was keeping me and knowing how much work that posting would entail. When I hung up, I called each of the three National Defense Agency vice presidents who assisted me, and each said the same thing: "You should take this job, for the good of the country. We'll do everything we can to cover your work here."

After thinking it over for some time, I called GSDF Chief of Staff Hibako, the most trustworthy of the uniformed vice presidents I had ever worked with at the National Defense Academy, to ask his opinion. "You should take the job," he said. "I'll do everything I can to support you. This is a once-in-a-lifetime opportunity to help rebuild the country." As usual, Hibako impressed me with his enthusiasm. Of course, in the military sphere the opinion of one's superior officer is all that really matters, so I called Defense Minister Kitazawa. He said, "Mr. Kan just told me. I think it's a fine decision."

The following day, Deputy Chief Cabinet Secretaries Fukuyama and Takino came to the National Defense Academy to give me more details. I was surprised to hear that the membership roster was already full. When I suggested that someone with more specialized skills might be better able to obtain an overall grasp of the situation, they told me that specialists were being gathered in subordinate working groups. I requested the addition of a few people who could work alongside me, and in the end the main body comprised sixteen members, with another nineteen in affiliated working groups. Acting Chair Mikuriya Takashi, Working Group Chief Iio Jun, and myself thereby took on management of the Reconstruction Design Council.

Five fundamental policies

Due to his outbursts of anger when faced with the existential crisis of a nuclear disaster, the prime minister came to be called "Kan the Irritable," but he behaved very differently in the Reconstruction Design Council. He attended almost every meeting, demonstrating their importance, but rarely spoke up. Even when council members directly addressed him with questions, Kan would say, "I'm here to listen, not to debate."

When I received my official appointment as council chair on April 11, Kan gave me no specific instructions; he simply handed me written notice of the cabinet decision. He did mention his concerns regarding the future of reconstruction plans should opposition parties regain complete control of the Diet: "No matter what plans you make, they're dead in the water if the opposition parties oppose them." Cabinet decisions clearly called for not just recovery, but creative reconstruction with an eye to the future. It is a fine thing for the government to desire a thorough reconstruction plan, but equally disappointing to see such plans crushed by political maneuvering in the Diet. Kan's Democratic Party possessed a good-sized majority in the Lower House but had failed to keep it in the Upper House election in July 2010. This divided Diet had been causing him much concern, and he worried about the future.

Fortunately, I had separately met with Liberal Democratic Party President Tanigaki Sadakazu and Kōmeitō Party President Yamaguchi Natsuo, where I asked for their cooperation with the recovery despite any political battles. I requested that each party bring its proposed reconstruction plans to the Reconstruction Design Council meetings, so that we could consider them from the perspective of the country as a whole, and both agreed to do so.

I also consulted with three friends and scholars in my field: Kitaoka Shinichi, Mikuriya Takashi, and Iio Jun. I asked for their comments on my draft, and consequently we crafted five proposed fundamental policies that I orally presented to Prime Minister Kan:

1. *The Reconstruction Design Council shall be nonpartisan, serving Japan and its people.*
   We shall seek nationwide wisdom, avoiding influence by specific factions or parties. We shall accept and respond to the compassion demonstrated by expanding support from people of the nation and the world.
2. *As a country, we shall create an overall plan, but we respect local ownership and initiative.*
   The people of the Tōhoku region have a particular attachment to their home. This is the origin of reconstruction, and afflicted municipalities are the core of every activity. We shall be receptive to local needs and opinions while forging an overall plan that

considers safety standards shared by Japanese society as a whole.

3. *We shall aim not at mere recovery, but at creative reconstruction.*
Our job is not to simply rebuild houses and towns that would be destroyed in the next tsunami. We shall remake homes, schools, and hospitals on higher ground, build strong, five-story or larger buildings for port and fishery facilities in towns along the sea, and utilize debris to create parks on hills that can be used as evacuation sites.

4. *The Japanese people must be called on for support and burden sharing.*
Recovery and reconstruction will call for unprecedented funds, including donations, government bonds, and the establishment of a disaster-recovery tax. We should end the self-restraint on our previously planned events and projects and not hesitate to organize festivals and other activities to heighten social connections in Japan, thereby strengthening relations and mutual cooperation.

5. *We shall prepare a blueprint that provides hope for Japan's future.*
In addition to safety and security standards, we shall promote town planning that emphasizes well-being through development of a clean-energy society and welfare for our aging society. We shall adopt latest models as nationwide standards for a new era. We note that this is a common concern for all regions of Japan, considering the possibility of a large tsunami due to a Nankai trough earthquake.

Along with producing a plan according to these five policies and presenting it to both the people of Japan and those from around the world who were lending us their support, we decided to implement specific policies with the support of the national government. When I explained this to the prime minister, he responded by saying, "You've already given this your deep consideration, I see," with no particular requests for changes or additions. He thereby left the actual content of the reconstruction plan up to us.

A raucous first meeting

Despite this, the first meeting of the Reconstruction Design Council in Response to the Great East Japan Earthquake, held on April 14, 2011, did not go smoothly.

The first issue on the table was the Fukushima nuclear disaster. We received word that Kan wanted the response to the disaster to remain

Figure 4.4. The first meeting of the Reconstruction Design Council in Response to the Great East Japan Earthquake. (From right) Prime Minister Kan Naoto and the author with other committee members (April 14, 2011)

the purview of the prime minister's office and not to be addressed by the council, incensing several members. One even stood and pounded on his desk, announcing that he would quit if forced to "abandon" Fukushima. Of course, the prime minister's words only applied to crisis management, which was understandable; the council did not include a single nuclear-power expert, and so had no ability to consider appropriate responses. It is clearly impossible to perform the same recovery activities in areas highly contaminated with radioactivity, but to summarize the debate that went on that day, the council had a strong desire to avoid cutting Fukushima off from recovery efforts being conducted in other regions; they demanded that it remain on an equal footing to the very end.

Even so, it seems extreme for committee members to engage in out-bursts so aggressive as to stall any progress the committee might make. Why should planning the recovery from an unprecedented natural disaster provoke such an unnatural state of excitement? Was it because so many committee members were from the disaster area, and therefore were over-whelmed by emotions? Or was it something else? In any case, the more heated the discussion became, the harder I tried to remain calm and keep the meeting on course.

The next objection to arise—shared by several members—was that the council included no government officials, current or retired, who could produce viable plans. Honestly, I was thankful this issue was being raised. Although there was a strong antibureaucratic movement in the Democratic Party of Japan administration, I, too, was concerned that it would be difficult to produce a good reconstruction plan without utilizing the expertise of bureaucrats. To replace this negativity with something positive, I promised to work hard to utilize bureaucratic expertise as best I could.

At a press conference held after that first meeting, I was asked about the possibility of a reconstruction tax. As council president, I had distributed my Five Policies, Item 4 of which specifically stated the need to not exclude consideration of just such a tax, and reporters had latched on to that. I told them the issue had not come up in our first meeting, but they pressed for my opinion on the subject. Emphasizing that this was merely a personal opinion, I said that piling the enormous costs of recovery atop Japan's fiscal deficit (already 200 percent of GDP) would heighten the risk of an international financial crisis, and that rather than pass those costs on to future generations through public debt, I considered it preferable that those living now shoulder the burden. Despite my disclaimer, the headline in the following day's newspaper read "Reconstruction Design Council President Advocates Tax Increase." I had suddenly become the bad guy.

The other committee members grilled me about this at our second meeting. It wasn't right for the president to discuss such matters with the press before raising them in council, they said. In my defense, I described how the press conference had progressed. "So, if the council decides against a tax increase, will you abide by that?" they asked. "Of course, I will. This is a democratic council," I said. Apparently, some council members were dead set against any kind of tax increase, so I suggested that we set aside any such discussion for the time. The more pressing matter was to determine what recovery plans should accomplish, and the extent of financial resources they would require. Without knowing those two things, any talk of whether to increase taxes would be meaningless.

That was when I realized that I had two duties: drawing up an outstanding recovery plan by the end of June, and getting all of the council members, including those who seemed antagonistic to it, to agree with it. Divisions within the council soon set off a media feeding frenzy, causing me to fear that our work would end in failure.[17]

The Seven Principles for the Reconstruction Framework

The Reconstruction Design Council in Response to the Great East Japan Earthquake had set sail on rough seas, but the Council's visit to the three primary affected prefectures in May 2011 calmed the waters; once members saw disaster sites for themselves, they shared a common base for understanding the situation.

Each council member selected a single prefecture to visit, but as council president I visited all three. With the assistance of GSDF Chief of Staff Hibako and North Eastern Army Commander Kimizuka (both formerly part of the leadership of the National Defense Academy who had assisted me in the past), I had been able to visit disaster sites by helicopter before the Reconstruction Design Council was organized, but there was much more to see and learn. Furthermore, there were many council members whom I did not yet know well, so traveling together seemed like a good opportunity to get to know them.

While I was traveling back and forth to the Tōhoku region, Acting Chair Mikuriya and working group chief Iio were preparing the "Seven Principles for the Reconstruction Framework." This was intended to serve as something like a council charter, expressing its basic spirit and policies. Considering the breadth of discussions that the council would engage in, such a lofty document seemed necessary.

We presented the principles for debate at the fourth council meeting on May 10. One participant expressed doubts regarding the seventh item, which called for solidarity of the people in supporting reconstruction, suggesting that this implied the establishment of a reconstruction tax. On the other hand, the fifth item called for the simultaneous pursuit of disaster recovery and revival of the Japanese economy, and Iwate governor Tasso Takuya protested that this would prevent the establishment of such a tax, since doing so carried the potential for economic damage. These objections were handled by changing the wording of each item. In the end, the following seven principles were established.

Seven Principles for the Reconstruction Framework

1. For us, the surviving, there is no other starting point for the path to recovery than to remember and honor the many lives that have been lost. Accordingly, we shall record the disaster for eternity, including through the creation of memorial forests and monu-

ments, and we shall have the disaster scientifically analyzed by a broad range of scholars to draw lessons that will be shared with the world and passed down to posterity.

2. Given the vastness and diversity of the disaster region, we shall make community-based reconstruction the foundation of efforts toward recovery. The national government shall support that reconstruction through general guidelines and institutional design.

3. To revive disaster-afflicted Tōhoku, we shall pursue forms of recovery and reconstruction that tap into the region's latent strengths and lead to technological innovation. We shall strive to develop this region's socioeconomic potential to lead Japan in the future.

4. While preserving the strong bonds of local communities, we shall construct disaster-resilient safe and secure communities and a natural-energy-powered region.

5. Japan's economy cannot be restored unless the disaster areas are rebuilt. The disaster areas cannot be truly rebuilt unless Japan's economy is restored. Recognizing these facts, we shall simultaneously pursue reconstruction of the afflicted areas and revitalization of the nation.

6. We shall seek an early resolution of the nuclear accident, and shall devote closer attention to support and recovery efforts for the areas affected by the accidents.

7. All of us living now shall view the disaster as affecting our own lives and shall pursue reconstruction with the spirit of solidarity and burden-sharing that permeates the entire nation.

I hoped that council meetings would go smoother after the spring holidays. Previous meetings had ended with each council member speaking in turn, or with a talk by some invited guest, such as Ishihara Nobuo (deputy secretary of state at the time of the Great Hanshin-Awaji Earthquake), Kaihara Toshitami (governor of Hyōgo prefecture at the time of the Great Hanshin-Awaji Earthquake), or representatives from major economic groups. In the hope of making this a bipartisan, nationwide initiative, we invited representatives from the opposition Liberal Democratic and Kōmeitō Parties to present their recommendations, but circumstances within the LDP prevented this from happening. Some questioned whether bipartisan cooperation for reconstruction could be maintained in such a turbulent political atmosphere.

Prime Minister Kan had requested our initial recommendations by the end of June, and a final report by year end, but we managed to produce our final report by the June deadline. People can press on as long as hope remains in even the grimmest situations, but year-end felt too far away. We thus did our best to produce our final recommendations as quickly as possible, so that they might serve as a beacon of hope.

Furthermore, to allow time for budgeting, Iio considered it essential to produce a proposal by June. To do so, as a rule we met for five hours every Saturday. This was a harsh schedule by the norms of today, but also served to democratize the council. The council was a forum for many diverse and controversial opinions, but I did not want to overmanage the agenda simply because time was short. Each member had to be treated as an expert, regardless of the emotional content of their opinion. I felt that thorough discussion of the effectiveness and limits of the ideas presented would eventually lead to mutual understanding, considering that all shared a desire for recovery of the disaster area. As the council chair, I did my best to accommodate even opinions that seemed hostile or disruptive, and to present my reasons for doing so.

Some members, particularly those in the media, could not wait for the end of June, and felt strongly that we needed to immediately make a statement to society. I agreed and did what I could to promote our efforts in postmeeting press conferences and by making requests to government representatives who attended our meetings. Unlike in the case of the Hanshin-Awaji Reconstruction Committee under Shimokōbe Atsushi, I had no intention of making concrete and perhaps timely proposals to a frustrated public at every meeting. We needed to take a broad approach to planning recovery from such a widespread, complex, and severe disaster, and for this basic goal I had to follow standard procedures. We took the time to establish the "Seven Principles" despite opposition from some members who wished to emphasize a speedy and timely proposal.

I tried to set a tone of calm and reasonable meetings in which all committee members could participate, but I am no master leader, and felt there was some roughness to our meetings. I was exhausted during the hour-long drive back to my residence at the Defense Academy after each meeting, but the discussions of the day would replay through my mind, making sleep difficult after I had gone to bed. On nights like that, I would change into workout clothes and head to the athletic field, despite the late hour, where I would run three to five laps around the 500-meter track. At 10:30 p.m. a trumpet would signal lights out, and I would watch windows go dark one by one. Something about exercise always improved my outlook, clearing away frustrations and helping me devise strategies for the next meeting.

Some ten staff from various ministries comprised the council's secretariat, but in late April I directly appealed to the prime minister, and after the spring holidays increased staffing to fifty. They provided vital support, such as classifying all statements made at previous council meetings into five categories, and summarizing the results in diagrams, tables, and booklets. Knowing that this would serve as a good basis for our final report, we presented the five overall categories of the summary for approval at the seventh council meeting on May 29.

The fight for a reconstruction plan

The summary was not well received within the council. "We're still just running around in circles," some said. Others argued the document was "nothing but fragments of past opinions," and insisted that "If we present this to the press, we'll be painted as fools!" With the exception of Seike Atsushi, an economist and President of Keiō University, almost everyone who spoke up wanted the document withdrawn. Perhaps out of a sense of responsibility, the secretariat sent me a memo saying, "We will not oppose a withdrawal."

But I had already made up my mind. These were the opinions of the group, after all, and there was no point in setting them aside to instead await instructions from heaven. I pushed the memo off to a corner of my desk. Sensing my mood, Acting Chair Mikuriya whispered, "You're going to stand up to them, right? I'll back you up."

Rather than engage in debate, I decided to proceed with the meeting. "I will take your opinions into consideration and discuss the matter with my assistants during the break," I said. "For now, there were several issues that subcommittees were looking into and are ready to report on, so I would like to hear from Mr. Iio regarding that."

This provided a needed cooling-off period; I could feel the mood in the room start to settle as members became engaged in the details of Iio's report.

During the break, rather than meeting with me as announced, Mikuriya and Iio engaged with opposing members, even standing in line for the toilet with them to get a chance to speak. After the break, I continued reports and discussions, and only returned to the issue of the five problem categories at the end, when there was little time left.

I began by saying, "I see two reasons for the unified opposition to this."

The heat that characterized the start of the meeting was now gone, and everyone was listening quietly. In the end, I obtained the group's understanding that the document would provide a framework for the council's final recommendations and promised that we would make the additions required to overcome its shortcomings. We were rapidly approaching the council's June deadline, so we did not have time to go back to the drawing board. I thereby got approval to use the draft as an important framework to be fleshed out by Mikuriya.

Prime Minister Kan had attended only the first half of that day's meeting, so he left with the impression that the council was in a state of rebellion. He was surprised when his secretary told him that everything had calmed down by evening.

Iio created a series of workshops to address important problems. These were mainly hosted by experts from study groups, and we invited not only council members but also midlevel ministry bureaucrats to provide them with intensive reviews. This allowed us to both fully apply bureaucrats' expertise and to request new responses to unexpected events as they arose. Unlike the typical image of bureaucrats, these individuals were not fixed in their ways, but rather seemed eager to do what they could for the good of the country. Through this process, Iio was assigned a series of tasks related to town planning for safety, recovery of the fishing and manufacturing industries, renewable energy, and comprehensive care in an aging society.

Knowing that our report would have historical significance, but that we social scientists were unlikely to come up with a suitably written document to that end, Special Advisor Umehara Takeshi (1925–2019) insisted that we should delegate authority for drafting a report to journalists and others in literary fields. The introduction and conclusion by Mikuriya, however, received high acclaim from Umehara and other committee members as truly fine writing.

Mikuriya and Iio presented a draft report on June 18 at our tenth meeting. Council members were generally receptive but proposed a variety of large and small corrections and edits. The corrected report was as long as a book, but the drafters promised to present a revised edition reflecting everyone's opinions to the extent possible at the next meeting.

A highly revised edition was presented at our eleventh meeting on June 22. Committee members responded with another mountain of desired changes, but this time they seemed to be smaller in scale. Miyagi prefectural governor Murai Yoshihiro made a proposal: "A never-ending series of minor corrections does nothing to help disaster areas. Actual disaster victims are anxious to see our ideas move toward implementation as soon as possible. We have already presented many opinions, so I move that we leave any further considerations up to the chairman." This proposal had the support of the council and was implemented.

At our twelfth meeting on June 25—our final substantial meeting—we presented our report, "Towards Reconstruction: Hope beyond the Disaster"[18] to the prime minister. Kan expressed his thanks for the council's hard work and announced that he would carefully consider our report "as if it were a Bible."

The report was also well received on television and in newspapers. Since its initial draft version of June 18, we had conducted rigorous information control to prevent misleading media coverage regarding preparations for our report. The media had seemed poised to pounce on our report, but when I conducted an embargoed press conference the day before its submission, I got a sense that journalists were impressed with the extent of care with which it was crafted.

In July, our recommendations were formalized as the basic policy of the central government, and despite the political changes underway, ruling and opposition parties established a system for implementing them with the needed financial resources within the year.

Contents of the reconstruction plan

The following describes the content of the recommendations[19] we proposed to Prime Minister Kan.

First, we proposed a definitive framework for safety-oriented city planning, avoiding Japan's historically common mistake of rebuilding homes and towns in the same way as before, only to have them swept away by the next tsunami.

There are two typical methods for doing so, the first being relocation to higher ground. When a tsunami hits, all people can do is flee. They must leave their homes and valuables behind. However, with relocation to higher ground ahead of time, people, along with their homes and valuables, will be safe. Partial relocation had been attempted following the Meiji and Shōwa Sanriku Tsunamis, but this time we recommended full national support for anyone who wished to relocate.

Today, it is quite common for new residential areas to be built in hilly areas. However, towns in the disaster area were heavily dependent on the sea and their ports, so some rebuilding had to occur in the same locations. This necessitated the second rebuilding strategy: multiple layers of defense from waves. Specific methods include the use of seawalls, breakwaters, artificial hills and forests, taller and stronger buildings, and secondary lines of defense such as roads or railways on embankments. Combinations of such disaster-mitigation strategies can improve town safety, and the country should fully support their construction.

The extreme depopulation and advanced aging in the disaster areas posed a particular challenge to reconstruction planning. Revitalization of industry and employment in those areas would be vital to reverse such trends. We therefore looked for ways to improve the fishing and agricultural industries, for example by establishing special economic zones for industry, retail, and tourism to increase the attractiveness and vitality of these regions. The primary targets for recovery were those living in the disaster areas, and the country needed to provide programs and financial resources to support motivated people there.

Unlike in the case of the Great Hanshin-Awaji Earthquake, governmental policy was for not just recovery, but creative reconstruction, so using the disaster area as a model for advanced approaches was appropriate. An aging society calls not only for safety, but for comprehensive care. The nuclear disaster also spurred demands for municipal production of renewable energy. With the aid of nonprofit organizations and intermediary support personnel, we hoped to bring human warmth to those living as evacuees while their towns were rebuilt. The hardships suffered by victims of the Fukushima nuclear disaster were particularly harsh and called for even more careful consideration.

Such extensive recovery efforts would require enormous financial resources, which we hoped the Japanese public as a whole would support. No part of the country is safe from natural disasters, after all, so those providing support today might end up needing it themselves in the future. Indeed, developing a national community in which help will always be extended to those in need is vital. We might even view support for a strong recovery not as a burden, but rather as an opportunity for revitalizing Japan's overall economy.

Government response

Regardless of what the council recommended, the government's response would ultimately determine whether our efforts were in vain. Unfortunately, the period after the Great East Japan Earthquake was not an ideal one for relying on a government response.

There were high hopes for the Democratic Party of Japan when it took control in 2009, but it did not remain in power for long. Prime Minister

Hatoyama Yukio resigned his seat to fellow party-member Kan within a year, and defeat in the House of Councilors elections in July 2010 resulted in a difficult-to-manage Diet partially under control of the opposition.

As mentioned above, it is significant that the Great East Japan Earthquake struck just as the prime minister was being pressured over his use of political funds. When I was appointed to lead the Reconstruction Design Council on April 11, the prime minister warned me that no plans would see the light of day without minority-party support. This was not only a political calculation but a practical one. In this sense, the need for a bipartisan approach is important.

Indeed, efforts to depose Prime Minister Kan began in earnest in May. This was not only a minority-party offensive, but also a rebellion from within the ruling party that culminated in a vote of no confidence on June 2. Kan maintained his position only by promising to withdraw if several projects, such as a special bill for budget enforcement, were accepted. The Reconstruction Design Council was forced to do its work while keeping an eye on this political environment.

But despite the ruthless political battles being waged, the disaster recovery received surprising nonpartisan support. On May 2, the Diet approved an initial supplementary budget of over four trillion yen for the disaster areas. This was a large sum, and when I visited the disaster area, I learned that this measure provided great hope for the people there. A supplemental allocation of two trillion yen was approved on July 25.

However, the Basic Act on Reconstruction that provided the legal basis for recovery efforts was delayed due to ruling- and opposition-party disagreements over establishment of the Reconstruction Agency. This disagreement reflected conflict over applying a Great Kantō Earthquake model versus a Great Hanshin-Awaji Earthquake model. As described in chapter 1, Gotō Shinpei's plans to reconstruct Tokyo under the leadership of the Reconstruction Bureau were quickly shot down, but his legend lived on. Shimokōbe Atsushi and other leaders of the Hanshin-Awaji Reconstruction Committee avoided establishing a new organization that might cause friction between existing government agencies, instead adopting policies in which overall government functions supported a recovery plan conducted under local leadership. However, Reconstruction Committee members from the private sector such as Sakaiya Taichi and politicians such as LDP members Obuchi Keizō insisted on creating a new organization to symbolize the remarkable and groundbreaking countermeasures.

As a result, recovery from the Great Hanshin-Awaji Earthquake proceeded quickly and efficiently, and was considered a success. Prime Minister Kan's office took a similar approach of implementing measures through government-wide support. However, Nukaga Fukushirō and others from the LDP called for establishment of a new organization. Having a majority in one house of the Diet made for a very powerful opposition party. To accommodate the LDP, establishment of the Reconstruction Agency was written into the Basic Act on Reconstruction. In the end, establishing a unified organization with multiple offices in different disaster areas ended up being a good idea, considering the wide area and compound nature of the Great East Japan Earthquake as compared with the Great Hanshin-Awaji Earthquake.

In any event, the delayed passage of the Basic Act on Reconstruction on June 24, 2011, set the stage for the Reconstruction Design Council recommendations, which were presented the following day and written into the Basic Act on Reconstruction on July 29 by administrative agencies under the central government. Aside from papers essentially written by bureaucrats, the wholesale incorporation into government policy of a council report prepared through debate among scholars and experts is a rare occurrence.

On the one hand, the recommendations of the Reconstruction Design Council were the result of debate among committee members, which in most cases guided its direction. On the other hand, the various workshops led by Iio to address major problems sought the participation of bureaucrats from related ministries and made proposals based on their expertise. The result of this process was a response to an unprecedented event that would have otherwise been out of reach but became achievable through the efforts of the central government. Ministries that had been consulted beforehand were able to smoothly produce the necessary administrative documents within about a month. Considering the heavily antibureaucratic outlook of the Democratic Party of Japan, I believe the Reconstruction Design Council did a good job of drawing on the know-how of bureaucratic organizations without being controlled by them.

On August 30, 2011, the Kan cabinet resigned in full, and the cabinet of Noda Yoshihiko (1957–) succeeded him on September 2. As fall deepened, I could not help feeling frustrated about the implementation of our plan, which seemed to have hardly started. It was as if the government intended to waste time until spring.

At a government meeting on November 10, I complained that we had already wasted two months on politics, and that we were progressing far too slowly. Very soon after, I heard that the central government would fully fund all costs related to relocation to higher ground.

This was very surprising; in the past, the national government had only funded three-fourths of the cost of mass relocations for disaster prevention, with local areas covering the rest. That remaining one-fourth is more significant than it might seem. The local portion of funding following the Great Hanshin-Awaji Earthquake amounted to an astronomical figure, and even today Hyōgo prefecture has not fully repaid the debt it incurred to cover it. Not wanting to see small local governments in the Tōhoku region suffer the same fate, I had pressed officials in the Ministry of Finance to cover something between 90 and 95 percent of costs. But for whatever reason, by late fall the figure had risen to 100 percent. While I appreciated their boldness, I worried a little about moral hazards. If disaster areas provided no support, wouldn't they lose all sense of responsibility? Wouldn't it be better to at least ask for a token 1 percent, or even 0.1 percent?

My understanding was that the financial resources for this had already been decided. In November and December, agreements between three parties—the Democratic Party of Japan, the Liberal Democratic Party, and the Kōmeitō—produced a series of results: a third supplementary budget, designation of a special recovery zone, plans for establishment of the Reconstruction Agency, and the funding of recovery through a 2.1 percent addition to income taxes over twenty-five years. This most extensive recovery effort in Japan's history was to take place under the supervision of the Reconstruction Agency, which was established on February 10, 2012. As noted above, success or failure would be determined by politicians, but from all appearances they were overcoming the tremendous pressure they were under to come up with the necessary schemes and funding.[20]

Having come this far, the ball was now in the court of regional governments in the disaster area.

The Reconstruction Design Council in Response to the Great East Japan Earthquake aimed not just at recovery, but at creative reconstruction that would provide a cutting-edge model for societies facing increased aging and falling birthrates. Such sweeping changes are best initiated within the disaster areas themselves. On the one hand, they have experienced such misery that restoring normality was a challenge. On the other hand, however, they are being given the opportunity to rebuild their hometowns with full national support.

5. Toward Building Safer Towns

Three types of recovery

I spent several days in late April 2015 in Iwate prefecture, visiting disaster areas along the Sanriku coast. I was surprised at the extent to which rebuilding was underway, with construction sites across the entire area. It had been a long time since I had last seen such extensive national efforts at land redevelopment.

Back in the fall of 2011, as chairman of the Reconstruction Design Council I was brazenly complaining to the prime minister that reconstruction was taking too long. Several months had been wasted during the transition to the Noda cabinet, and I feared that rebuilding would not begin before winter came to the disaster area. This was no simple issue, since people first had to be moved out of emergency shelters and rubble had to be cleared away. True rebuilding of the towns still seemed still far off.

Areas that had been flooded by the tsunami were designated as danger zones from which residential and commercial buildings must be moved. In the most extreme cases, over 100 landowners were associated with a single structure, making it nearly impossible to obtain agreements from all. Obtaining high ground suitable for building was also difficult. Those in temporary housing were as a rule supposed to remain there no more than two years, but ultimately some would need to remain for two, three, or even five times that long.

At times, I felt we would never reach our goals, but now, in our fifth spring since the earthquake, the situation finally seems to be improving. New towns are being built. That began in earnest in 2014, but the media curiously did little reporting on the subject, so the public remains largely unaware of the current state of the reconstruction.

I noted three categories of postdisaster town planning[21] while touring disaster areas in Iwate prefecture:

> *A. New towns developed after total destruction*
> Towns in this category were completely swallowed by the tsunami, including their municipal offices, and today are being totally rebuilt with safety in mind. Typical examples are Yamada, Ōtsuchi, and Rikuzentakata in Iwate prefecture.
> *B. Towns recovering from coastal-district destruction*
> Towns in this category suffered tsunami damage in core areas, but flooding extended only to part of the town or only up to the first floor of buildings, leaving many structures intact. Municipal buildings might have been damaged, but continued to function and support compound disaster mitigation, such as the construction of seawalls, breakwaters, greenbelts, and second layer of defense such as raised embankments. Examples from this category include major cities in Iwate prefecture, such as Miyako, Kamaishi, and Ōfunato. In some cases, such as Kamaishi, new

Figure 4.5. Placing a sign at the entrance to the newly established Miyagi Recovery Bureau (February 10, 2012)

town centers were built by clearing land where tsunami-damaged homes formerly stood.

C. *Rapid recovery of towns with less damage*

Because tsunami frequently strike the Sanriku coast, many towns already had solid seawalls and breakwaters. These proved to be highly effective in northern Iwate, where maximum wave heights were much lower than they were to the south. Examples include Hirono, Kuji, and Fudai. The tsunami crested seawalls in places such as Noda, Tanohata, and Iwaizumi, but even so damage was limited in comparison with other areas. Noda and Tanohata each lost over thirty people in the disaster, and inundation extended deep inland to residential areas, but rebuilding is generally proceeding smoothly.

Some cases straddle categories A and B. I included Miyako, Kamaishi, and Ōfunato in category B, but these are major cities along the San-

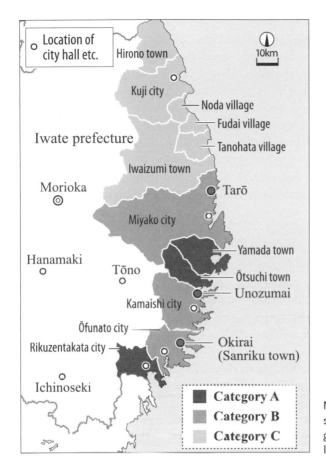

Map 4.1. Disaster-stricken local governments along the Iwate prefecture coast

riku coast, and each has expanded by merging with neighboring towns. In many cases, the city center falls in category B, but merged peripheral towns were completely destroyed. Examples include Tarō in northern Miyako, Unozumai in northern Kamaishi, Okirai in northern Ōfunato, and Ogatsu in Ishinomaki.

As described above, Tarō did not follow Ministry of Home Affairs relocation policies, despite having been destroyed in both the Meiji and Shōwa Sanriku Tsunamis, instead electing to construct an X-shaped "Great Wall" of dual-layered seawalls. This structure did an admirable job of repulsing the tsunami resulting from the 1960 Valdivia Earthquake, but in the Great East Japan Earthquake the wave crested both seawalls at their intersection and took the homes and lives of those trying to flee.

Today, Tarō is in the process of rebirth. The ten-meter seawall that protected the western part of town for so long was left in place, but the town shifted toward higher western ground near the mountains along National Highway 45. All residences have been removed from the completely destroyed eastern part of the town (Otobe), leaving only the remains of the Kankō Hotel as a memorial. A new residential area (the Sannō Housing Development) is being carved out of the hills to the north. It had previously been considered impossible to find land suitable for relocation from Tarō, but technological improvements and deep financial resources proved to be the key.

Unozumai is an old town that is now part of Kamaishi. It lies adjacent to the Ōtsuchi Bay, two inlets north from the Kamaishi Bay. The town was completely destroyed by the wave, making it the site of both the miracle and the tragedy of Kamaishi.

The miracle occurred when students at soccer practice on the athletic field at Kamaishihigashi Junior High School saw a crack open up in the ground. Following their training, students started to run inland along the hills. Seeing them, other teachers directed the remaining students to do the same. Next to the junior high was Unozumai Elementary School, where instructors first evacuated students to upper floors, but after seeing the older students heading for the hills decided to do the same, forming a long line of evacuees. Thanks to this early evacuation, they escaped the tsunami that arrived 35 minutes later by moving to even higher ground than the usual evacuation site.

While the autonomous approach to tsunami evacuation practiced by schools yielded this miracle, the local disaster prevention center taught and practiced standard procedures. Many residents fled to this center, but the tsunami rose to the second floor, killing some sixty people. Today the entire town is being redeveloped, and the 2019 Rugby World Cup was held at the Memorial Stadium completed in 2018 on the former sites of the elementary and junior high schools.

The Okirai Bay in northern Ōfunato was the site where the tsunami first hit land, approximately thirty minutes after the earthquake struck. Okirai, located deep within the bay, was totally destroyed, and as described earlier, it was another site of both a miracle (the elementary school) and a tragedy (the elderly care home). Thirty minutes is a dreadfully short time for support personnel to perform their duties. When I visited the city, I said a prayer for the dedicated staff who lost their lives trying to save residents at the elderly care home.

As the above examples show, the central areas of larger cities fell into category B, while merged areas along inlets generally fell into category A and are being rebuilt from total destruction. When I traveled down the Sanriku coast in 2015 for my inspection tour, I found myself speechless when viewing the devastation left by floods and fires in Yamada and Ōtsuchi but impressed in equal measure by the activity surrounding the reconstruction of those towns, evidenced by the constant coming and going of dump trucks. The Ōtsuchi municipal offices were swallowed by the tsunami, and the loss of the mayor was the only death in the line of duty among municipal governments, but current mayor Ikarigawa Yutaka described to me how things have changed now that reconstruction is fully underway. According to him, "people seem a little nicer now."

Towns on artificial hills

Rikuzentakata is the city most dramatically changed by the Great East Japan Earthquake. A fifteen-meter wave completely inundated the town, which lies on a broad plain, but today the area is a flurry of construction activity. A mountain on the far side of the river has been converted to gravel, which is carried by an enormous conveyor belt to the city center, where the belt splits in five directions to carry landfill being used to raise the entire plain.

Our report from the Reconstruction Design Council recommended both relocation to higher ground and multiple lines of defense against natural disaster as key components of rebuilding safer cities. Nearly all towns in the disaster area are pursuing some combination of both, but some are doing so to an extent exceeding even our own expectations.

To fulfill our call for multiple lines of defense, towns are combining disaster-mitigation strategies such as seawalls, breakwaters, seaside parks, and secondary embankments. So far, this follows our recommendations. However, we are also seeing things like the creation of high artificial hills with towns built atop them. In the case of Rikuzentakata, such artificial hills are being built to heights averaging ten meters. This makes me slightly nervous, since homes on a soft foundation tend to be vulnerable to earthquakes. I've heard that contemporary engineering techniques make artificial hills safe up to a height of around ten meters, and indeed I saw huge roller trucks being used to compress them. Upgrades to the north-south highways along the Sanriku coast and to roads between Morioka and Miyako and between Hanamaki and Kamaishi are progressing rapidly, to the great benefit of the region.

There is no doubt that safer towns are now appearing along the Sanriku coast, a welcome development considering that area's long history of tsunami destruction. The problem, however, is whether these towns will have enough vitality to halt the increased aging and depopulation that have characterized the region.

The seas in that area are quite bountiful, and catches are reportedly recovering. However, the natural disaster hitting an already aging society has robbed the fishing industry of the workers it needs. Business owners seeking to expand their business are therefore turning to increased mechanization and robotics to exploit the rich seas of the area.

Now that the "hard" aspects of reconstruction are coming together, we will increasingly need to turn to "soft" issues such as how to invite the bustle of productivity while retaining the charming qualities one desires in a home town.[22]

Recovery processes that produced results

After leaving Iwate, I visited disaster areas in Miyagi and Fukushima prefectures from June 8 to 13, 2015. Setting aside the evacuation area in Fukushima, I saw common features in all three prefectures. The Japanese government had designated the five years following the Great East Japan Earthquake as a period of intensive recovery, but up until some point in 2014 I worried that things were progressing too slowly and too casually. However, by 2015—the final year of "intensive" recovery—the rebuilding of new towns had begun in earnest, and the sound of construction could be heard throughout disaster areas in the Tōhoku region.

The harsher the initial conditions of a given town, the more large-scale reconstruction becomes. I earlier referred to towns that were completely inundated, resulting in extensive loss of life and destruction of municipal offices that would normally serve as the focal point for recovery, as "category A" disaster sites. Such towns were now highly focused on civil-engineering projects. Examples include Ōtsuchi, Yamada, and Rikuzentakata in Iwate prefecture, and Minamisanriku and Onagawa in Miyagi.

The town center of Minamisanriku was inundated by a fifteen-meter wave, and Shizugawa Hospital, located near the sea, was flooded up to its fourth floor, drowning seventy patients inside. Forty-three people who had taken refuge atop the three-story Disaster Prevention Measures Office building, twelve meters above ground, were swept away by the tsunami; the only survivors were eleven people who had climbed an antenna. When I visited the town one month after the disaster, Mayor Satō Jin told me that they had established a policy of moving all residents in flat areas to three adjacent elevated areas.

During this visit, four years after the earthquake, I could see that reconstruction was proceeding well. Particularly surprising on this visit was that the plain, which is sandwiched between two rivers, was already bordered by ten-meter embankments, and large artificial hills were near completion. The town is also planning a new shopping arcade. I assumed that as in the case of Rikuzentakata, Minamisanriku must be following the national policy, but Satō told me that was not the case; mining mountains to develop sites for relocation in Minamisanriku had produced four million cubic meters of gravel, which was being used to raise plains. The town is also building a large memorial park around the destroyed Disaster Prevention Office building, which may be left in place in remembrance of the disaster. I look forward to seeing the new town, which is largely being designed by noted architect Kuma Kengo.

The terms "L1" and "L2" are frequently heard in regard to improving town safety in disaster areas. A tsunami expected to occur once per 100 years, such as the Shōwa Sanriku Tsunami that claimed approximately 3,000 lives, is an "L1" event. A truly enormous event expected to occur once every 1,000 years, like the Great East Japan Earthquake (approximately 20,000 fatalities), is called an "L2" event. Hard structures such as seawalls are effective countermeasures against L1 events, but total protection against L2 events is impossible; the only protection is a combination of soft countermeasures that make escape easier. That said, by moving all houses to higher ground, Minamisanriku seems to have come closest to finding a way to address L2 events.

Onagawa, which has a population of slightly over 10,000, was hit by an 18.5-meter tsunami that destroyed six buildings and inundated the city hall. Sitting 14.8 meters above sea level, the Onagawa Nuclear Power Plant only narrowly escaped disaster, but 8.7 percent of the town's population lost their lives, the highest fatality rate in the disaster area. This was largely due to the town's geography: the tsunami had the most momentum in coves facing the Pacific Ocean.

Suda Yoshiaki, a Miyagi Prefectural Assembly member who became mayor of Onagawa after the earthquake, is bringing the town together and making use of nonprofit organization activities and other resources for reconstruction. The railway connecting the town with Ishinomaki and Sendai is now repaired, and a promenade connecting the train station and the port provides a gathering spot for artists and others from the town and elsewhere. The town is thus showing great promise for the future. Homes are all being moved to higher ground, and civil engineering is ongoing.

Although I saw similar circumstances among the disaster areas I visited in Miyagi prefecture, I learned that in many cases differences in leadership and reconstruction policy led to quite different recovery processes. Like Onagawa, the neighboring town of Ogatsu is surrounded by mountains and ocean and became part of Ishinomaki through a merger. In addition to its aquatic resources, Ogatsu commands 90 percent of the domestic market for inkstones. The tsunami killed 236 of the town's 4,300 residents, but even more devastating was the fact that half the remaining population relocated soon after the earthquake. That outflow has not abated, and today the population is only one-third what it was before the earthquake. Construction is belatedly starting to improve town safety by moving residences to higher ground, but any actions must await approval by the far-off Ishinomaki city hall, which runs the risk of decreasing morale. I could not help comparing Ogatsu with Onagawa, which was progressing so well. One bright point, however, is the Moriumius project, a private initiative headed by former businessman Tachibana Takashi to rebuild a destroyed elementary school around the principles of sustainability and utilization of local resources.

Among municipalities in the disaster area, Ishinomaki suffered the most casualties—3,971, accounting for 2.5 percent of its population of 160,000. Its harbor at the foot of Mount Hiyori and its industrial zone were destroyed, the residential area inland from them was flooded, and towns like Ogatsu that it had merged with were heavily damaged as well. Ishinomaki was also the site of the Ōkawa Elementary School tragedy, in which 84 students and faculty were killed by the tsunami. No one visiting the area can help but wonder why evacuation to the nearby hills was not possible. Some have called for the remains of the school to be left as a memorial, but if such plans are realized it will surely be the saddest memorial in existence.

Besides Ishinomaki, Higashimatsushima lost 2.7 percent of its population (1,152 people) and Kesennuma lost 1.95 percent (1,433). Both lost vital infrastructure as well, nearly making them category A disaster sites. However, since the cities were not totally destroyed and both are actively rebuilding, a category B designation is perhaps more apt. The same can be said of Miyako, Kamaishi, and Ōfunato in Iwate prefecture.

Kesennuma experienced the destruction of its Shishiori district, at the innermost part of the bay, and of the Asahi district, sandwiched between the bay and the Ōkawa River. Furthermore, a fuel tank exploded, spreading fires to the city and nearby hills of Ōshima via burning debris in the bay. The city hall thankfully escaped the flooding, and the hilly terrain kept broad areas dry. Most civil-engineering projects in the area are focused

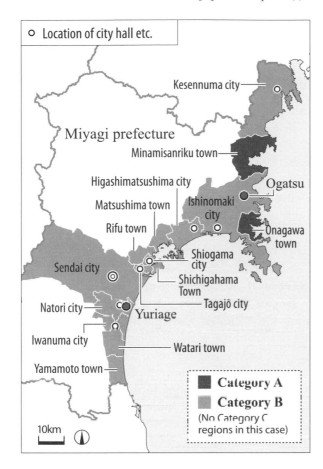

○ Location of city hall etc.

Miyagi prefecture

Kesennuma city ─○

Minamisanriku town ─

Higashimatsushima city
Ogatsu
Matsushima town
Ishinomaki
city
Rifu town
Ōnagawa
town
Sendai city
Shiogama
city
Shichigahama
Town
Natori city ─
Tagajō city
Yuriage
Iwanuma city
Watari town
Yamamoto town ─

▪ **Category A**
▪ **Category B**
(No Category C regions in this case)

10km

Map 4.2. Disaster-stricken local governments along the Miyagi prefecture coast

on Shishiori and Asahi, and the city is implementing further initiatives to increase local appeal, such as promoting itself as a "shark town" and finding ways to reduce the unsightliness of its tall seawalls.

Two seaside districts in Higashimatsushima were destroyed, Ōmagari and Nobiru. Both districts are being relocated inland to the hills, but the most significant feature of the reconstruction is an initiative led by Mayor Abe Hideo for improved communication with citizens in what he calls "regional decentralization." The scheme establishes processes for dialog with residents of the city's eight districts on issues such as disaster preparation, debris removal, and relocation. Such resident-led reconstruction is proving to be fast and effective.

The same can be said for Iwanuma, where six seaside communities along the dunes were struck by the tsunami. Then-mayor Iguchi Tsuneaki established separate policies related to evacuation sites and temporary housing for each. In the Great Hanshin-Awaji Earthquake, the policy of preferentially placing people with disabilities and the elderly in temporary housing—intended as a humanitarian approach—had the result of severing community ties, leading to solitary deaths and even suicides. From that lesson, Iwanuma decided to establish evacuation centers and temporary housing on a village-by-village basis.

When doing so, municipal authorities placed an emphasis on discussions with district residents. A retired professor from the area led a council to coordinate the six villages, and this council decided to create a new town in the Tamaura district, where the elementary and junior high school were located. The town was built over filled-in former rice paddies and includes rows of houses and a shopping center. Now under the leadership of Mayor Kikuchi Hiroo, Iwanuma provides a model case for recovery from a major disaster.

Strong leaders can make all the difference at moments of crisis. The remarkable response by Tachiya Hidekiyo, mayor of Sōma in Fukushima prefecture, from the time of the disaster through the recovery process illustrates the truth of this proposition. On the evening of the tsunami, the mayor gathered municipal staff and key persons from the city. At a meeting that lasted until 3 a.m., they decided on an overall plan for what to deal with immediately versus in the medium to long term, and clearly wrote their plans out on a large sheet of paper. They announced they would start by giving 30,000 yen (approximately US$270) in cash to those who had lost their homes in the tsunami and gathered disaster victims to quickly gain an understanding of the situation. To avoid the dreary scene of rows of prefab housing, they instead built wooden structures that could be used as their permanent homes. They also constructed a new type of elderly care facility that provided a community for its residents. The mayor—who was also a doctor and head of the local hospital—proved to be an excellent leader in these initiatives.

However, when insightful leadership turns into aggressive leadership, there can be adverse effects. Natori city, located north of Iwanuma, had a historic and charming port district called Yuriage, which was destroyed. No doubt attempting to express strong top–down leadership and a powerful sense of duty, city officials neglected to sufficiently consult with residents or provide a process in which they could feel a part of decision-making. The resulting city policies divided the community between supporters and opponents.

The Yuriage reconstruction plan has gone through multiple revisions, but now has finally attained consensus and is starting to get underway. Society today demands both leadership and democratic processes.

Visiting areas in Fukushima that were polluted by the nuclear disaster, I found myself speechless, feeling the pain of those forced to flee their homes. Even there, however, I saw promising changes. The Jōban Expressway and National Highway 6 have been reopened, and connecting roads between the two are now usable. The evacuation area has been gradually shrinking through repeated decontamination efforts. Next steps include securing intermediate storage facilities for the nuclear waste generated in the cleanup.

In the case of the Great Hanshin-Awaji Earthquake, only one-third of those who evacuated from Kobe to faraway locations returned to the city. The situation may be even more severe for those from Fukushima, but Japan is a resilient society and I am confident Japan will prove to be a society that can support its residents no matter where they live.

FIVE

Living in an Age of Seismic Activity

1. The Lisbon Earthquake

The Lisbon Earthquake as a historical model

In this book so far, I have compared three earthquakes that occurred during Japan's modern period, as well as related disasters including the Great Edo Fire of Meireki and the Meiji and Shōwa Sanriku Tsunamis. However, we can certainly benefit from also considering disasters that occurred overseas.

Few countries have experienced cataclysmic events in population-dense social centers to the extent that Japan has, but of course catastrophes do occur in other countries. One example is the 1755 earthquake and tsunami that struck Lisbon, the capital of the prosperous global empire of Portugal, resulting in fires that made a mark on humanity that persists even today. This enormous earthquake had huge significance in Western history, and references to the Lisbon Earthquake were common even in Japan after the Great East Japan Earthquake. Perhaps the people of Japan felt a sense of common fate as they, too, experienced a great disaster in the face of a national decline.

If that is the case, the sentiment was based on misunderstanding. The crisis management and emergency response after the Lisbon Earthquake, not to mention the two decades of rebuilding that followed, serve as excellent historical models. Lisbon turned misfortune to its advantage, rebuilding into a magnificent capital that greatly improved on what had existed before. In the nineteenth century, however, Portugal met defeat in the Napoleonic

Wars, and eventually found itself unable to compete with newly industrialized countries in northern Europe such as Holland and England. It was not the earthquake that led to the country's decline; even the best of recoveries cannot counter the tide of long-term historical trends.

In 2015, 260 years after the Lisbon Earthquake and 20 years after the Great Hanshin-Awaji Earthquake, I visited Lisbon with Professor Kawata Yoshiaki, then with Kansai University, to attend an international symposium cosponsored by the city of Lisbon and the Hyogo Earthquake Memorial 21st Century Research Institute. Between workshops I was able to attend a memorial ceremony held on 1 November, and also to visit ruins and museums in the city, allowing me to relive that past cataclysm, on the second and third days in between the symposium and various workshops.

In what follows, I will reflect on the Lisbon Earthquake and the recovery that followed and consider modern Japan's response to major earthquakes in light of that example.

In the Atlantic Ocean, over 1,000 kilometers from Portugal, a north-to-south crack runs along a tectonic plate, and at right angles to that is an east-to-west rupture that enters the Mediterranean from the Gibraltar Strait. Here, the African continent slides to the east and west. (This is a marked difference from the behavior of Asian Plates, where the Indian Continent slips under the Himalayas, and the Pacific and Philippine oceanic plates slide beneath the Japanese archipelago.) It was in this rupture, around 200 kilometers offshore from Portugal, that an earthquake of around M 8.6 occurred at 9:30 a.m. on November 1, 1755.

This was All Saint's Day, a time when churchgoers were attending mass. Today one can visit the remains of the Carmo Convent, where the sight of the roofless church invites visions of its collapse on the worshippers in attendance. In Europe, this event led humanists to question the benefit of appeals to God, and Jesuits to strengthen their assuredness of divine punishment.

Three tremors occurred over a span of around ten minutes, and forty minutes later a tsunami measuring five to ten meters high traveled up the Tagus River and struck Lisbon. This was followed by fires that burned in the capital for six days. Most buildings in the city were destroyed by some combination of earthquake, tsunami, and fire.

Top-class crisis management and emergency response

Portuguese King José I (1714–77; reigned 1750–77) was fortunately in the Belém Palace when the event occurred, and thus avoided injury, but was so overcome by the disaster that he did not return to the city. Instead he delegated all authority for reconstruction and recovery to his confident cabinet member Sebastião de Carvalho, who later came to be known as the Marquês of Pombal. This proved to be a wise decision. Pombal had extensive international experience, having learned about reconstruction in the 1666 Great Fire of London, and about dealing with religious superstitions in Vienna. When José I asked him what they should do, he reportedly replied, "Bury the dead and heal the living."

Pombal traveled to the disaster area by wagon and immediately took command. He convinced the church of the necessity of water burials to avoid plague, and had the military and citizens dispose of corpses by throwing them into the Tagus River. He set up tents amid the collapsed buildings to serve as support and evacuation centers, and provided water, food, and medical treatment to the survivors. He deployed the military to keep the peace, and had thieves and looters hung in city plazas. He furthermore established price controls for food and building materials. Even by today's standards, this was top-class crisis management and emergency response.

Japan's handling of similar crisis situations has been far different. Crisis management and emergency response after the Great Kantō Earthquake were delayed due to the absence of a prime minister, allowing massacres by vigilantes. In the Great Hanshin-Awaji Earthquake, both the Hyōgo prefectural government and the prime minister's office lacked good information systems, and therefore did not recognize the seriousness of the situation for half a day. First responders such as police and firefighters fought bravely, but initial deployment of the Self-Defense Forces came late. Crisis management and emergency response to the Great Hanshin-Awaji Earthquake, too, can thus be classified as a failure.

Thankfully, both the government and first responders learned lessons from the Great Hanshin-Awaji Earthquake and were able to rapidly respond to the Great East Japan Earthquake and Tsunami. Even so, TEPCO's response to the nuclear power plant accident was slow, and the government was inadequately prepared to provide needed support. In contrast, as seen above, Lisbon's response two and a half centuries before that was praiseworthy.

Recovery in Lisbon

The recovery that followed the Lisbon Earthquake is also noteworthy. Pombal forbade residents from rebuilding on their own, instead instructing engineers to propose five reconstruction plans. He approved one that called for rebuilding the devastated Baixa district into a city center with large streets laid out on a grid. Large plazas were built at the mountain and seaside ends of the district, greatly beautifying the capital.

The venue for the symposium I attended in Lisbon was a church that had been converted into a bank near the seaside plaza. In its basement were countless pine pilings coated in resin to prevent decomposition in water, topped by a wooden framework to strengthen the building's foundation. This technology was also used in Venice, but I still considered it a brilliant countermeasure against ground liquefaction, and something from which Japan can learn.

Pombal not only addressed building foundations, but also standardized construction of four-story buildings; to improve earthquake resistance, these were required to have a wooden external framework called a "birdcage," along which stone walls were piled. Many were later extended to five or even six stories. The twenty years of dictatorial power that Pombal was granted allowed him to apply all the techniques and technologies of his time, resulting in an entirely new city.

In the case of Japan, while Gotō Shinpei's plans for rebuilding a new imperial capital following the Great Kantō Earthquake were abandoned amid political strife, the Reconstruction Bureau and Tokyo's municipal

TABLE 5.1 Earthquake response in Lisbon and the three major earthquakes in Japan

		Lisbon Earthquake	Great Kantō Earthquake	Great Hanshin-Awaji Earthquake	Great East Japan Earthquake	
Date of occurrence		November 1, 1755	September 1, 1923	January 17, 1995	March 11, 2011	
Deaths		60,000+	105,385	6,434	19,418; 2,592 missing	
Disaster type		Earthquake, tsunami, fire	Earthquake, fire	Earthquake	Earthquake, tsunami	Nuclear accident
Response rating	Crisis management	A	D	C	A	D
	Emergency response	A	C	B	A	C
	Recovery	—	B	A	—	—
	Creative reconstruction	A+	A	A	A+	—

Notes: Deaths of the Great Hanshin-Awaji Earthquake and the Great East Japan Earthquake are including disaster-related deaths.

Source: Disaster Management Cabinet Office, *1923 Great Kantō Earthquake Disaster Report*, Vol. 1, National Institutes of Natural Sciences National Astronomical Observatory of Japan (Ed.), *Chronological Scientific Tables 2017*, etc.

government were nonetheless able to accomplish extensive urban planning and development.

After the Great Hanshin-Awaji Earthquake, national funds were applied only to restoration; any efforts to improve on the status quo had to be funded through local resources. However, local governments were set on creative reconstruction, and successfully produced disaster museums, think tanks, art and cultural centers, and other assets that will be passed on for years to come.

Following the Great East Japan Earthquake, creative reconstruction became national policy, and now coastal municipalities are implementing large-scale civil-engineering projects to create much safer cities. Thanks to the public's acceptance of a recovery tax, the region is receiving generous reconstruction assistance. In places like Minamisanriku in Miyagi prefecture, all residences are being relocated to higher ground, flat areas are being reformed as artificial hills up to ten meters high, and shopping arcades are being built. These new towns are being rebuilt to withstand once-in-a-thousand-year tsunamis (L2), rather than the once-in-hundred-year events (L1) that typically informed reconstruction before.

However, the areas contaminated in the nuclear accident represent the opposite of creative reconstruction. Units 1 through 4 of the Fukushima Daiichi Plant are currently being decommissioned, but former residents of the surrounding area are still unable to return to their homes.

The decline of a nation

Pombal not only rebuilt Lisbon into an earthquake-resistant city, he worked to revitalize industries that the earthquake had pushed toward decline. This was accomplished through tremendous financial support from other European countries, as well as a reconstruction tax imposed on Brazil, Portugal's largest colony. Pombal also conducted broad surveys to grasp the extent of damage, a notable accomplishment representing the birth of scientific approaches to disaster recovery.

However, the fact that Lisbon accomplished one of the most remarkable recoveries in history was not enough to stave off the nation's long-term fate. Portugal is a small country occupying one corner of the Iberian Peninsula, and although it had attained greatness through the bounty of its colonies, it lost Brazil due to the Napoleonic Wars. As a result, it was not the Portuguese, but northern European countries such as the United Kingdom that led Europe into the modern era through innovative industry.[1]

In Japan, the reconstruction that has taken place since the Great East Japan Earthquake has been the most extensive in the nation's history, perhaps even comparable to Lisbon's, although the nuclear accidents were a significant setback. What remains to be seen, however, is whether Japan will be able to avoid a similar decline in the long term. Deviating from this path will require sustainable economic success. To that end, we must regain our previous high level of technology and find a way to end our current population decline.

Even if Japan cannot attain the status of a powerful country, we must at least strive to become a highly attractive country from a cultural perspective. Western Europe is a regional community that shares similar values and protects smaller and midsized nations that comprise it. In East Asia, however, several countries do not share these values and have different political systems, including dictatorships and authoritarian governments. As such, Japan, has to pay special attention to diplomacy and security to protect our existence.

In that sense, it may be difficult for postdisaster Japan to escape Portugal's fate, considering that long-term economic and geopolitical trends are rarely affected by disaster recovery.

Historically speaking, Japan has shown a remarkable propensity for bouncing back from disaster and learning from other cultures, as evidenced by the Battle of Baekgang in the seventh century, the forced opening of Japan's borders in the nineteenth century, and defeat in World War II. This gives me hope that full recovery will eventually come, even if it is hard to say exactly when.

2. The Current State of Disaster Response

Restoration or recovery

To consider how disaster countermeasures can be further improved, I would like to review the problems discussed in this book so far and summarize the current situation. First, let us consider the questions of whether to pursue simple restoration or creative reconstruction, and whether public funds should be applied to public functions only, or also to private property and the recovery of individual livelihoods.

As we have already seen, despite Gotō Shinpei's setbacks after the Great Kantō Earthquake, creative reconstruction was at the core of Tokyo's development. After the Great Hanshin-Awaji Earthquake, Hyōgo prefectural governor Kaihara Toshitami called for a locally led reconstruction plan as a symbol of decentralization theory, a point with which the Murayama cabinet agreed. Both parties also agreed on a system that relied not on new agencies like the Reconstruction Bureau of the Great Kantō Earthquake era, but rather on government-wide support of the disaster-affected areas.

However, some disagreements remained. While the governor carried the banner of creative reconstruction, the national government set limits under what was called the "Gotōda doctrine." National funds could only be used for restoration to a pre-earthquake state; anything new would have to be built using local funds. The idea was that disaster areas should not take advantage of their misfortune to further local development. On the basis of conformity with the existing legal system, the central government forbade use of national funds to establish special disaster zones or restore the lifestyles of individual residents.

By the time of the Great East Japan Earthquake, however, the national and regional governments had become better at listening to the needs of disaster areas. Hyōgo and Kobe, with the consent of the national government, established a 900-billion-yen reconstruction fund to finance projects that disaster areas considered vital, but could not normally be paid for with national funds. The National Association of Governors helped collect twenty-five million signatures nationwide in favor of providing support for individuals, motivating politicians to establish the "Act Concerning Support for Reconstructing Livelihoods of Disaster Victims" three years after the earthquake. This legislation provided victims with up to one million yen to help rebuild their lives, later expanded by amendments to three million yen. Such application of funds beyond the public sector is commonplace overseas and is even considered natural according to international standards of morality.

Indeed, the United Nations and the international community as a whole have taken up the slogan "build back better" as a guideline for recovery from disasters. The Cabinet meeting held one month after the Great East Japan Earthquake that called for not just recovery, but creative reconstruction with an eye to the future shows recognition of this shift in international trends, and a marked difference with the responses to the Great Kantō and Great Hanshin-Awaji Earthquakes.

National support was not provided to victims of the Great Hanshin-Awaji Earthquake, leaving Hyōgo prefecture to help survivors rebuild their lives through programs such as medical and psychological care for vulnerable populations. The value of such programs was widely recognized after the Great East Japan Earthquake, and the central government moved quickly to establish a headquarters to manage them, thereby becoming an important pillar of recovery efforts. This shift demonstrates a maturation of public perception with regard to what support is needed after a disaster.[2]

International support

While I was unable to sufficiently address the topic in this book, the international support Japan received after the Great East Japan Earthquake deserves at least some mention.

Since I have been involved in disaster recovery myself, whenever I visit a foreign country, I always make a point of acknowledging the extraordinary support they have provided. In many cases, the response is something like "Not at all—we've received quite generous assistance from Japan in the past, so we owe it to you." These conversations have convinced me that Japan's postwar policies of promoting international cooperation through overseas development assistance and other means in this area have not been a mistake.

Of course, the foremost example of international disaster recovery support for Japan is Operation Tomodachi. The restoration of Sendai Airport and landing operations at Ōshima, among other accomplishments, showed the outstanding abilities of the U.S. military. At the time, Japan-U.S. relations were strained by the chaotic and inexperienced administration of the Democratic Party of Japan, and territorial issues had worsened relations with neighboring countries. However, the United States showed its willingness to be there for Japan by bringing the aircraft carrier USS *Ronald Reagan* in for disaster response and sailing the USS *Essex* and other ships through the Sea of Japan as a strategic message to countries in the region.

Japan's disaster-response capacity will inevitably fall short in the event of a huge disaster, such as an earthquake at the Nankai trough or one beneath Tokyo. In such a situation, international assistance from the United States and other countries will be crucial.

The role of the Emperor

Following all three great earthquakes that struck Japan in modern times, it was the Emperor who displayed the clearest support for the survivors and played the largest role in preserving national unity.

After the Great Kantō Earthquake, Prince Hirohito—then regent for his ill father, the Taishō Emperor (1879–1926; reigned 1912–26)—actively patrolled the affected area. Describing the fire destruction of Tokyo, on

September 12 he noted that the scene "feels like one big graveyard."³ As Emperor, Hirohito was a creative reconstructionist, as seen in the declaration he drafted with Itō Miyoji.

Hirohito performed additional surveys of other afflicted areas in Tokyo in the coming weeks, and described his shock to Imperial Household Minister Makino Nobuaki (1861–1949), saying, "the scope of the disaster is enormous—the more I see, the sadder I become." He moved Makino by announcing that he would postpone his own wedding, which had been scheduled to take place that autumn.⁴

As shown by donations from the Emperor since before the prewar, it is a tradition of the Imperial family to stand beside the people of Japan when they are thrown into misfortune, cheering them on. Support for disaster victims by the Heisei Emperor (Akihito, 1933–; reigned 1989–2019) has been even closer and more heartfelt. This was first demonstrated in 1990, when he visited victims of the eruption of Mount Unzen. Both Akihito and Empress Michiko visited crowded disaster shelters, where they crouched down to the height of residents to speak with them and shake their hands. It was surprising enough to see the noblest couple in Japan behaving like this, but similar scenes have unfolded at all disaster sites since as well.

Two weeks after the Great Hanshin-Awaji Earthquake, the Imperial couple visited disaster sites, taking care not to get in the way. Such heartfelt behavior deeply impressed residents, leading Hokudan mayor Kokubo to write, "Their visit helped to heal broken hearts, pulling people together. Nerves were becoming frayed, but the Imperial couple soothed them." Hyōgo governor Kaihara wrote that for several years afterward he was frequently invited to the Imperial Palace to give detailed updates on the status of disaster recovery.⁵

The Heisei Emperor is the first Japanese emperor who took to heart the postwar constitution's description of his role as "a symbol of Japanese unity." Through reconciliation with foreign countries that Japan harmed in World War II, Japan has become a stable member of the international community in good standing. Domestically, however, people continue to suffer from disasters, disease, and disability, so the maintenance of national unity is an ongoing process. The Emperor and Empress have played an important role in all of these processes.

Their deep empathy and dedication to victims continued after the Great East Japan Earthquake. In a video message released five days after the earthquake, the Emperor stated, "It is my sincere hope that . . . each and every Japanese will continue to care for the afflicted areas and the people for years to come and, together with the afflicted, watch over and support their path to recovery." An essay by Grand Chamberlain Kawashima Yutaka well described how more than anyone the Emperor lived up to these ideals.[6]

In the most disastrous of circumstances, the Emperor and Empress wholeheartedly engage in various activities for the sake of national integrity. By doing so, cherishing the people of the nation and the world and wishing them well, they provide a basis for our national ethics.

Beyond safe towns

The Great East Japan Earthquake hit just as Japan was emerging from the "lost two decades" that followed the collapse of the bubble economy in the early 1990s. Despite the poor timing, however, the disaster area was provided with generous support, and towns in the areas hit by tsunami are being rebuilt for improved safety. The financial resources for doing so are also now secure, thanks to the Japanese people's acceptance of a recovery tax.

While historically significant advances to improve safety are taking place, cause for concern remains. One particular worry is Japan's social trend toward decreased population, and especially in the disaster area, fewer children and more elderly. It is in a sense ironic that such safety improvements are coming not while these towns are in a period of increasing population and industry, but in a period of decline. Another vital issue in the future will therefore be finding ways to make such areas more attractive to new residents from across the country.

Some may consider it better to delay town relocation in the name of rapid recovery, instead immediately reconstructing residences and shopping districts where they are and improving evacuation routes to ensure that residents could quickly escape from tsunamis. Today, however, recognition of the importance of safety and security has increased, so few people are willing to continue living in tsunami zones. Indeed, this has led to even more rapid depopulation of such areas. Waiting too long to relocate, as residents forget the danger and become accustomed to the convenience of living on the seaside, is an invitation to another disaster. We must thus strive to improve both safety and attractiveness.

The first step toward increasing regional attractiveness is revitalizing industry. Of course, while restoring commerce is vital, it is not all that must be done. Towns must be beautiful and in harmony with nature, they must hold festivals and other cultural activities, and, most important of all, they must be home to a warm community that values its residents. A new value system is therefore also essential in the present era.

Preparing for a Nankai Trough Earthquake

It is worth noting that in Japan, where disaster response has tended to consist of patchwork attempts to catch up with incidents, new laws such as the 2013 Basic Act for National Resilience have made it easier to prepare for the next catastrophe.

Kushimoto in Wakayama prefecture is currently relocating to higher ground in preparation for a tsunami resulting from a Nankai Trough Earthquake. In Minami, Tokushima prefecture, too, residents are planning to relocate in cooperation with the University of Tokushima, but it remains unclear how such a project will be funded; the national government offers no financial resources for preemptive relocations.

Following the Great East Japan Earthquake, the Japanese government increased taxes to generate the revenue to pay for reconstruction and future preparedness. In particular, an extra 2.1 percent was added to the income tax for the next twenty-five years. Personally, I think the tax should be continued, with the revenue used to establish a disaster agency that will proactively take precautionary measures in probable disaster areas as quickly and effectively as possible. Japan tends to use a lot of money for reconstruction and recovery following a disaster, but it is cheaper to prepare ahead of time, and what's more, society makes out better because more lives and property can be saved. Historically, tsunamis tend to strike certain areas. In the recovery following the Great East Japan Earthquake, the Sanriku coast of Tōhoku, one of the areas that experiences tsunamis, was strengthened to better withstand them. However, in the part of the country along the coast of a future Nankai Trough Earthquake and Tsunami situation, with the exception of Shizuoka prefecture, little has been done. I visited Kōchi prefecture to see how its residents are preparing. As one heads toward Kuroshio from the Kōchi plain, the mountains come closer to the beach. Here and there are new signs indicating tsunami evacuation routes. I heard that the national government was funding up to 70 percent of the costs for evacuation-route maintenance.

A tsunami will hit the Kōchi coast just ten minutes after an earthquake, so there is no time to evacuate from the plains to the hills. Residents have constructed steel evacuation towers in response. After an agreement that the national government would fund 70 percent of the construction costs, over 100 of these towers were built.

Government reports predict that Kuroshio will be hit by a thirty-four-meter tsunami within ten minutes of a powerful earthquake in the Nankai trough. I was impressed by the way in which local governments in Kōchi prefecture were turning this dire prediction into an opportunity for promoting safety and community-wide cooperation. However, I could not help but think that the bigger issue was how to protect the 340,000 residents of the prefectural capital, Kōchi city.

In contrast to preparations for a Nankai Trough Earthquake, which are being based on worst-case scenarios, those planning for an earthquake directly beneath Tokyo have not considered how to handle the loss of function in Japan's capital city. This mirrors the case of Hyōgo prefecture and Kobe, which in 1974 received reports of the possibility of an intensity VII earthquake but prepared only for an intensity V event.

The focus in Tokyo has been limited to a M 7–class earthquake in a fault directly below the city, not in an oceanic plate like that in the Great Kantō Earthquake. That may indeed be the most pressing concern, but it blocks considerations of a disaster that will eventually come and rationalizes Japan's failure to seriously address overconcentration of resources in Tokyo. The population concentration there today is nearly ten times what it was at the time of the Great Kantō Earthquake, yet central government agencies refuse to face the fact that natural disasters are accompanied by social disasters, and thus have continued to maintain the centralization of population and government functions in Tokyo. The government has furthermore failed to carry out preliminary national preparations for a cataclysmic disaster and has not established a disaster-management agency to enable integrated functioning in crises.

I can only hope that the era of the combined failure of Japan's political establishment and government bureaucracy to consider worst-case scenarios and implement adequate crisis management will not last much longer.

Afterword

If asked to specify the primary influence on my approach to disaster response, I could only point to my experience in the Great Hanshin-Awaji Earthquake. This was a pivotal event in my life, one that took the life of a dear advisee along with 6,000 of my fellow countrymen.

As a historian and political scientist, my goal in writing this book was to perform an overall comparative analysis of three major disasters in modern Japanese history, but I also tried to pay close attention to the misery experienced by every one of the victims, because I myself have shared that experience. So even as a specialist, I try not to lose sight of the people living in such exceptional times; there is something about disasters that pulls one back from abstract theory.

After officials certified that our home in Nishinomiya was completely destroyed, my wife and two daughters evacuated to the home of close friends in Hiroshima. In stark contrast to the common image of harsh refugee life, what I saw was them unexpectedly enjoying their survival time. I stood in front of their house the following morning, watching as her new schoolmates walked my six-year-old daughter to her first day of first grade at Koiue Elementary School. Watching her bounce happily as she hopped up the outside stairs near the neighborhood park wearing a red backpack someone had lent her, I could not hold back my tears. I knew that Kobe had not been abandoned, and that the people of Hiroshima and indeed the entire nation were there to warmly take us in.

When I was appointed Chairperson of the Reconstruction Design Council in Response to the Great East Japan Earthquake, my mission was clear: I was to do everything within reason to support those in the disaster-affected area.

Anyone living in Japan, and for that matter, in the world, can potentially become a disaster victim. In Japan's case, as a nation subject to disasters, it is vital that we strengthen our bonds. As the Seven Principles for the Reconstruction Framework state, the only way to overcome great disasters is for all those living in Japan to cooperate and share the burden of recovery. Extending a helping hand to those in need is furthermore an affirmation of one's own existence. As fate would have it, I was born at the start of an era of disasters and became personally involved in both the Great Hanshin-Awaji and Great East Japan Earthquakes, deepening my conviction that this is the case. Even so, I cannot help but wonder why disaster seems to follow me so closely.

After my tenure as president of the National Defense Academy, I became Chancellor of the Prefectural University of Kumamoto, which was my post when the Kumamoto Earthquake struck in April 2016. I was at my home in Nishinomiya, Hyōgo prefecture, when that earthquake hit, and the day after a stronger one hit on April 16 (later described as the main shock, with the one two days before as a foreshock), my old friend Governor Kabashima Ikuo telephoned to ask me to join him in Kumamoto to help with the reconstruction there. I thus became Chairperson of the Expert Group for Reconstruction and Recovery from the Kumamoto Earthquake.

The Great Hanshin-Awaji Earthquake was followed by the Tottori, Chūetsu, and Iwate-Miyagi Earthquakes in a geographically clockwise progression leading to the Great East Japan Earthquake, but the Kumamoto Earthquake has undeniably triggered a new phase of seismic activity in southwestern Japan. In particular, I hope that residents throughout Japan can go beyond myths regarding safety from earthquakes so as to better prepare for the next disaster.

This book is an adaptation of a regular column titled "The Era of Great Disasters" that appeared in the *Mainichi Shimbun* newspaper over three years and eight months, starting in 2012. While writing that column, I received an extraordinary amount of support from Kishi Toshimitsu and the rest of the *Mainichi* editorial staff. I am also thankful for the warm support of Umeyama Akio at Mainichi Shimbun Publishing while creating this book.

I will refrain from a making a long list of acknowledgements, but of course this book could not have been created without the help of many people. In particular, I express my deep gratitude to the late Kaihara Toshitami, the former president of my other workplace, the Hyogo Earthquake Memorial 21st Century Research Institute, and to the many groups working toward disaster preparedness and mitigation, including the Reconstruction Design Council in Response to the Great East Japan Earthquake and the Reconstruction Agency.

I dedicate this book to all those working for the safety of the residents of Japan.

Iokibe Makoto
June 2016

Notes

INTRODUCTION

1. Sangawa Akira. *Jishin no nihonshi: Daichi wa nani o katarunoka*, zōhoban [Earthquake and the History of Japan: What the Earth Would Say?, enlarged ed.]. (Tokyo: Chuokoron-shinsha, 2011).

2. Morimoto Kōsei. *Shōmu tennō: Seme wa warehitori ni ari* [Emperor Shōmu: I Am the One to Blame]. (Tokyo: Kodansha, 2010).

3. Shizenkagaku kenkyūkikō Kokuritsu Tenmondai [National Institutes of Natural Sciences National Astronomical Observatory of Japan] (Ed.). *Rika Nenpyō 2017* [Chronological Scientific Tables 2017]. (Tokyo: Maruzen, 2016).

CHAPTER 1

1. There are various ways to measure earthquake strength (seismic scales). Most commonly, "magnitude" correlates with the amount of energy released at the epicenter, and thus measures the earthquake's potential for causing ground movement. In contrast, "intensity" measures the force of ground movement at a given location, and thus varies according to factors such as distance from the epicenter and local geography.

2. Ikeda Tetsurō. *Shinsai yobō chōsakai hōkoku*, 100 [Earthquake Prevention Research Committee Report, Vol. 100]. (1925).

3. Yoshimura Akira. *Sanriku kaigan ōtsunami* [Great Tsunami of the Sanriku Coast]. (Tokyo: Bungeishunju, 1970).

4. Chūō bōsaikaigi [Disaster Management Cabinet Office]. *1923 Kantō daishinsai hōkokusho*, 1 [1923 Great Kantō Earthquake Disaster Report, Vol. 1]. (2006).

5. Ibid.

6. Ibid.

7. Yoshimura Akira. *Kantō daishinsai* [The Great Kantō Earthquake]. (Tokyo: Bungeishunju, 1973).

8. Yokohama-shi shishi hensangakari (Ed.). *Yokohama-shi shinsaishi*, 1 [History of Yokohama City Earthquake Disaster, Vol. 1]. (Yokohama: Yokohama-shi shishi hensangakari, 1926).

9. Chūō bōsaikaigi. *1923 Kantō daishinsai hōkokusho*, 1.

10. Yoshimura. *Kantō daishinsai.*

11. Chūō bōsaikaigi. *1923 Kantō daishinsai hōkokusho*, 1. Shizenkagaku kenkyūkikō Kokuritsu Tenmondai [National Institutes of Natural Sciences National Astronomical Observatory of Japan] (Ed.). *Rika Nenpyō 2017* [Chronological Scientific Tables 2017]. (Tokyo: Maruzen, 2016). etc.

12. Ibid.

13. Yamamoto Sumiyoshi. *Edo no kaji to hikeshi* [Fires and Firefighting in Edo]. (Tokyo: Kawade shobo shinsha, 1993).

14. Chūō bōsaikaigi [Disaster Management Cabinet Office]. *1657 Meireki no edo taika hōkokusho* [Report on the 1657 Great Meireki Edo Fire]. (2004).

15. Murosaki Yoshiteru. "Hakodate taika (1934) to Sakata taika (1976)" [The Hakodate (1934) and Sakata (1976) Fires]. In Hyogo Earthquake Memorial 21st Century Research Institute. *Saigai taisaku zensho* 1: *Saigai gairon* [Compendium of Disaster Prevention, Vol. 1: The Basics of Disaster]. (Kobe: Hyogo Earthquake Memorial 21st Century Research Institute, 2011).

16. Ikeda. *Shinsai yobō chōsakai hōkoku*, 100.

17. Chūō bōsaikaigi [Disaster Management Cabinet Office]. *1923 Kantō daishinsai hōkokusho*, 2 [1923 Great Kantō Earthquake Disaster Report, Vol. 2]. (2008).

18. Tokyo-shi (Ed.). *Tokyo shinsairoku* [Record of the Tokyo Earthquake and Disaster]. (Tokyo: Tokyo-shi, 1926).

19. Hyogo Earthquake Memorial 21st Century Research Institute Research & Investigation Center. *Risubon jishin to sono bunmeishiteki igi no kōsatsu* [Examination of the Lisbon Earthquake and Its Historical Significance for Civilization]. (Kobe: Hyogo Earthquake Memorial 21st Century Research Institute, 2015).

20. Chūō bōsaikaigi. *1923 Kantō daishinsai hōkokusho*, 2.

21. Yoshimura. *Kantō daishinsai.*

22. Keishichō [Metropolitan Police Department]. *Taishō daishin kasaishi* [History of the Great Taishō Earthquake and Fires]. (Tokyo: Keishichō, 1925).

23. Chūō bōsaikaigi. *1923 Kantō daishinsai hōkokusho*, 2.

24. Naimushō shakaikyoku [Ministry of Home Affairs, Department of Social Affairs]. *Taishō shinsaishi, naihen* [Report on the Taishō Earthquake, Supplement]. (Tokyo: Naimushō shakaikyoku, 1923).

25. Investigation by Zainichi Chōsen Dōhōimonkai [The Committee for the Consolation of Korean Compatriots].

26. Hatano Masaru, and Iimori Akiko. *Kantō daishinsai to nichibei gaikō* [The Great Kantō Earthquake and Japan-US Diplomacy]. (Tokyo: Soshisha, 1999). Naimushō shakaikyoku [Ministry of Home Affairs, Department of Social Affairs]. *Taishō shinsaishi, gaihen* [Report on the Taishō Earthquake, Supplement]. (Tokyo: Naimushō shakaikyoku, 1923).

27. Tsurumi Yūsuke. *Gotō Shinpei*, Vol. 4. (Tokyo: Keiso shobo, 1967). Ko hakushaku Yamamoto kaigun taishō denki hensankai [Committee for the Biography of the late Admiral Yamamoto] (Ed.). *Hakushaku Yamamoto Gonnohyōe den*, 2

[Biography of Count Yamamoto Gonnohyōe, Vol. 2]. (Tokyo: Yamamoto Kiyoshi, 1938).

28. Kinshichi Norio. "Risubon daishinsai to keimōtoshi no kensetsu" [The Lisbon Earthquake and Construction of the City of Enlightenment]. In *JCAS renkei kenkyūseika hōkoku*, Vol. 8. (2005).

29. Tsurumi. *Gotō Shinpei*, Vol. 4. Goto Shinpei kenkyūkai [Gotō Shinpei Research Group] (Ed.). *Shinsai fukkō: Gotō Shinpei no 120 nichi: Toshi wa shimin ga tsukuru mono* [Earthquake Recovery: 120 Days of Gotō Shinpei: The Town Is Meant for Its Residents]. (Tokyo: Fujiwara-shoten, 2011).

30. Kunaichō [Imperial Household Agency]. *Shōwa tennō jitsuroku* [Records of the Shōwa Emperor, Vol. 3]. (Tokyo: Tokyo shoseki, 2015), p. 930.

31. Takahashi Shigeharu (Ed.). *Teito fukkōshi*, 1–3 [A History of the Reconstruction of the Imperial City, Vols. 1–3]. (Tokyo: Teito fukkō chōsa kyōkai, 1930).

32. Ibid., chapter 5.

33. Ibid., chapter 6.

34. Tsutsui Kiyotada. *Teito fukkō no jidai: Kantō daishinsai igo* [Era of Imperial City Reconstruction: The Great Kantō Earthquake and Beyond]. (Tokyo: Chuokoron-shinsha, 2011).

35. Gotō Shinpei kenkyūkai (Ed.). *Shinsai fukkō*.

36. Chūō bōsaikaigi [Disaster Management Cabinet Office]. *1923 Kantō daishinsai hōkokusho*, 3 [1923 Great Kantō Earthquake Disaster Report, Vol. 3]. (2009). Taikakai (Ed.). *Naimushō shi*, 3 [History of the Ministry of Home Affairs, Vol. 3]. (Tokyo: Chiho zaimu kyōkai, 1971). Soeda Yoshiya. *Naimushō no shakaishi* [Social History of the Ministry of Home Affairs]. (Tokyo: University of Tokyo Press, 2007). Takahashi (Ed.). *Teito fukkōshi*, 1–3.

CHAPTER 2

1. Hyogo Earthquake Memorial 21st Century Research Institute. *Saigai taisaku zensho 1: Saigai gairon* [Compendium of Disaster Prevention, Vol. 1: The Basics of the Disaster]. (Kobe: Hyogo Earthquake Memorial 21st Century Research Institute, 2011). Fukao Yoshio and Ishibashi Katsuhiko (Eds.). *Hanshin Awaji daishinsai to jishin no yosoku*. [Great Hanshin-Awaji Earthquake and Forecast of Earthquake]. (Tokyo: Iwanami shoten, 1996). Hanshin Awaji daishinsai chōsa hōkoku henshūiinkai (Ed.). *Hanshin Awaji daishinsai chōsa hōkoku*, 1–25 [Report on the Hanshin–Awaji Earthquake Disaster, 1–25]. (Tokyo: Japanese Geotechnical Society, Japan Society of Civil Engineers, Japan Society of Mechanical Engineers, Architectural Institute of Japan, & Seismological Society of Japan, 1996–2000).

2. Keisatsuchō [National Police Agency] (Ed.). *Keisatsu hakusho Heisei 7 nenban* [Police White Paper 1995]. (Tokyo: Ministry of Finance, 1995), p. 43.

3. Japan Association for Fire Science and Engineering. *1995 nen hyōgo-ken nanbu jishin ni okeru kasai ni kansuru chōsa hōkokusho* [A Survey of Fires in the 1995 Southern Hyōgo Prefecture Earthquake]. (Tokyo: Japan Association for Fire Science and Engineering, 2011).

4. Ibid.

5. Hanshin-Awaji daishinsai kinen kyōkai [Great Hanshin-Awaji Earthquake Memorial Association] (Ed.). "Hanshin-Awaji daishinsai kinen kyōkai Ōraru Hisutorī" [Oral Histories from Survivors, Collected by the Great Hanshin-Awaji Earthquake Memorial Association]. The Collection of the Disaster Reduction and Human Renovation Institution Library (Kobe), hereafter, "HAOH."

6. Nihon Shōbō Kyōkai [Japan Firefighters Association] (Ed.). *Hanshin Awaji daishinsaishi* [Accounts of the Great Hanshin-Awaji Earthquake]. (Tokyo: Nihon Shōbō Kyōkai, 1996).

7. Interview with Hokudan mayor Kokubo Masao (on August 7, 2002, at Hokudan town hall). In HAOH.

8. Stated by Volunteer Fire Brigade Deputy Chief Handa Yasuhiro. In Nihon Shōbō Kyōkai (Ed.). *Hanshin Awaji daishinsaishi*.

9. Interview with Nishinomiya Education Director (later, mayor) Yamada Satoru (on August 25, 2005, at Nishinomiya city hall). In HAOH.

10. As told by Maezawa Tomoe, chairwoman of the Hyōgo Women's Fire Prevention Group Liaison Council. In Nihon Shōbō Kyōkai (Ed.). *Hanshin Awaji daishinsaishi*.

11. Oda Chizuko, assistant head nurse at the Kobe University Medical College Hospital Intensive Care Unit. In Nihon Shōbō Kyōkai (Ed.). *Hanshin Awaji daishinsaishi*.

12. Miyake Masashi, vice chair of the Nagata Ward Nishidai Tozaki Self-Governance Union Council. In Nihon Shōbō Kyōkai (Ed.). *Hanshin Awaji daishinsaishi*.

13. Mentioned by Kawai Tomokazu, chief of the Ashiya City Fire Brigade. In Nihon Shōbō Kyōkai (Ed.). *Hanshin Awaji daishinsaishi*.

14. An article in the *Yomiuri Shimbun* newspaper, February 19, 1995.

15. Interviews with Hyōgo Prefectural Police Chief Takitō Kōji (on September 19, 2002, at West Japan Railway Company Headquarters) and National Police Commissioner Kunimatsu Takaji (on October 7, 2004, in Tokyo at Sompo Japan Insurance Headquarters). In HAOH. See an article in the *Mainichi Shimbun* newspaper, March 12, 1995.

16. Sekizawa Ai. "Jishinkasai no higai keigen taisaku" [Measures for Mitigating Damage Due to Earthquake Fires]. In Hyogo Earthquake Memorial 21st Century Research Institute. *Saigai taisaku zensho, 2: Okyūtaiō* [Compendium of Disaster Prevention, Vol. 2: The Emergency Response]. (Kobe: Hyogo Earthquake Memorial 21st Century Research Institute, 2015).

17. Shōbōchō [Fire and Disaster Management Agency] (Ed.). *Hanshin Awaji daishinsai no kiroku, 2* [Records of the Great Hanshin-Awaji Earthquake, Vol. 2]. (Tokyo: Gyosei Corporation, 1996).

18. Sekizawa, "Jishinkasai no higai keigen taisaku."

19. Shōbōchō [Fire and Disaster Management Agency] (Ed.). *Hanshin Awaji daishinsai no kiroku, bekkan shiryōhen* [Records of the Great Hanshin-Awaji Earthquake, Supplemental Edited Records volume]. (Tokyo: Gyosei Corporation, 1996).

20. Japan Association for Fire Science and Engineering. *1995 nen hyōgo-ken nanbu jishin ni okeru kasai ni kansuru chōsa hōkokusho*.

21. Shōbōchō. *Hanshin Awaji daishinsai no kiroku, 2*.

22. Interview with Kobe Fire Department Chief Kamikawa Shōjirō (on

December 6, 1999, at Hanshin-Awaji daishinsai kinen kyōkai). In HAOH. The Iwai Forum Head Office for Hanshin-Awaji Reconstruction. *Iwai fōramu kōwashū,* 3 [A Collection of Conversations at Iwai Forum, Vol. 3]. (2006).

23. Interview with the Himeji Regiment Commander Hayashi Masao (on July 29, 2005, at Kōchi prefectural office). In HAOH. Matsushima Yūsuke. *Hanshin daishinsai jieitai kaku tatakaeri* [How Japan Self-Defense Forces Dealt with the Great Hanshin-Awaji Earthquake]. (Tokyo: Jiji Press, 1996). See Bōeichō rikujō bakuryōkanbu [Japan Defense Agency Ground Staff Office]. *Hanshin Awaji daishinsai saigai haken kōdōshi* [Records of Actions Taken during the Dispatch for the Great Hanshin-Awaji Earthquake Disaster: From 1995 January 17th to April 27th]. (Tokyo: Rikujō jieitai dai 10 shidan [Japan Ground Self-Defense Force 10th Division], 1995).

24. Interview with the prefecture's Disaster Prevention Section head Noguchi Kazuyuki (on June 22, 1998, at Hanshin-Awaji daishinsai kinen kyōkai). In HAOH. Archived notes by the head of the Governor's Secretariat Saitō Tomio (on February 8, 2010). Interview with Commander Hayashi (on July 29, 2005). Bōeichō rikujō bakuryōkanbu, ibid.

25. Interviews with Regiment Commander Kurokawa Yūzō (on September 17, 2005, in Moriyama city in Shiga prefecture at his home). In HAOH. GSDF Middle Army Commander Matsushima Yūsuke (on October 6, 2004, in Tokyo at Daikin Headquarters). In HAOH. Matsushima. *Hanshin daishinsai jieitai kaku tatakaeri.* Bōeichō rikujō bakuryōkanbu, ibid.

26. Nihon Shōbō Kyōkai (Ed.). *Hanhin Awaji daishinsaishi.* Kobe University of Mercantile Marine, *Shindo 7 no hōkoku: Sonotoki Kobe shōsendaigaku dewa* [The Report of the Intensity VII: What Happened at Kobe University of Mercantile Marine]. (Kobe: Kobe University of Mercantile Marine, 1996).

27. Recollections by Hakuō Dorimitory Student Council Chair Arita Toshiaki. In Nihon Shōbō Kyōkai (Ed.). *Hanshin Awaji daishinsaishi,* pp. 352–53.

28. Kawata Yoshiaki, "Daikibo jishin saigai ni yoru jinteki higai no yosoku" [Predicting Human Casualties in a Large-scale Earthquake Disaster]. In *Shizen saigai kagaku,* Vol. 16. (1997).

29. According to 2006 figures by Shōbōchō [Fire and Disaster Management Agency], on May 19, 2006.

30. No documents have captured disaster-related deaths in their entirety. The numbers cited here were acquired by the author speaking with related officials and others.

31. Hanshin Awaji daishinsai chōsa hōkoku henshūiinkai (Ed.). *Hanshin Awaji daishinsai chōsa hōkoku,* 1–25.

32. An article in the *Kobe Shimbun* newspaper, evening edition, June 26, 1974.

33. Ibid.

34. Interviews with Itami mayor Matsushita Tsutomu (on January 25, 2007, at Hanshin-Awaji daishinsai kinen kyōkai). In HAOH. Amagasaki mayor Miyata Yoshio (on December 9, 2006, at Hanshin-Awaji daishinsai kinen kyōkai). In HAOH. Amagasaki ultimately lost 49 people in the earthquake, and Itami lost 22.

35. Interviews with Ashiya mayor Kitamura Harue (on September 19, 2003, at Hanshin-Awaji daishinsai kinen kyōkai). In HAOH. Ashiya deputy mayor Gotō Tarō (on August 7, 2003, at Hanshin-Awaji daishinsai kinen kyōkai). In HAOH.

Iokibe Makoto. "Kikikanri: Gyōsei no taiō" [Crisis Management: Administrative Response]. In Asahi Shimbun (Ed.). *Hanshin-Awaji daishinsaishi: 1995 nen Hyōgo-ken nanbu jishin* [Collected Records of the Great Hanshin-Awaji Earthquake: The Southern Hyōgo Earthquake in 1995]. (Tokyo: Asahi Shimbun, 1996). Takayose Shōzō. *Hanshin daishinsai to jichitai no taiō* [Local Government Response to the Great Hanshin Earthquake]. (Tokyo: Gakuyo shobo, 1996).

36. Interviews with Kobe mayor Sasayama Kazutoshi (on February 5, 2001, at Kobe International House). In HAOH. Departmental Director Yamashita Akihiro (on November 18, 1999, at Kobe city hall). In HAOH. Hyōgo prefectural governor Kaihara Toshitami (on April 15, 1995, at Hyōgo chiiki seisaku kenkyū kikō, and on October 5, 2001, at Hyōgo prefectural office). In HAOH.

37. Interviews with Nishinomiya mayor Baba Junzō (on October 3, 2002, at Nishinomiya city hall). In HAOH. Education Director Yamada (on August 25, 2005).

38. Interviews with Hyōgo prefectural governor Kaihara (on October 5, 2001). Vice Governor Ashio Chōji (on August 30, 2000, at Minato Bank Headquarters). In HAOH. Section head Noguchi (on June 22, 1998). Saitō Memo.

39. Oral history with Hyōgo prefectural governor Kaihara Toshitami. In Iokibe Makoto. "Kikikanri."

40. Kaihara Toshitami. *Hyōgo-ken chiji no Hanshin-Awaji daishinsai: 15 nen no kiroku* [The Governor of Hyōgo prefecture in the Great Hanshin-Awaji Earthquake: 15 Years of Records]. (Tokyo: Maruzen, 2009).

41. Keisatsuchō (Ed.). *Keisatu hakusho Heisei 7 nenban*.

42. Interviews with Prime Minister Murayama Tomiichi (on February 19, 2003), Chief Cabinet Secretary Igarashi Kōzō (on June 3, 2003), and Deputy Chief Cabinet Secretary Ishihara Nobuo (on April 8, 2003). Murayama Tomiichi (Oral History), Yakushiji Katsuyuki (Ed.). *Murayama Tomiichi kaikoroku* [Memoirs of Murayama Tomiichi]. (Tokyo: Iwanami shoten, 2018). Igarashi Kōzō. *Kantei no rasenkaidan: Shiminha kanbōchōkan funtōki* [Caracole in the Prime Minister's Office: Struggles of a Grassroots Official of the Cabinet]. (Tokyo: Gyosei Corporation, 1997), Ishihara Nobuo (Oral History), Mikuriya Takashi and Watanabe Akio (Eds.). *Shushōkantei no ketsudan: Naikaku kanbō fukuchōkan Ishihara Nobuo no 2600 nichi* [A Decision at the Prime Minister's Office—2600 Days of Deputy Cabinet Chief Ishihara Nobuo]. (Tokyo: Chuokoron sha, 2002). Yamakawa Katsumi. "Hanshin Awaji daishinsai ni okeru Murayama shushō no kikikanri rīdāshippu" [Crisis Management Leadership of Prime Minister Murayama at Great Hanshin-Awaji Earthquake]. In *The Law Review of Kansai University.* (Osaka: Kansai Daigaku Hogakukai, 1997). Iokibe, "Kikikanri."

43. Interviews with Prime Minister Murayama (on February 19, 2003) and Cabinet Minister Ozato Sadatoshi (on August 21, 2002).

44. Hanshin-Awaji daishinsai kinen kyōkai [Great Hanshin-Awaji Earthquake Memorial Association] (Ed.). *Tobe Fenikkusu: Sōzōteki fukkō eno gunzō* [Fly Phoenix: Toward the Creative Reconstruction]. (Kobe: Hanshin-Awaji daishinsai kinen kyōkai, 2005).

45. Ibid.

46. Interviews with Prime Minister Murayama (on February 19, 2003), Chief Cabinet Secretary Igarashi (on June 3, 2003), and former National Land Agency

Administrative Vice-Minister Shimokōbe Atsushi (on May 11, 2000). Kaihara. *Hyōgo-ken chiji no Hanshin-Awaji daishinsai.*

47. Mikuriya Takashi, Kanai Toshiyuki, and Makihara Izuru (Interview). "Hanshin-Awaji shinsai fukkō iinkai" (1995–1996) iinchō Shimokōbe Atsushi "Dōji Shinkō" Ōraru hisutorī, 1 [Interview with Shimokōbe Atsushi Synchronized Oral History]. *C.O.E. Project for Oral History and Policy Enrichment*, Vol. 1. (Tokyo: National Graduate Institute for Policy Studies, GRIPS, 2002).

48. Hanshin-Awaji daishinsai kinen kyōkai. *Tobe Fenikkusu.*

49. Ibid. Mikuriya Takashi, Kanai Toshiyuki, and Makihara Izuru (Interview). "Hanshin-Awaji shinsai fukkō iinkai" (1995–1996) iinchō Shimokōbe Atsushi "Dōji Shinkō" Ōraru hisutorī, 2 [Interview with Shimokōbe Atsushi Synchronized Oral History]. *C.O.E. Project for Oral History and Policy Enrichment*, Vol. 2. (Tokyo: National Graduate Institute for Policy Studies, GRIPS, 2002).

50. Murayama. *Murayama Tomiichi kaikoroku.*

51. As told to the author by former Prime Minister Murayama Tomiichi (on January 17, 2015, in Kobe).

52. Hanshin-Awaji daishinsai kinen kyōkai. *Tobe Fenikkusu.*

CHAPTER 3

1. Specifically, according to Keisatsucho [National Police Agency]. Higashi-nihon daishinsai to keisatsu [Police in the Great East Japan Earthquake]. (Tokyo: Keisatsuchō, 2012), 14,308 (90.6 percent) of deaths were drownings, while only 667 (4.2 percent) were due to collapsed buildings and 145 (0.9 percent) to fires.

2. Shizenkagaku kenkyūkiko Kokuritsu Tenmondai [National Institutes of Natural Sciences National Astronomical Observatory of Japan] (Ed.). *Rika Nenpyō 2017 [Chronological Scientific Tables 2017].* (Tokyo: Maruzen, 2016), p.760.

3. Kawata Yoshiaki. "Kyodai saigai to shiteno Higashinihon daishinsai" [The Great East Japan Earthquake as a Massive Disaster]. In Faculty of Societal Safety Sciences, Kansai University (Ed.). *Higashinihon daishinsai fukkō 5 nenme no kenshō: Fukkō no jittai to bōsai, gensai, shukusai no tenbō* [Analysis of the Reconstruction: Five Years from the Great East Japan Earthquake: The Status of Reconstruction and Prospect for Disaster Prevention, Natural Disaster Reduction, and Cutback to Disaster]. (Kyoto: Minervashobo, 2016).

4. For further information related to tsunami measurements, see Shōbōchō [Fire and Disaster Management Agency]. *Higashinihon daishinsai kirokushū: 2013 nen 3 gatsu* [Records of the Great East Japan Earthquake: March 2013]. (Tokyo: Shōbōchō, 2013). Regarding seafloor earthquake activity see Okada Yoshimitsu. "2011 nen Tōhoku chihō taiheiyō oki jishin no gaiyō" [Outline of the 2011 off the Pacific Coast of Tōhoku Earthquake]. In *Natural Disaster Research Report of the Natural Research Institute for Earth Science and Disaster Resilience*, No. 48. (2012).

5. Nihon kishō kyōkai [Japan Weather Association]. "Jishin tsunami no gaiyō, dai 3 pō" [Overview of the Earthquake and Tsunami, Report 3]. In *Saigai to bōsai, bōhan tōkei dētashū, 2014* [Data Book of a Disaster, Crime Prevention, and Disaster Prevention, 2014]. (2014).

6. Naimushō daijinkanbō toshikeikakuka [Ministry of Home Affairs Town

Planning Division]. Sanriku tsunami ni yoru higaichōson no fukkōkeikaku hōkoku [Municipal Reconstruction Plan for Damage Caused by the Sanriku Tsunami]. (1934), hereafter, "the Home Ministry report."

7. Shōbōchō taisakuhonbu [Fire and Disaster Management Agency Response Headquarters]. *Higashinihon daishinsai, Dai 149 hō* [149th Report on the Great East Japan Earthquake]. (Tokyo: Shōbōchō, 2014).

8. Murai Shunji. *Higashinihon daisaigai no kyōkun: Tsunami kara tasukatta hito no hanashi* [Lessons from the Great East Japan Earthquake: A Story of Tsunami Survivors]. (Tokyo: Kokon shoin, 2011).

9. Kahoku Shimpo Publishing hensyūkyoku. *Futatabi tachiagaru! Kahoku Shimpōsha, Higashinihon daishinsai no kiroku* [We Stand Up Again! The Document of the Great East Japan Earthquake by Kahoku Shimpo Publishing]. (Tokyo: Chikuma shobo, 2012).

10. NHK Great East Japan Earthquake Project. *Shōgenkiroku Higashinihon daishinsai* [Recorded Testimonies from the Great East Japan Earthquake]. (Tokyo: NHK Publishing, 2013).

11. Murai. *Higashinihon daisaigai no kyōkun.*

12. Kahoku Shimpo Publishing hensyūkyoku. *Futatabi tachiagaru!*

13. According to an investigation by Kokudokōtsūshō kaijikyoku [Ministry of Land, Infrastructure, Transport and Tourism Maritime Bureau] in August 2012. In Iokibe Makoto. "Higashinihon daishinsai." In Hyogo Earthquake Memorial 21st Century Research Institute. *Saigai taisaku zensyo bessatsu* [Compendium of Disaster Prevention, Additional Volume]. (Kobe: Hyogo Earthquake Memorial 21st Century Research Institute, 2015).

14. Mori Kahee, socioeconomic historian. In Yamashita Fumio. *Aishi Sanriku Ōtsunami: Rekishi no kyōkun ni manabu* [Sad Stories of Sanriku Tsunami: Learn from the Lesson of History]. (Tokyo: Kawade shobo shinsha, 2011).

15. Nakamura Shigehisa, Kyoto University Disaster Prevention Research Institute. In Yamashita. *Aishi Sanriku Ōtsunami.*

16. The Home Ministry report.

17. Yamashita. *Aishi Sanriku Ōtsunami.*

18. Chūō bōsaikaigi [Disaster Management Cabinet Office]. *1896 nen meiji-sanriku tsunami* [Lessons, The 1896 Meiji Sanriku Tsunami]. (2005).

19. Yamashita. *Aishi Sanriku Ōtsunami.*

20. The Home Ministry report.

21. Yamashita. *Aishi Sanriku Ōtsunami.*

22. The Home Ministry report.

23. Ibid.

24. Ibid.

25. Kitahara Itoko. *Tsunami saigai to kindai nihon* [Tsunami Disaster and Modern Japan]. (Tokyo: Yoshikawa, 2014).

26. Yamashita. *Aishi Sanriku Ōtsunami.* Iwate-ken. *Iwate-ken kaishō jōkyō chōsasho* [Tidal Wave Status Report]. (1896). Takayama Fumihiko. *Ōtsunami o ikiru: Kyodai bōchōtei to Tarō 100 nen no itonami* [The Life with Tsunami: A Hundred Years in Tarō with the Enormous Coastal Levee]. (Tokyo: Shinchosha Publishing, 2012).

27. NHK Great East Japan Earthquake Project. *Shōgenkiroku Higashinihon daishinsai.*

28. Shōbōchō taisakuhonbu [Fire and Disaster Management Agency Response Headquarters], on March 7, 2014.

29. NHK Special Group of Reporters. *Kyodai tsunami: Sonotoki hito wa dō ugoitaka* [Great Tsunami—How People Reacted]. (Tokyo: Iwanami shoten, 2013).

30. Minami Sanriku shōbōsho, Watari shōbōsho, Kobe-shi shōbōkyoku, and Kawai Ryūsuke (Eds.). *Higashinihon daishinsai: Shōbō taiin shitō no ki: Tsunami to gareki no naka de* [The Great East Japan Earthquake: Mortal Combat of the Firefighters: Among the Tsunami and Heaps of Rubble]. (Tokyo: Junposha, 2012).

31. Keisatsuchō [National Police Agency]. *Higashinihon daishinsai ni okeru keisatsukatsudō ni kakaru kenshō sochi* [Verification of the Police Activity in the Great East Japan Earthquake]. (Tokyo: Keisatsuchō, 2011).

32. Fukushima-ken keisatsu honbu [Fukushima prefecture police] (Sup.). *Fukushima ni ikiru, Fukushima o mamoru: Keisatsukan to kazoku no shuki* [Memoirs of a Police Officer and His Family: We Live in Fukushima, We Save Fukushima]. (Fukushima: Fukushima-ken keisatsu gojokai, 2012).

33. Ibid.

34. Ibid.

35. Keisatsuchō. *Higashinihon daishinsai ni okeru keisatsukatsudō ni kakaru kenshō sochi.* Keisatsuchō [National Police Agency]. *Higashinihon daishinsai ni tomonau keisatsu sochi* [Police Activities and the Great East Japan Earthquake]. (Tokyo: Keisatsuchō, 2014).

36. Kunitomo Akira, commander of the Tagajō regiment. In Takino Takahiro. *Dokyumento: Jieitai to Higashinihon daishinsai* [Document: Japan Self-Defense Forces and the Great East Japan Earthquake]. (Tokyo: POPLAR Publishing, 2012). To allow members of his regiment to "be able to write truthfully," he had them write anonymously.

37. Interview with Commander of the Northeastern Army Kimizuka Eiji and his lecture at the National Defense Academy (on January 20, 2012). Sudō Akira. *Jieitai kyuen katsudō nisshi: Tohoku chiho Taiheiyo oki jishin no genba kara* [The Daily Logs of the Japan Self-Defense Forces Rescue Activities in the Disaster Site of the Great East Japan Earthquake]. (Tokyo: Fusosha, 2011). General Kimizuka was later promoted to army chief of staff and passed away in December 2015, having retired in 2013. One of the above U.S. military members even published an obituary about Kimizuka honoring his work immediately after his passing.

38. Japan Society for Defense Studies. Jieitai saigaihaken no jittai to kadai [The Reality and the Challenges of the Disaster Relief Operations by Japan Self-Defense Forces]. *Defense Studies*, Vol. 46. (2012). Hibako Yoshifumi. *Sokudō hissui: Higashinihon daishinsai rikujō bakuryōchō no zenkiroku* [The Necessity to Respond Quickly: Activity Logs in the Great East Japan Earthquake by Chief of Staff, Ground Self-Defense Force]. (Tokyo: Manegimentosha, 2015).

39. Interview with GSDF Chief of Staff Hibako Yoshifumi.

40. Interviews with Chief of Staff Hibako and Chief of Staff, Joint Staff Oriki Ryōichi.

41. Takashima Hiromi. *Bujin no honkai: FROM THE SEA: Higashinihon daishinsai ni okeru kaijō jieitai no katsudōkiroku* [Samurai's True Worth: Activity Logs of Japan Maritime Self-Defense Force in the Great East Japan Earthquake]. (Tokyo: Kodansha, 2014).

42. Ōhata Akihiro (Ed.). *Higashinihon daishinsai kinkyūtaiō 88 no chie: Kokkōshō shodō no kiroku* [Eighty-Eight Words of Wisdom from the Emergency Response to the Great East Japan Earthquake: A Record of the Initial Action in Ministry of Land, Infrastructure, Transport, and Tourism]. (Tokyo: Bensei Publishing, 2012). Shinsai taiō seminā jikkōiinkai. 3.11 daishinsai no kiroku [March 11th: Record of the Disaster]. (2012).

43. Nihon sekijūjisha [Japanese Red Cross Society]. *Higashinihon daishinsai: Kyūgokatsudō kara fukkōshien made no zenkiroku* [The Great East Japan Earthquake: A Complete Record from Rescue Operation to Restoration Assistance]. (2015). Kumamoto sekijūji Byōin [Japanese Red Cross Kumamoto Hospital]. *Fukkō eno kiseki: Higashinihon daishinsai 82 jikan no kyūgokiroku* [The Road to Reconstruction: The Rescue Record of 82 hours in the Great East Japan Earthquake]. (2014). I Seishi (Ed.). "Tokushū: Saigaiiryō to higasinihon daishinsai" [Disaster Medical Care and the Great East Japan Earthquake]. In *Resident*, July 2012. (Tokyo: Igaku shuppan, 2012). Miyagi-ken. *Higashinihon daishinsai: Miyagi-ken no hassaigo 1 nenkan no saigaitaiō no kiroku to sono kenshō* [The Great East Japan Earthquake: A Year-After Analysis of the Disaster Response in Miyagi Prefectural Government]. (2015). Retrieved from https://www.pref.miyagi.jp/site/kt-kiroku/kt-kensyou3.html

44. Aoki Eiichi (Ed.), Muramatsu Michio, and Tsunekawa Keiichi (Sup.). *Daishinsai ni manabu shakaikagaku, 6: Fukkyū fukkō e mukau chiiki to gakkō* [Learning from the Great Disasters, Vol. 6: Neighbors and Schools Making Progress on Reconstruction]. (Tokyo: Toyo Keizai, 2015). Shōbōchō [Fire and Disaster Management Agency]. *Higashinihon daishinsai kirokushū: 2013 nen 3 gatsu* [Records of the Great East Japan Earthquake: March 2013]. (Tokyo: Shōbōchō, 2013).

45. According to a report by Associate Professor Zenkyō Masahiro of Kwansei Gakuin University at Hyogo Earthquake Memorial 21st Century Research Institute. Zenkyō Masahiro. "Saigaiji sōgo ōen kyōtei wa kinōshitaka: Hisai jichitai sābei o mochiita bunseki" [Did Mutual Support Agreements in Disasters Function? An Analysis of Surveys Conducted with Affected Communities]. In Iokibe Makoto (Sup.), Ōnishi Yutaka (Ed.). *Saigai ni tachimukau jichitaikan renkei: Higashinihon daishinsai ni miru kyōryokuteki gabanansu no jittai* [Cooperation between Municipalities in Response to Disasters: The Actual Situation of Cooperative Governance in the Great East Japan Earthquake]. (Kyoto: Minervashobo, 2017).

46. Hyōgo-ken fukkō shienka [Hyōgo prefecture Reconstruction Support division]. *Higashinihon daishinsai ni kakaru shien* [The Great East Japan Earthquake Support Activities]. (2015).

47. Union of Kansai Government's Fujimori Tatsu and Hyōgo prefecture government's Fudeyasu Keiichi. Hyōgo-ken. *Higashinihon daishinsai: Hyōgo-ken no sien 1 nen no kiroku* [The Great East Japan Earthquake: The Activity Report of Hyōgo Prefecture's Disaster Relief Assistance]. (2012). Retrieved from https://web.pref.hyogo.lg.jp/kk41/faq/higashinihonn1.html. Kōmoto Hiroko, Shigekawa Kishie, and Tanaka Satoshi. "Hiaringu chōsa ni yoru saigaiōen, juengyōmu ni kansuru kōsatsu: Higashinihon daishinsai no jirei" [A Hearing Survey of Disaster Relief Activities After the Great East Japan Earthquake]. In *Institute of Social Safety Science Journal*, Vol. 20. (2013).

48. Sōmushō [Ministry of Internal Affairs and Communications]. Retrieved from http://www.soumu.go.jp/

49. Hyogo Earthquake Memorial 21st Century Research Institute. *Dai 2 kai jichitai saigaitaisaku zenkokukaigi hōkokusho* [The Second National Conference Report for the Disaster Prevention Strategy for the Local Government]. (Kobe: Hyogo Earthquake Memorial 21st Century Research Institute, 2013).

50. Fujisawa Retsu. "Kokyō o sasaeru kigyō" [Corporate Support of the Public]. In Okamoto Masakatsu (Ed.). *Higashinihon daishinsai: Fukkō ga nihon o kaeru: Gyōsei, kigyō, NPO no mirai no katachi* [The Great East Japan Earthquake Reconstruction Changes Japan: The Future of Administration, Corporation, and NPO]. (Tokyo: Gyosei Corporation, 2016).

51. Ibid.

52. Tōno-shi. *Tōno-shi kōhōsien katsudō kenshō kirokushi* [The Activity Logs of Tōno City's Logistic Support]. (Tōno: Tōno-shi, 2013).

CHAPTER 4

1. Kotaki Akira. *Higashinihon daishinsai: Kinkyū saigaitaisaku honbu no 90 nichi: Seihu no syodō ōkyu taiō wa ikani nasaretaka* [90 Days in Emergency Response Headquarters: Government's Initial Reaction to the Great East Japan Earthquake]. (Tokyo: Gyosei Corporation, 2013). Kan Naoto. *Tōden fukushima genpatsu jiko: Sōri daijin toshite kangaeta koto* [Tokyo Electric Power Company Holdings Fukushima Daiichi Nuclear Power Station Accident—What I Thought as Prime Minister]. (Tokyo: Gentosha Literary Publication, 2012). Fukuyama Tetsurō. *Genpatsu jiko: Kantei karano shōgen* [The Nuclear Accident: Testimonies for the Prime Minister's Office]. (Tokyo: Chikumashobo, 2012). Funabashi Yōichi. *Kauntodaun merutodaun*, 1 [Countdown Meltdown, Vol. 1]. (Tokyo: Bungeishunju, 2012). Kimura Hideaki. *Kenshō Fukushima genpatsu jiko: Kantei no 100 jikan* [Study of the Fukushima Nuclear Accident: 100 Hours in the Prime Minister's Office]. (Tokyo: Iwanami shoten, 2012).

2. Kitazawa Toshimi. *Nihon ni jieitai ga hitsuyōna riyū* [The Reasons Why Japan Needs the Self-Defense Forces]. (Tokyo: Kadokawa, 2012). Hibako Yoshifumi. *Sokudō hissui: Higashinihon daishinsai rikujō bakuryōchō no zenkiroku* [The Necessity to Respond Quickly: Activity Logs in the Great East Japan Earthquake by Chief of Staff, Ground Self-Defense Force]. (Tokyo: Manegimentosha, 2015).

3. Fukuyama. *Genpatsu jiko*.

4. Kyodo News nuclear accident crew, and Takahashi Hideki (Eds.). *Zendengen sōsitsu no kioku: Shōgen Fukushima daiichi genpatsu: 1000 nichi no shinjitsu* [Loss of Electricity: The Truth of 1000 Days in Fukushima Daiichi Nuclear Power Station]. (Tokyo: Shodensha, 2015).

5. Fukushima nuclear power plant accident record team (Ed.). *Fukushima genpatsujiko: Tōden terebikaigi 49 jikan no kiroku* [Tokyo Electric Power Company Holdings Fukushima Daiichi Nuclear Power Station Accident: The Record of 49-Hour-Teleconference]. (Tokyo: Iwanami shoten, 2013).

6. Kadota Ryūshō. *Shi no fuchi o mita otoko: Yoshida Masao to Fukushima daiichi-genpatsu no 500 nichi* [A Man at the Brink of Death: Yoshida Masao's 500 Days at Fukushima Daiichi Nuclear Power Station]. (Tokyo: PHP Institute, 2012). Kyodo News Nuclear Accident Crew, and Takahashi, *Zendengen sōsitsu no kioku*. Funabashi. *Kauntodaun merutodaun*, 1. Fukushima Nuclear Power Plant Accident Record Team

(Ed.), Miyazaki Tomomi, Kimura Hideaki, and Kobayashi Gō. *Fukushima genpatsu jiko: Taimurain 2011–2012* [Fukushima Daiichi Nuclear Power Station Accident: Timeline 2011–2012]. (Tokyo: Iwanami shoten, 2013).

7. Kyodo News Nuclear Accident Crew, and Takahashi, ibid.

8. Hatano Masaru, and Iimori Akiko. *Kantō daishinsai to nichibei gaikō* [The Great Kantō Earthquake and Japan–US Diplomacy]. (Tokyo: Soshisha, 1999).

9. America-Japan Society (Ed.). *Mouhitotsu no nichibei kōryūshi: Nichibei kyōkai shiryō de yomu 20 seiki* [A New History of Japan-US Interactions: The 20th Century as Seen in the Documents from the America-Japan Society]. (Tokyo: Chuokoron-shinsha, 2012).

10. Murakami Tomoaki. "Jieitai no saigaikyūen katsudō: Sengonihon ni okeru kokubō to bōsai no sōkoku" [Disaster Rescue Activities of National Defense Army: Postwar Rivalry between National Defense and Disaster Prevention and Rescue]. In Iokibe Makoto (Sup.), Katayama Yutaka (Ed.). *Bōsai o meguru kokusaikyōryoku no arikata* [International Cooperation in Disaster Prevention]. (Kyoto: Minervashobo, 2017).

11. Tsunekawa Keiichi (Ed.), Muramatsu Michio, and Tsunekawa Keiichi (Sup.). *Daishinsai ni manabu shakaikagaku, 7: Daishinsai genpatsukikika no kokusaikankei* [Learning from the Natural Disasters, Vol. 7: International Relations under the Crisis of Great Earthquake and Nuclear Power Plant]. (Tokyo: Toyo Keizai, 2015). Nakabayashi Hironobu. "Beigun ni yoru nihonkokunai deno saigaikyūen: Hanshin Awaji daishinsai ikō no tenkai" [Disaster Rescue by US Military in Japan: Evolution after Great Hanshin-Awaji Earthquake]. In *Institute of Social Safety Science Journal*, Vol. 30. (2017). Robert D. Eldridge. "Higashinihon daishinsai ni okeru beigun no tomodachi sakusen: Kokusaishien to bōsai kyōryoku no arikata" [Operation Tomodachi of the U.S. Military during the Great East Japan Earthquake: A Paradigm of International Support and Disaster Prevention Support]. In Iokibe Makoto (Sup.), Katayama Yutaka (Ed.). *Bōsai o meguru kokusaikyōryoku no arikata*.

12. Funabashi Yōichi. *Kauntodaun merutodaun, 2* [Countdown Meltdown, Vol. 2]. (Tokyo: Bungeishunju, 2012).

13. Robert D. Eldridge. *Operation Tomodachi: The Incredible Story of the United States Marine Corps' Response to the Great East Japan Earthquake of 2011 and the Relationship It Built with Ōshima, the Island It Helped Save.* (Osaka: Reed International, 2018). Robert D. Eldridge. *Preparing for Japan's Next Major Disaster: New Approaches to Civil-Military Cooperation in Japan as Proposed by U.S. Marine Corps' Participants in "Operation Tomodachi."* (Osaka: Reed International, 2018).

14. Eldridge, *Operation Tomodachi*. Eldridge, *Preparing for Japan's Next Major Disaster*. Prefectures that formally agreed to work with the Marine Corps included Shizuoka, Kōchi, Wakayama, Mie, and Okinawa.

15. As told to author by Prime Minister Kan Naoto (on March 20, 2011, at the National Defense Academy of Japan).

16. Interviews with Deputy Chief Cabinet Secretary Fukuyama Tetsurō (on May 13, 2014) and Deputy Chief Cabinet Secretary Takino Kinya (on May 14, 2014). Independent Investigation Commission on the Fukushima Daiichi Nuclear Accident (Ed.). *Fukushima genpatsujiko dokuritsu kenshōiinkai chōsa kenshō hōkokusho* [Investigative Report of Independent Investigation Commission on the Fukushima Daiichi Nuclear Accident]. (Tokyo: Discover 21, 2012).

17. Higashinihon daishinsai fukkōkōsō kaigi [The Reconstruction Design Council in Response to the Great East Japan Earthquake]. "Fukkō eno teigen: Hisan no naka no kibō" [Towards Reconstruction: Hope beyond the Disaster]. In *Report to the Prime Minister of the Reconstruction Design Council in Response to the Great East Japan Earthquake, 25 June 2011*. (2011). Retrieved from https://www.cas.go.jp/jp/fukkou/pdf/fukkouhenoteigen.pdf

18. Higashinihon daishinsai fukkōkōsō kaigi. "Fukkō eno teigen."

19. Ibid.

20. Iokibe Makoto. "Higashinihon daishinsai fukkōkōsō kaigi no yakuwari" [The Role of the Reconstruction Design Council in Response to the Great East Japan Earthquake]. In Hyogo Earthquake Memorial 21st Century Research Institute. *Saigai taisaku zensho bessatsu* [Compendium of Disaster Prevention, Additional Volume]. (Kobe: Hyogo Earthquake Memorial 21st Century Research Institute, 2015). Iio Jun. "Fukkō taisaku honbu to fukkō kihonhō, fukkōchō no hossoku" [The Start of the Reconstruction Task Force, Reconstruction Basic Law, and Reconstruction Agency]. In Hyogo Earthquake Memorial 21st Century Research Institute. *Saigai taisaku zensho bessatsu*. Hayashi Toshiyuki. "Higashinihon daishinsai fukkōzaisei (fukkōkikin)" [Great East Japan Earthquake Reconstruction Finance (Reconstruction Fund)]. In Hyogo Earthquake Memorial 21st Century Research Institute. *Saigai taisaku zensho bessatsu*.

21. I benefited from the paper by Reconstruction Design Council working group member Iwate University Professor Hirota Junichi, which describes the categorization of disaster areas.

22. I benefited from the insights and information provided by officials from Fukkōchō [Reconstruction Agency], Iwate prefecture, and cities, towns, and villages along the coast, Professor Hirota Junichi of Iwate University, and Tezuka Sayaka, an assistant for reconstruction in Kamaishi city, among many others.

CHAPTER 5

1. Kazumori Tetsuo. "Risubon jishin no kinkyūtaiō to fukkyū fukkō" [The Immediate Response to the Lisbon Earthquake: Its Restoration and Reconstruction]. In Hyogo Earthquake Memorial 21st Century Research Institute. *Saigai taisaku zensho bessatsu* [Compendium of Disaster Prevention, Additional Volume]. (Kobe: Hyogo Earthquake Memorial 21st Century Research Institute, 2015). Hyogo Earthquake Memorial 21st Century Research Institute Research & Investigation Center. *Risubon jishin to sono bunmeishiteki igi no kōsatsu* [Examination of the Lisbon Earthquake and Its Historical Significance for Civilization]. (Kobe: Hyogo Earthquake Memorial 21st Century Research Institute, 2015).

2. Hanshin-Awaji daishinsai kinen kyōkai [Great Hanshin-Awaji Earthquake Memorial Association] (Ed.). *Tobe Fenikkusu: Sōzōteki fukkō eno gunzō* [Fly Phoenix: Toward Creative Reconstruction]. (Kobe: Hanshin-Awaji daishinsai kinen kyōkai, 2005). Okamoto Masakatsu (Ed.). *Higashinihon daishinsai: Fukkō ga nihon o kaeru: Gyōsei, kigyō, NPO no mirai no katachi* [The Great East Japan Earthquake: Reconstruction Changes Japan: The Future of Administration, Corporation, and NPO]. (Tokyo: Gyosei Corporation, 2016).

3. Kunaichō [Imperial Household Agency]. *Shōwa tennō jitsuroku* 3 [Records of the Shōwa Emperor, Vol. 3]. (Tokyo: Tokyo shoseki, 2015), p. 932.

4. Hatano Masaru, and Iimori Akiko. *Kantō daishinsai to nichibei gaikō* [The Great Kantō Earthquake and Japan-US Diplomacy]. (Tokyo: Soshisha, 1999).

5. Kaihara Toshitami. *Hyōgo-ken chiji no Hanshin-Awaji daishinsai: 15 nen no kiroku* [The Governor of Hyōgo prefecture in the Great Hanshin-Awaji Earthquake: 15 Years of Records]. (Tokyo: Maruzen, 2009).

6. Kawashima Yutaka. "Tennō Kōgō ryōheika 5 nenkan no inori" [Five-Year Prayers of Emperor and Empress]. In *Bungeishunju*, April 2016. (2016).

References

America-Japan Society (Ed.). (2012). *Mouhitotsu no nichibei kōryūshi: Nichibei kyōkai shiryō de yomu 20 seiki* [A New History of Japan-U.S. Interactions: The 20th Century as Seen in the Documents from the America-Japan Society]. Tokyo: Chuokoron-shinsha.

Aoki, Eiichi (Ed.), Muramatsu Michio, and Tsunekawa Keiichi (Sup.). (2015). *Daishinsai ni manabu shakaikagaku, 6: Fukkyū fukkō e mukau chiiki to gakkō* [Learning from the Great Disasters, Vol. 6: Neighbors and Schools Making Progress on Reconstruction]. Tokyo: Toyo Keizai.

Boeichō rikujō bakuryōkanbu [Japan Defense Agency Ground Staff Office]. (1995). *Hanshin Awaji daishinsai saigai haken kōdōshi* [Records of Actions Taken during the Dispatch for the Great Hanshin-Awaji Earthquake Disaster: From 1995 January 17th to April 27th]. Tokyo: Rikujō jieitai dai 10 shidan [Japan Ground Self-Defense Force 10th Division].

Chūō bōsaikaigi [Disaster Management Cabinet Office]. (2004). *1657 Meireki no edo taika hōkokusho* [Report on the 1657 Great Meireki Edo Fire].

Chūō bōsaikaigi [Disaster Management Cabinet Office]. (2005). *1896 nen meiji-sanriku tsunami* [Lessons, The 1896 Meiji Sanriku Tsunami].

Chūō bōsaikaigi [Disaster Management Cabinet Office]. (2006, 2008, 2009). *1923 Kantō daishinsai hōkokusho*, 1–3 [1923 Great Kantō Earthquake Disaster Reports, Vols. 1–3].

Eldridge, Robert D. (2017). "Higashinihon daishinsai ni okeru beigun no tomodachi sakusen: Kokusaishien to bōsai kyōryoku no arikata" [Operation Tomodachi of the U.S. Military during the Great East Japan Earthquake: A Paradigm of International Support and Disaster Prevention Support]. In Iokibe Makoto

(Sup.), Katayama Yutaka (Ed.). *Bōsai o meguru kokusaikyōryoku no arikata* [International Cooperation in Disaster Prevention]. Kyoto: Minervashobo.

Eldridge, Robert D. (2018). *Operation Tomodachi: The Incredible Story of the United States Marine Corps' Response to the Great East Japan Earthquake of 2011 and the Relationship It Built with Ōshima, the Island It Helped Save*. Osaka: Reed International.

Eldridge, Robert D. (2018). *Preparing for Japan's Next Major Disaster: New Approaches to Civil-Military Cooperation in Japan as Proposed by U.S. Marine Corps' Participants in "Operation Tomodachi."* Osaka: Reed International.

Fujisawa, Retsu. (2016). "Kokyō o sasaeru kigyō" [Corporate Support of the Public]. In Okamoto Masakatsu (Ed.). *Higashinihon daishinsai: Fukkō ga nihon o kaeru: Gyōsei, kigyō, NPO no mirai no katachi* [The Great East Japan Earthquake Reconstruction Changes Japan: The Future of Administration, Corporation, and NPO]. Tokyo: Gyosei Corporation.

Fukao, Yoshio, and Ishibashi Katsuhiko (Eds.). (1996). *Hanshin Awaji daishinsai to jishin no yosoku*. [The Great Hanshin-Awaji Earthquake and Earthquake Forecasting]. Tokyo: Iwanami shoten.

Fukushima-ken keisatsu honbu [Fukushima prefecture police] (Sup.). (2012). *Fukushima ni ikiru, Fukushima o mamoru: Keisatsukan to kazoku no shuki* [Memoirs of a Police Officer and His Family: We Live in Fukushima, We Save Fukushima]. Fukushima: Fukushima-ken keisatsu go jokai.

Fukushima Nuclear Power Plant Accident Record Team (Ed.). (2013). *Fukushima genpatsujiko: Tōden terebikaigi 49 jikan no kiroku* [Tokyo Electric Power Company Holdings Fukushima Daiichi Nuclear Power Station Accident: The Record of the 49-Hour-Teleconference]. Tokyo: Iwanami shoten.

Fukushima Nuclear Power Plant Accident Record Team (Ed.), Miyazaki Tomomi, Kimura Hideaki, and Kobayashi Gō. (2013). *Fukushima genpatsu jiko: Taimurain 2011–2012* [Fukushima Daiichi Nuclear Power Station Accident: Timeline 2011–2012]. Tokyo: Iwanami shoten.

Fukuyama, Tetsurō. (2012). *Genpatsu jiko: Kantei karano shōgen* [The Nuclear Accident: Testimonies from the Prime Minister's Office]. Tokyo: Chikumashobo.

Funabashi, Yōichi. (2012). *Kauntodaun merutodaun, 1–2* [Countdown Meltdown, Vols. 1 and 2]. Tokyo: Bungeishunju.

Gotō Shinpei kenkyūkai [Gotō Shinpei Research Group] (Ed.). (2011). *Shinsai fukkō: Gotō Shinpei no 120 nichi: Toshi wa shimin ga tsukuru mono* [Earthquake Recovery: 120 Days of Gotō Shinpei: The Town Is Meant for Its Residents]. Tokyo: Fujiwara-shoten.

Hanshin Awaji daishinsai chōsa hōkoku henshūiinkai (Ed.). (1996–2000). *Hanshin Awaji daishinsai chōsa hōkoku, 1–25* [Report on the Hanshin–Awaji Earthquake Disaster, 1–25]. Tokyo: Japanese Geotechnical Society, Japan Society of Civil

Engineers, Japan Society of Mechanical Engineers, Architectural Institute of Japan, and Seismological Society of Japan.

Hanshin-Awaji daishinsai kinen kyōkai [Great Hanshin-Awaji Earthquake Memorial Association] (Ed.). (2005). *Tobe Fenikkusu: Sōzōteki fukkō eno gunzō* [Fly Phoenix: Toward Creative Reconstruction]. Kobe: Hanshin-Awaji daishinsai kinen kyōkai.

Hanshin-Awaji daishinsai kinen kyōkai [Great Hanshin-Awaji Earthquake Memorial Association] (Ed.). "Hanshin-Awaji daishinsai kinen kyōkai Ōraru Hisutorī" [Oral Histories from Survivors, Collected by the Great Hanshin-Awaji Earthquake Memorial Association]. The Collection of the Disaster Reduction and Human Renovation Institution Library (Kobe).

Hatano, Masaru, and Iimori Akiko. (1999). *Kantō daishinsai to nichibei gaikō* [The Great Kantō Earthquake and Japan-U.S. Diplomacy]. Tokyo: Soshisha.

Hayashi, Toshiyuki. (2015). "Higashinihon daishinsai fukkōzaisei (fukkōkikin)" [Great East Japan Earthquake Reconstruction Finance (Reconstruction Fund)]. In Hyogo Earthquake Memorial 21st Century Research Institute. *Saigai taisaku zensho bessatsu* [Compendium of Disaster Prevention, Additional Volume]. Kobe: Hyogo Earthquake Memorial 21st Century Research Institute.

Hibako, Yoshifumi. (2015). *Sokudo hissui: Higashinihon daishinsai rikujō bakuryōchō no zenkiroku* [The Necessity to Respond Quickly: Activity Logs in the Great East Japan Earthquake by Chief of Staff, Ground Self-Defense Force]. Tokyo: Manegimentosha.

Higashinihon daishinsai ukkōkōsō kaigi [The Reconstruction Design Council in Response to the Great East Japan Earthquake]. (2011). "Fukkō eno teigen: Hisan no naka no kibō" [Towards Reconstruction: Hope beyond the Disaster], In *Report to the Prime Minister of the Reconstruction Design Council in Response to the Great East Japan Earthquake, June 25, 2011*. Retrieved from https://www.cas.go.jp/jp/fukkou/pdf/fukkouhenoteigen.pdf

Hyogo Earthquake Memorial 21st Century Research Institute. (2011). *Saigai taisaku zensho 1: Saigai gairon* [Compendium of Disaster Prevention, Vol. 1: The Basics of the Disaster]. Kobe: Hyogo Earthquake Memorial 21st Century Research Institute.

Hyogo Earthquake Memorial 21st Century Research Institute. (2013). *Dai 2 kai jichitai saigaitaisaku zenkokukaigi hōkokusho* [The Second National Conference Report for the Disaster Prevention Strategy for Local Governments]. Kobe: Hyogo Earthquake Memorial 21st Century Research Institute.

Hyogo Earthquake Memorial 21st Century Research Institute (Ed.). (2015). *Tobe Fenikkusu 2* [Fly Phoenix II: Construction for Disaster Prevention and Natural Disaster Reduction]. Kobe: Hyogo Earthquake Memorial 21st Century Research Institute.

Hyogo Earthquake Memorial 21st Century Research Institute Research & Investigation Center. (2015). *Risubon jishin to sono bunmeishiteki igi no kōsatsu* [Examination of the Lisbon Earthquake and Its Historical Significance for Civilization]. Kobe: Hyogo Earthquake Memorial 21st Century Research Institute.

Hyōgo-ken. (2012). *Higashinihon daishinsai: Hyōgo-ken no sien 1 nen no kiroku* [The Great East Japan Earthquake: The Activity Report of Hyōgo Prefecture's Disaster Relief Assistance]. Retrieved from https://web.pref.hyogo.lg.jp/kk41/faq/higashinihonn1.html

Hyōgo-ken fukkō shienka [Hyōgo prefecture Reconstruction Support division]. (2015). *Higashinihon daishinsai ni kakaru shien* [The Great East Japan Earthquake Support Activities].

I, Seishi (Ed.). (2012). "Tokushū: Saigaiiryō to higasinihon daishinsai" [Disaster Medical Care and the Great East Japan Earthquake]. In *Resident*, July 2012. Tokyo: Igaku shuppan.

Igarashi, Kōzō. (1997). *Kantei no rasenkaidan: Shiminha kanbōchōkan funtōki* [Caracole in the Prime Minister's Office: Struggles of a Grassroots Official of the Cabinet]. Tokyo: Gyosei Corporation.

Iio, Jun. (2015). "Fukkō taisaku honbu to fukkō kihonhō, fukkōchō no hossoku" [The Start of the Reconstruction Task Force, Reconstruction Basic Law, and Reconstruction Agency]. In Hyogo Earthquake Memorial 21st Century Research Institute. *Saigai taisaku zensho bessatsu* [Compendium of Disaster Prevention, Additional Volume]. Kobe: Hyogo Earthquake Memorial 21st Century Research Institute.

Ikeda, Tetsurō. (1925). *Shinsai yobō chōsakai hōkoku*, 100 [Earthquake Prevention Research Committee Report, Vol. 100].

Independent Investigation Commission on the Fukushima Daiichi Nuclear Accident (Ed.). (2012). *Fukushima genpatsujiko dokuritsu kenshōiinkai chōsa kenshō hōkokusho* [Investigative Report of Independent Investigation Commission on the Fukushima Daiichi Nuclear Accident]. Tokyo: Discover 21.

Iokibe, Makoto. (1996). "Kikikanri: Gyōsei no taiō" [Crisis Management: Administrative Response]. In Asahi Shimbun (Ed.). *Hanshin-Awaji daishinsaishi: 1995 nen Hyōgo-ken nanbu jishin* [Collected Records of the Great Hanshin-Awaji Earthquake: The Southern Hyōgo Earthquake in 1995]. Tokyo: Asahi Shimbun.

Iokibe, Makoto. (2013). "Kunimachi rondan: Kumamoto demo daijishin no sonae o" [Local and Nationwide Debate: Let Kumamoto Be Ready for a Great Earthquake Disaster]. In *Kumamotonichinichi Shimbun*, 3 November 2013.

Iokibe, Makoto. (2015). "Higashinihon daishinsai." In Hyogo Earthquake Memorial 21st Century Research Institute. *Saigai taisaku zensho bessatsu* [Compendium of Disaster Prevention, Additional Volume]. Kobe: Hyogo Earthquake Memorial 21st Century Research Institute.

Iokibe, Makoto. (2015). "Higashinihon daishinsai fukkōkōsō kaigi no yakuwari" [The Role of the Reconstruction Design Council in Response to the Great East Japan Earthquake]. In Hyogo Earthquake Memorial 21st Century Research Institute. *Saigai taisaku zensho bessatsu* [Compendium of Disaster Prevention, Additional Volume]. Kobe: Hyogo Earthquake Memorial 21st Century Research Institute.

Ishihara, Nobuo (Oral History), Mikuriya Takashi, and Watanabe Akio (Eds.). (2002). *Shushōkantei no ketsudan: Naikaku kanbō fukuchōkan Ishihara Nobuo no 2600 nichi* [A Decision at the Prime Minister's Office—2600 Days of Deputy Cabinet Chief Ishihara Nobuo]. Tokyo: Chuokoron sha.

Iwate-ken. (1896). *Iwate-ken kaishō jōkyō chōsasho* [Tidal Wave Status Report].

Japan Association for Fire Science and Engineering. (2011). *1995 nen hyōgo-ken nanbu jishin ni okeru kasai ni kansuru chōsa hōkokusho* [A Survey of Fires in the 1995 Southern Hyōgo Prefecture Earthquake]. Tokyo: Japan Association for Fire Science and Engineering.

Japan Society for Defense Studies. (2012). Jieitai saigaihaken no jittai to kadai [The Reality and the Challenges of the Disaster Relief Operations by Japan Self-Defense Forces]. *Defense Studies*, Vol. 46.

Kadota, Ryūshō. (2012). *Shi no fuchi o mita otoko: Yoshida Masao to Fukushima daiichi-genpatsu no 500 nichi* [A Man at the Brink of Death: Yoshida Masao's 500 Days at Fukushima Daiichi Nuclear Power Station]. Tokyo: PHP Institute.

Kahoku Shimpo Publishing henshūkyoku. (2012). *Futatabi tachiagaru! Kahoku Shimpōsha, Higashinihon daishinsai no kiroku* [We Stand Up Again! The Document of the Great East Japan Earthquake by Kahoku Shimpo Publishing]. Tokyo: Chikuma shobo.

Kaihara, Toshitami. (2009). *Hyōgo-ken chiji no Hanshin-Awaji daishinsai: 15 nen no kiroku* [The Governor of Hyōgo prefecture in the Great Hanshin-Awaji Earthquake: 15 Years of Records]. Tokyo: Maruzen.

Kan, Naoto. (2012). *Tōden fukushima genpatsu jiko: Sōri daijin toshite kangaeta koto* [Tokyo Electric Power Company Holdings Fukushima Daiichi Nuclear Power Station Accident—What I Thought as Prime Minister]. Tokyo: Gentosha Literary Publication.

Kawashima, Yutaka. (2016). "Tennō Kōgō ryōheika 5 nenkan no inori" [Five-Year Prayers of Emperor and Empress]. In *Bungeishunju*, April 2016.

Kawata, Yoshiaki. (1997). "Daikibo jishin saigai ni yoru jinteki higai no yosoku" [Predicting Human Casualties in a Large-scale Earthquake Disaster]. In *Shizen saigai kagaku*, Vol. 16.

Kawata, Yoshiaki. (2016). "Kyodai saigai to shiteno Higashinihon daishinsai" [The Great East Japan Earthquake as a Massive Disaster]. In Faculty of Societal Safety Sciences, Kansai University (Ed.). *Higashinihon daishinsai fukkō 5 nenme no kenshō: Fukkō no jittai to bōsai, gensai, shukusai no tenbō* [Analysis of the Reconstruction: Five Years from the Great East Japan Earthquake: The Status of Reconstruction and Prospect for Disaster Prevention, Natural Disaster Reduction, and Cutback to Disaster]. Kyoto: Minervashobo.

Kazumori, Tetsuo. (2015). "Risubon jishin no kinkyūtaiō to fukkyū fukkō" [The Immediate Response to the Lisbon Earthquake: Its Restoration and Reconstruction]. In Hyogo Earthquake Memorial 21st Century Research Institute. *Saigai taisaku zensho bessatsu* [Compendium of Disaster Prevention, Additional Volume]. Kobe: Hyogo Earthquake Memorial 21st Century Research Institute.

Keisatsuchō [National Police Agency] (Ed.). (1995). *Keisatu hakusho Heisei 7 nenban* [Police White Paper 1995]. Tokyo: Ministry of Finance.

Keisatsuchō [National Police Agency]. (2011). *Higashinihon daishinsai ni okeru keisatsukatsudō ni kakaru kenshō sochi* [Verification of the Police Activity in the Great East Japan Earthquake]. Tokyo: Keisatsuchō.

Keisatsuchō [National Police Agency]. (2012). *Higashinihon daishinsai to keisatsu* [Police in the Great East Japan Earthquake]. Tokyo: Keisatsuchō.

Keisatsuchō [National Police Agency]. (2014). *Higashinihon daishinsai ni tomonau keisatsusochi* [Police Activities and the Great East Japan Earthquake]. Tokyo: Keisatsuchō.

Keishichō [Metropolitan Police Department]. (1925). *Taishō daishin kasaishi* [History of the Great Taishō Earthquake and Fires]. Tokyo: Keishichō.

Kimura, Hideaki. (2012). *Kenshō Fukushima genpatsu jiko: Kantei no 100 jikan* [Study of the Fukushima Nuclear Accident: 100 Hours in the Prime Minister's Office]. Tokyo: Iwanami shoten.

Kinshichi, Norio. (2005). "Risubon daishinsai to keimōtoshi no kensetsu" [The Lisbon Earthquake and Construction of the City of Enlightenment]. In *JCAS renkei kenkyūseika hōkoku*, Vol. 8.

Kitahara, Itoko. (2014). *Tsunami saigai to kindai nihon* [Tsunami Disaster and Modern Japan]. Tokyo: Yoshikawa.

Kitazawa, Toshimi. (2012). *Nihon ni jieitai ga hitsuyōna riyū* [The Reasons Why Japan Needs the Self-Defense Forces]. Tokyo: Kadokawa.

Ko hakushaku Yamamoto kaigun taishō denki hensankai [Committee for the Biography of the late Admiral Yamamoto] (Ed.). (1938). *Hakushaku Yamamoto Gonnohyōe den*, 2 [Biography of Count Yamamoto Gonnohyōe, Vol. 2.]. Tokyo: Yamamoto Kiyoshi.

Kobe Shimbun newspaper article, evening edition, 26 June 1974.

Kobe University of Mercantile Marine. (1996). *Shindo 7 no hōkoku: Sonotoki Kobe shōsendaigaku dewa* [The Report of the Intensity VII: What Happened at Kobe University of Mercantile Marine]. Kobe: Kobe University of Mercantile Marine.

Kokudokōtsūshō kaijikyoku [Ministry of Land, Infrastructure, Transport and Tourism Maritime Bureau]'s investigation in August 2012. In Iokibe. "Higashinihon daishinsai."

Kōmoto, Hiroko, Shigekawa Kishie, and Tanaka Satoshi. (2013). "Hiaringu chōsa ni yoru saigaiōen, juengyōmu ni kansuru kōsatsu: Higashinihon daishinsai no jirei" [A Hearing Survey of Disaster Relief Activities After the Great East Japan Earthquake]. In *Institute of Social Safety Science Journal*, Vol. 20.

Kotaki, Akira. (2013). *Higashinihon daishinsai: Kinkyū saigaitaisaku honbu no 90 nichi: Seihu no shodō ōkyu taiō wa ikani nasaretaka* [90 Days in Emergency Response Headquarters: Government's Initial Reaction to the Great East Japan Earthquake]. Tokyo: Gyosei Corporation.

Kumamoto sekijūji Byōin [Japanese Red Cross Kumamoto Hospital]. (2014). *Fukkō eno kiseki: Higashinihon daishinsai 82 jikan no kyūgokiroku* [The Road to Reconstruction: The Rescue Record of 82 hours in the Great East Japan Earthquake].

Kunaichō [Imperial Household Agency]. (2015). *Shōwa tennō jitsuroku*, 3 [Records of the Shōwa Emperor, Vol. 3] Tokyo: Tokyo shoseki.

Kyodo News Nuclear Accident Crew, and Takahashi Hideki (Eds.). (2015). *Zendengen sōsitsu no kioku: Shōgen Fukushima daiichi genpatsu: 1000 nichi no shinjitsu* [Loss of Electricity: The Truth of 1,000 Days in Fukushima Daiichi Nuclear Power Station]. Tokyo: Shodensha.

Mainichi Shimbun newspaper article, March 12, 1995.

Matsuba, Kazukiyo. (2012). *Teito fukkōshi o yomu* [A Study of the History of Imperial City Reconstruction]. Tokyo: Shinchosha Publishing.

Matsushima, Yūsuke. (1996). *Hanshin daishinsai jieitai kaku tatakaeri* [How Japan Self-Defense Forces Dealt with the Great Hanshin-Awaji Earthquake]. Tokyo: Jiji Press.

Mikuriya, Takashi, Kanai Toshiyuki, and Makihara Izuru (interview). (2002). "Hanshin-Awaji shinsai fukkō iinkai" (1995–1996) iinchō Shimokōbe Atsushi "Dōji Shinkō" Ōraru hisutorī, 1–2 [Interview with Shimokōbe Atsushi Synchronized Oral History]. *C.O.E. Project for Oral History and Policy Enrichment*, Vols. 1 and 2. Tokyo: National Graduate Institute for Policy Studies.

Minami Sanriku shōbōsho, Watari shōbōsho, Kobe-shi shōbokyoku, and Kawai Ryūsuke (Eds.). (2012). *Higashinihon daishinsai: Shōbō taiin shitō no ki: Tsunami to gareki no naka de* [The Great East Japan Earthquake: Mortal Combat of the Firefighters: Among the Tsunami and Heaps of Rubble]. Tokyo: Junposha.

Miyagi-ken. (2015). *Higashinihon daishinsai: Miyagi-ken no hassaigo 1 nenkan no saigaitaiō no kiroku to sono kenshō* [The Great East Japan Earthquake: A Year-

After Analysis of the Disaster Response in Miyagi Prefectural Government]. Retrieved from https://www.pref.miyagi.jp/site/kt-kiroku/kt-kensyou3.html

Morimoto, Kōsei. (2010). *Shōmu tennō: Seme wa warehitori ni ari* [Emperor Shōmu: I Am the One to Blame]. Tokyo: Kodansha.

Murai, Shunji. (2011). *Higashinihon daisaigai no kyōkun: Tsunami kara tasukatta hito no hanashi* [Lessons from the Great East Japan Earthquake: A Story of Tsunami Survivors]. Tokyo: Kokon shoin.

Murakami, Tomoaki. (2017). "Jieitai no saigaikyūen katsudō: Sengonihon ni okeru kokubō to bōsai no sōkoku" [Disaster Rescue Activities of National Defense Army: Postwar Rivalry between National Defense and Disaster Prevention and Rescue]. In Iokibe Makoto (Sup.), Katayama Yutaka (Ed.). *Bōsai o meguru kokusaikyōryoku no arikata* [International Cooperation in Disaster Prevention]. Kyoto: Minervashobo.

Murayama, Tomiichi (Oral History), Yakushiji Katsuyuki (Ed.). (2018). *Murayama Tomiichi kaikoroku* [Memoirs of Murayama Tomiichi]. Tokyo: Iwanami shoten.

Murosaki, Yoshiteru. (2011). "Hakodate taika (1934) to Sakata taika (1976)" [The Hakodate (1934) and Sakata (1976) Fires]. In Hyogo Earthquake Memorial 21st Century Research Institute. *Saigai taisaku zensho 1: Saigai gairon* [Compendium of Disaster Prevention, Vol. 1: The Basics of Disaster]. Kobe: Hyogo Earthquake Memorial 21st Century Research Institute.

Naimushō shakaikyoku [Ministry of Home Affairs, Department of Social Affairs]. (1923). *Taishō shinsaishi, naihen* [Report on the Taishō Earthquake, Supplement]. Tokyo: Naimushō shakaikyoku.

Naimushō shakaikyoku [Ministry of Home Affairs, Department of Social Affairs]. (1923). *Taisho shinsaishi, gaihen* [Report on the Taishō Earthquake, Supplement]. Tokyo: Naimushō shakaikyoku.

Naimushō daijinkanbo toshikeikakuka [Ministry of Home Affairs Town Planning Division]. (1934). Sanriku tsunami ni yoru higaichōson no fukkōkeikaku hōkoku [Municipal Reconstruction Plan for Damage Caused by the Sanriku Tsunami].

Nakabayashi, Hironobu. (2017). "Beigun ni yoru nihonkokunai deno saigaikyūen: Hanshin Awaji daishinsai ikō no tenkai" [Disaster Rescue by US Military in Japan: Evolution after Great Hanshin-Awaji Earthquake]. In *Institute of Social Safety Science Journal*, Vol. 30.

NHK Great East Japan Earthquake Project. (2013). *Shōgenkiroku Higashinihon daishinsai* [Recorded Testimonies from the Great East Japan Earthquake]. Tokyo: NHK Publishing.

NHK Special Group of Reporters. (2013). *Kyodai tsunami: Sonotoki hito wa dō ugoitaka* [Great Tsunami—How People Reacted]. Tokyo: Iwanami shoten.

Nihon kishō kyōkai [Japan Weather Association]. (2014). "Jishin tsunami no gaiyō, dai 3 pō" [Overview of the Earthquake and Tsunami, Report 3]. In *Saigai to bōsai, bōhan tōkei dētashū, 2014* [Data Book of a Disaster, Crime Prevention, and Disaster Prevention, 2014].

Nihon sekijūjisha [Japanese Red Cross Society]. (2015). *Higashinihon daishinsai: Kyūgokatsudō kara fukkōshien made no zenkiroku* [The Great East Japan Earthquake: A Complete Record from Rescue Operation to Restoration Assistance].

Nihon Shōbō Kyōkai [Japan Firefighters Association] (Ed.). (1996). *Hanshin Awaji daishinsaishi* [Accounts of the Great Hanshin-Awaji Earthquake]. Tokyo: Nihon Shōbō Kyōkai.

Ōhata, Akihiro (Ed.). (2012). *Higashinihon daishinsai kinkyūtaiō 88 no chie: Kokkōshō shodō no kiroku* [Eighty-Eight Words of Wisdom from the Emergency Response to the Great East Japan Earthquake: A Record of the Initial Action in Ministry of Land, Infrastructure, Transport and Tourism]. Tokyo: Bensei Publishing.

Okada, Yoshimitsu. (2012). "2011 nen Tōhoku chihō taiheiyō oki jishin no gaiyō" [Outline of the 2011 off the Pacific Coast of Tōhoku Earthquake]. In *Natural Disaster Research Report of the Natural Research Institute for Earth Science and Disaster Resilience*, No. 48.

Okamoto, Masakatsu (Ed.). (2016). *Higashinihon daishinsai: Fukkō ga nihon o kaeru: Gyōsei, kigyō, NPO no mirai no katachi* [The Great East Japan Earthquake: Reconstruction Changes Japan: The Future of Administration, Corporation, and NPO]. Tokyo: Gyosei Corporation.

Sangawa, Akira. (2011). *Jishin no nihonshi: Daichi wa nani o katarunoka*, zōhoban [Earthquake and the History of Japan: What the Earth Would Say?, enlarged ed.]. Tokyo: Chuokoron-shinsha.

Sekizawa, Ai. (2015). "Jishinkasai no higai keigen taisaku" [Measures for Mitigating Damage Due to Earthquake Fires]. In Hyogo Earthquake Memorial 21st Century Research Institute. *Saigai taisaku zensho 2: Ōkyūtaiō* [Compendium of Disaster Prevention, Vol. 2: The Emergency Response]. Kobe: Hyogo Earthquake Memorial 21st Century Research Institute.

Shinsai taiō seminā jikkōiinkai. (2012). 3.11 daishinsai no kiroku [March 11th: Record of the Disaster].

Shizenkagaku kenkyūkikō Kokuritsu Tenmondai [National Institutes of Natural Sciences National Astronomical Observatory of Japan] (Ed.). (2016). *Rika Nenpyō 2017* [Chronological Scientific Tables 2017]. Tokyo: Maruzen.

Shōbōchō [Fire and Disaster Management Agency] (Ed.). (1996). *Hanshin Awaji daishinsai no kiroku, 2* [Records of the Great Hanshin–Awaji Earthquake, Vol. 2]. Tokyo: Gyosei Corporation.

Shōbōchō [Fire and Disaster Management Agency] (Ed.). (1996). *Hanshin Awaji daishinsai no kiroku, bekkan shiryōhen* [Records of the Great Hanshin-Awaji Earthquake, Supplemental Edited Records Volume]. Tokyo: Gyosei Corporation.

Shōbōchō [Fire and Disaster Management Agency]. (2013). *Higashinihon daishin-*

sai kirokushū: 2013 nen 3 gatsu [Records of the Great East Japan Earthquake: March 2013]. Tokyo: Shōbōchō.

Shōbōchō [Fire and Disaster Management Agency], on May 19, 2006.

Shōbōchō taisakuhonbu [Fire and Disaster Management Agency Response Headquarters]. (2014). *Higashinihon daishinsai, Dai 149 hō* [149th Report on the Great East Japan Earthquake]. Tokyo: Shōbōchō.

Shōbōchō taisakuhonbu [Fire and Disaster Management Agency Response Headquarters], on March 7, 2014.

Soeda, Yoshiya. (2007). *Naimushō no shakaishi* [Social History of the Ministry of Home Affairs]. Tokyo: University of Tokyo Press.

Sudō, Akira. (2011). *Jieitai kyūen katsudō nisshi: Tōhoku chihō Taiheiyō oki jishin no genba kara* [The Daily Logs of the Japan Self-Defense Forces Rescue Activities in the Disaster Site of the Great East Japan Earthquake]. Tokyo: Fusosha.

Taikakai (Ed.). (1971). *Naimushō shi*, 3 [History of the Ministry of Home Affairs, Vol. 3]. Tokyo: Chiho zaimu kyōkai.

Takahashi, Shigeharu (Ed.). (1930). *Teito fukkōshi*, 1–3 [A History of the Reconstruction of the Imperial City, Vols. 1–3]. Tokyo: Teito fukkō chōsa kyōkai.

Takashima, Hiromi. (2014). *Bujin no honkai: FROM THE SEA: Higashinihon daishinsai ni okeru kaijō jieitai no katsudōkiroku* [Samurai's True Worth: Activity Logs of Japan Maritime Self-Defense Force in the Great East Japan Earthquake]. Tokyo: Kodansha.

Takayama, Fumihiko. (2012). *Ōtsunami o ikiru: Kyodai bōchōtei to Tarō 100 nen no itonami* [The Life with Tsunami: A Hundred Years in Tarō with the Enormous Coastal Levee]. Tokyo: Shinchosha Publishing.

Takayose, Shōzō. (1996). *Hanshin daishinsai to jichitai no taiō* [Local Government Response to the Great Hanshin Earthquake]. Tokyo: Gakuyo shobo.

Takino, Takahiro. (2012). *Dokyumento: Jieitai to Higashinihon daishinsai* [Document: Japan Self-Defense Forces and the Great East Japan Earthquake]. Tokyo: POPLAR Publishing.

The Iwai Forum Head Office for Hanshin-Awaji Reconstruction (2006). *Iwai fōramu kōwashū*, 3 [A Collection of Conversations at Iwai Forum, Vol. 3].

Tokyo denryoku Fukushima genshiryoku hatsudensho jiko chōsa iinkai. (2012). *Kokkai jikochō hōkokusho* [The Report to the Accident Investigation for the National Diet]. Tokyo: Tokuma shoten Publishing.

Tokyo denryoku Fukushima genshiryoku hatsudensho ni okeru jiko chōsa kenshō iinkai. (2012). *Seifu jikochō chūkan hōkokusho* [The Governmental Accident Investigation: The Interim Report]. Tokyo: Media Land.

Tokyo denryoku Fukushima genshiryoku hatsudensho ni okeru jiko chōsa kenshō iinkai. (2012). *Seifu jikochō saishū hōkokusho* [The Governmental Accident Investigation: The Final Report]. Tokyo: Media Land.

Tokyo-shi (Ed.). (1926). *Tokyo shinsairoku* [Record of the Tokyo Earthquake and Disaster]. Tokyo: Tokyo-shi.

Tokyo-to Suginami-ku. (2012). *3.11 Higashinihon daishinsai kara 1 nen: Suginami-ku no ayumi* [A Year from March 11th: The Advancement in Suginami]. Tokyo: Tokyo-to Suginami-ku.

Tōno-shi. (2013). *Tōno-shi kōhōsien katsudō kenshō kirokushi* [The Activity Logs of Tōno City's Logistic Support]. Tōno: Tōno-shi.

Tsunekawa, Keiichi (Ed.), Muramatsu Michio, and Tsunekawa Keiichi (Sup.). (2015). *Daishinsai ni manabu shakaikagaku, 7: Daishinsai genpatsukikika no kokusaikankei* [Learning from the Natural Disasters, Vol. 7: International Relations Under the Crisis of the Great (East Japan) Earthquake and Nuclear Power Plant Accident]. Tokyo: Toyo Keizai.

Tsurumi, Yūsuke. (1967). *Gotō Shinpei*, Vol. 4. Tokyo: Keiso shobo.

Tsutsui, Kiyotada. (2011). *Teito fukkō no jidai: Kantō daishinsai igo* [Era of Imperial City Reconstruction: The Great Kantō Earthquake and Beyond]. Tokyo: Chuokoron-shinsha.

Yamakawa, Katsumi. (1997). "Hanshin Awaji daishinsai ni okeru Murayama shushō no kikikanri rīdāshippu" [Crisis Management Leadership of Prime Minister Murayama at Great Hanshin-Awaji Earthquake]. In *The Law Review of Kansai University*. Osaka: Kansai Daigaku Hogakukai.

Yamamoto, Sumiyoshi. (1993). *Edo no kaji to hikeshi* [Fires and Firefighting in Edo]. Tokyo: Kawade shobo shinsha.

Yamashita, Fumio. (2011). *Aishi Sanriku Ōtsunami: Rekishi no kyokun ni manabu* [Sad Stories of Sanriku Tsunami: Learn from the Lessons of History]. Tokyo: Kawade shobo shinsha.

Yokohama-shi shishi hensangakari (Ed.). (1926). *Yokohama-shi shinsaishi, 1* [History of Yokohama City Earthquake Disaster, Vol. 1]. Yokohama: Yokohama-shi shishi hensangakari.

Yomiuri Shimbun newspaper article, February 19, 1995.

Yoshimura, Akira. (1970). *Sanriku kaigan ōtsunami* [Great Tsunami of the Sanriku Coast]. Tokyo: Bungeishunju.

Yoshimura, Akira. (1973). *Kantō daishinsai* [The Great Kantō Earthquake]. Tokyo: Bungeishunju.

Zenkyō, Masahiro. (2017). "Saigaiji sōgo ōen kyōtei wa kinōshitaka: Hisai jichitai sābei o mochiita bunseki" [Did Mutual Support Agreements in Disasters Function? An Analysis of Surveys Conducted with Affected Communities]. In Iokibe Makoto (Sup.), Ōnishi Yutaka (Ed.). *Saigai ni tachimukau jichitaikan renkei: Higashinihon daishinsai ni miru kyōryokuteki gabanansu no jittai* [Cooperation between Municipalities in Response to Disasters: The Actual Situation of Cooperative Governance in the Great East Japan Earthquake]. Kyoto: Minervashobo.

Index